CW00832813

Towards Building a British Islam: New Muslims' Perspectives

Despite the current negative image of Islam in the European context there has been a steady growth of converts to Islam over the past few decades, especially in Britain. British converts are a highly diverse group, with different social, economic and educational backgrounds. In recent years this group, or community, has grown in confidence and become increasingly active in influencing positive Islamic discourse in Britain. The book sheds light on the intellectual and spiritual contributions of some of the prominent figures of this group of 'new Muslims', and assesses their efforts in shaping Islam in British society; among those the study looks at are: Martin Lings, Gai Eaton, Tim Winter and Hamza Yusuf.

The research also investigates the potential benefit 'new Muslims' can bring to bridge the gap between Muslim communities and wider British society, thus helping in the process of building mutual trust, greater cooperation and positive understanding among all parties in Britain. The work will help readers to become aware of the evolution of a 'British Islam' that is more open, rooted in British values and spiritual traditions, and forms a part of the continually changing British religious landscape.

Towards Building a British Islam

New Muslims' Perspectives

Haifaa A. Jawad

continuum

Continuum International Publishing Group

The Tower Building	80 Maiden Lane
11 York Road	Suite 704
London, SE1 7NX	New York, NY 10038

www.continuumbooks.com

British Library Cataloguing-in-Publication Data
A catalogue record for this book is available from the British Library.

ISBN: HB: 978-0-8264-9684-3

Library of Congress Cataloguing-in-Publication Data
Jawad, H. A.
Towards building a British Islam : new Muslims' perspectives/Haifaa A. Jawad.
    p. cm.
Includes bibliographical references and index.
ISBN 978-0-8264-9684-3 (hdbk.)
1. Muslim converts–Great Britain. 2. Conversion–Islam–Case studies.
3. Muslims–Great Britain. 4. Islam–Great Britain.
I. Title.
BP65.G7J38 2011
297.5'740941–dc23   2011019461

Typeset by Deanta Global Publishing Services, Chennai, India
Printed and bound in Great Britain

To Little Anas with that Angelic face,
rest in peace with the Spirit

Contents

Foreword

By Dr. Khaled Abou El Fadl, Alfi Distinguished Professor of
Islamic Law, UCLA School of Law

Despite the critical importance of the subject, the history and growth of Islam
in Britain has received scant attention in Western scholarship. More particularly, the history of conversions to Islam in Britain, why people convert, and
what impact converts have upon British life has been a neglected subject.

Haifaa Jawad has done the scholarly community an immeasurable service
by writing this wonderfully inspired, informative, and well-written book. At
a time when most of what is published about Muslims in Europe, and
especially about converts, does not rise above the level of alarmist bigotry or
pitiful apologetics, Jawad presents the first sociologically grounded and
morally balanced study of the stories of British converts to Islam and the
multifaceted and diverse roles that they play in their native societies. Jawad's
study is invaluable in that it carefully and sympathetically allows the subjects
of her study to present their own narratives, in their own unique voices,
without treating her study either with presumptuous skepticism or uncriti-
cal indulgence. This book, however, is not about exemplary case studies of
some notable Muslim converts and their reasons and impact. Jawad's
contribution is of far greater import and significance. In this concise and
poignant book, Jawad offers an engaging introduction to the religion of
Islam as it is understood and practised by its followers, and also an overview
of the history of Muslims and Europe. Not surprisingly, this book will be of
great value to Muslims and non-Muslims alike, to academics and scholars,
and most of all to any reader who is interested in the future of Islam and the
West. Jawad's scholarship calmly but steadfastly unpacks so many stereotypes held by both Muslims and non-Muslims about converts, their reasons,
and roles in Britain. In my view, those who give Jawad's scholarship its due
and read her work carefully will discover that the greatest contribution of
this book is that, perhaps unwittingly, it offers hope: hope for a world of
shared humanity, shared values, and understanding and tolerance.

Acknowledgements

I am grateful to the following people for their help and support in the process of working on this book. Yahya Birt for his valuable time to accommodate my requests to interview him many times and discuss with him certain aspects of British Islamic history and the woks of some prominent British converts; his kind and valuable advice were extremely helpful. Yasin Dotten for his encouragement, Laura MacDonald for her swift response to my queries, Ian Draper for his time to discuss issues on the convert community, Tim Winter for his recommendation to some valuable sources, Reza Shah Kazemi for his valuable comments on Martin Lings chapter, and Hamza Yusuf for giving me some of his valuable time to discuss certain issues related to Islam in Britain. My last acknowledgement goes to my sister Suzan, and brothers Jamal and Emad for their support and understanding.

October 2011

Introduction

There is an increasing interest in the role of converts to Islam in Western Europe. This has come about as a result of the growing number of 'new Muslims' in most Western European countries, especially in Britain. The interest is focused primarily on the potential role that these converts might play in the societies in which they live. Despite the importance of the subject, no comprehensive study on the theme of this book has so far been undertaken in Britain. The present volume therefore aims to fill this gap by investigating the intellectual and spiritual contributions of several prominent members of this convert group, with a focus on the British convert community. However, before embarking on the main topic of the book, we need to put the subject into perspective and look at the phenomenon of conversion in a wider context.

Conversion: Brief Summary

Religious conversion is a broad and complex phenomenon: it may be a conversion from one religion to another, a shift from one group to another within a particular tradition or a dramatic increase in devotion and commitment to one's inherited religious tradition (a 'born again' experience is often likened to a religious 'conversion'). Conversion experiences vary considerably in different cultures, historical periods and social and economic circumstances.[1] Conversion to Islam is increasingly attracting attention not only in Britain[2], but worldwide; it is said that Islam is the fastest growing religion in the modern world and that despite the negative image and adverse publicity that the faith is confronted with, the number of people converting to Islam is steadily rising. There are no reliable figures about the numbers of converts worldwide, or even about numbers in individual Western European countries, primarily because census polls in most of these countries do not ask about religious affiliation. In Britain, where religious affiliation was actually included in the 2001census, the question was confined to religious background only; the issue of religious conversion was omitted. Moreover, most mosques and Islamic centres in Britain do not issue certificates of conversion; nor do they keep proper and accurate record of the number of persons who convert to Islam – let alone data which contains age group or social, economic or educational status – which makes any attempt to predict even approximate numbers too haphazard[3].

Conversion in an Islamic Context

It must be stressed that there is no term for 'conversion' in the Arabic language; rather, the emphasis is on the idea of becoming a Muslim, that is, 'submitting' to God in the form prescribed by His final revelation. Hence, to understand conversion to Islam requires an understanding of the word 'Islam' itself; Islam denotes an act of submission and envisages not only 'the acceptance of the outward forms of any one particular prophet's practice, not even that of the 'Seal of the Prophets', Muhammad. Rather, the word represents that pure worship of, and obedience to, the Divine that is exemplified in the lives of all of these prophets, from Noah, through Abraham, Moses and Jesus, to the Seal of the Prophets, Muhammad.'[4] Hence, to accept Islam is in reality 'to take on the ancient, Abrahamic, way of worship, albeit given the specific detailed requirements reflected in the outward practice of the seal of the prophets, Muhammad.'[5]

Furthermore, from an Islamic standpoint, conversion is also a remembrance and an affirmation of the primordial testimony to the Lordship of God, as the Quran says, 'When your Lord brought forth from the Children of Adam, from their lions, their seed, and made them testify of themselves. He said: 'Am I not your Lord?' They said, "Yea, we testify!" That was lest you should say on the Day of Resurrection: "Of this we were unaware."'[6] As such, those who embrace Islam often refer to themselves as 'reverts' rather than converts. Apart from the inner and spiritual transformation, which is essential, becoming a Muslim legally entails public acceptance of the declaration of faith in front of at least two witnesses, this being the first pillar of Islam. Once this is publicly stated, it is assumed that the 'new Muslim' would live according to Islamic rules and regulations dictated by God and the Prophet Muhammad. This involves the performance of the ritual prayer five times a day, payment of the annual alms-tax of Zakat, fasting throughout the month of Ramadan and performing the pilgrimage to Mecca at least once in a lifetime. In addition, the new Muslim is obliged to stop consuming alcohol, eating pork and non-halal meat and abide by the prohibitions related to issues such as stealing, committing adultery and murder. Although not obligatory, most new Muslims tend to take on Islamic names.[7] Some of those who decide against adopting a Muslim name indicate that they do so on the basis of maintaining their social acceptability and avoiding discrimination at work; in a personal conversation with David Wanies, former Head of Religious Studies at Lancaster University, who himself is a convert, he stated that some lecturers and teachers who prefer to keep their original names do so for pedagogical reasons.[8]

For women, becoming Muslim also entails a radical change in their appearance. Islamic law instructs women to dress modestly and this includes covering the hair. The hijab has come to be seen no longer as an innocent act by a woman intent on maintaining her cultural or religious identity but as a threatening symbol of a pathologically anti-western ideology. The following statements by Muslim women demonstrate what this can lead to: 'People would shout, "Go back to your own country;" I had someone spit at me once when I was standing at the bus stop at College.'[9] Covering the head may also prove to be an obstacle towards upward social mobility, especially among educated British and other European women, and, for this reason, some of them choose not to wear the hijab. From personal experience, I know of at least two university lecturers who have decided against wearing the hijab and a third one who wore it for a while but then decided to give up wearing it. She informed me that her motives for no longer wearing the hijab were twofold: first, social acceptability: 'I have been treated like them,' she said, (meaning immigrants and refugees). Second, she was concerned about job security and promotion; in a private conversation she told me that she had lost an opportunity for a senior position at a certain university primarily because of her hijab.[10] For women converts, the hijab brings not only outside rejection and hostility but also strong family opposition. This might jeopardize family ties, which are already under strain as a result of their conversion. A typical response is: 'You chose your religion over us . . . people will discriminate against you. You are making yourself a third-rate citizen. You have basically painted a bull's-eye on you saying "shoot me".'[11] Family reactions can vary, however. Some reject it: 'My mum said, "If you are happy, I am happy" – but obviously she was not. My dad said it and he meant it; that was the difference between them.'[12] Others cautiously accept it: 'My mom loves me so much she [will] buy me scarves sometimes. My grandmother gave me a beautiful, velvet-embroidered scarf. They will respect my prayer, but at the same time ask, "Why are you so fanatical?"'[13]

Motives for Conversion to Islam

As stated above, despite many misconceptions about the faith, especially in the West, conversion to Islam is on the rise. And although there are no reliable figures with regard to numbers, certain observations have been made. The number of British (and other European) citizens who are embracing Islam or have shown interest in doing so is increasing, and, unexpectedly, the rate of conversion to Islam apparently surges at times when there are strong anti-Muslim feelings, such as those which followed the Bosnian conflict, the Gulf war and the Rushdie affair.[14] After September 11, 'the number of conversions has risen in the UK, US and across Europe. A Dutch Islamic centre claims a tenfold increase, whilst a steady stream of converts are reported at the new Muslim project in Leicester.'[15] This has also been witnessed in mosques in cities such as London, Manchester and Glasgow. The process is reinforced by the availability of internet facilities for a wide range of audiences who have direct access to communities that are portrayed in a stereotyped manner.[16] One such comment by an internet 'surfer' attracted to Islam by what he discovered on the internet is the following: 'I began to visit the religious folders on AOL and the usernet-groups, where I found discussions on Islam to be the most intriguing. [I learnt] that Muslims were not the bloodthirsty, barbaric terrorists that news media and the televangelists paint them to be.'[17] The same can be said of the period after the invasion of, first, Afghanistan and then Iraq in 2003.

In the past, the dominant group of those who embraced Islam was of either African–Caribbean or African–American origin, whereas, in recent years, a large number of white people have become Muslim. In Britain, some of them come from affluent backgrounds, such as Joe Ahmed-Dobson, the son of the former cabinet minister, Frank Dobson; Mathew Wilkinson, a former headboy of Eton; Nicholas Brandt, the son of an investment Banker; Jonathan Birt, the son of the former director-general of the BBC, John Birt; the son and daughter of Lord Justice Scott, who investigated the arms-to-Iraq deal; Emma Clark, the great-granddaughter of the former Liberal prime minister, Herbert Asquith; and, very recently, Lauren Booth, the sister-in-law of the former prime minister, Tony Blair.

Despite the stereotypes that portray Muslim women as oppressed and mistreated, it has been noted that more women are converting to Islam than men; for example, in Britain, women converts outnumber men by two to one while in America they outnumber them by four to one.[18] The majority of the women are white, young and unmarried. The director of the Florida Chapter of the Council on American-Islamic Relations states:

'In the past there were more African-Americans coming into Islam, now I am seeing an influx of white Caucasian females.'[19] In Britain, as mentioned above, it is interesting to note that some of these women come from middle-class backgrounds such as the daughter of Lord Justice Scott, Jemima Goldsmith and the TV presenter, Kristiane Backer. The numbers may not be so significant, but the fact of conversion itself, especially among the elite, is revealing (and to some, utterly incomprehensible), given the extremely negative image of Islam in the West and the consequent tensions and difficulties generated by conversion to this religion. The question that needs to be asked is the following.

Why, then, are these women embracing Islam against all the odds?

Large numbers of Western women who convert to Islam do so on account of personal relationships such as marriage to Muslim men. However, more recently – and increasingly – they are embracing Islam primarily because of their convictions. In 2002, the Muath Trust in Birmingham reported that, of seventeen women who converted to Islam, eight of them did so through marriages while the remaining nine came to Islam as the result of personal search.[20] Taking a closer look at their convictions, the appeal of Islam to Western women can be attributed to a wide range of factors. One can begin with the familiar idea of Islam as a form of liberation theology offering an accessible language of protest for marginalized groups in society[21] such as women, who are in general excluded from public life and who consequently struggle to achieve happiness: 'I was looking for peace, I had a rough past. My teenage years were not great; I was bullied at school, people called me fat and ugly, and I was looking for something to make me happy. I tried to go to Church once a week but . . . I did not feel in place there. [Islam] gives you a purpose in your life. The Koran is like a guide to help you: when you read it, it makes you feel better.'[22]

Arguably, the nature of the religion itself and its simplicity appeal strongly to the religious consciousness of people who are drawn to its emphasis on the simple message of monotheism. It thus attracts those who are 'confused by Christological and Trinitarian controversies.'[23] As another convert seeks to explain, 'Something vital seemed to be missing from my life and nothing would fill this vacuum. Being a Christian did not do anything for me, and I began to question the validity of only remembering God one day a week. As with many other Christians too, I had become disillusioned with the hypocrisy of the church and was becoming increasingly unhappy with the concept of Trinity and the deification of Jesus.'[24] British and other European women coming from a tradition that is historically dominated by a male clergy and characterized by a strong aversion to and fear of the feminine, a tradition in which the concept, God qua Father (a supreme male figure), dominates the overall understanding of the Ultimate Reality – such women can discover in Islam an appealing alternative, with its emphasis on totality and integration. Despite its patriarchal features, they find in Islam an equilibrium on the plane of the 'heart' in its relationship with God. We shall return to this subject later. The following testimony by a female convert hints at the kind of equilibrium to which Islam gives access: 'There was an inner void that was not completely satisfied with academic success or human relationships. I had spent my life longing for a truth in which heart would be compatible with mind, action with thought, intellect with emotion. I found that reality in Islam.'[25]

In view of current social trends which foster widespread moral uncertainty, those aspects of Islamic teaching relating to morality, modesty, security, a sense of belonging, a sense of identity, close family ties, care and community and deference for the elderly, as well as traditional notions of respect for women have proven to be very popular among Western women. We hear the voices of women who say: 'I am now more confident, happy and satisfied. I have achieved the fulfilment I was looking for.' Commenting on the supposedly outmoded traditional respect for women, one convert states: 'You seem to be really looked after. [Pious] Muslim men really respect you; they do everything for you. You are highly thought of and protected.'[26] These sentiments are echoed by another woman, who extols the capacity to participate in more traditional family and community values, 'a feeling of belonging to a family . . . when with Muslim friends . . . closeness, love, kindness, caring: these are the benefits I have gained.' Another convert goes further, considering current liberal social cultural trends to be 'false': 'Islam made me feel the need to discipline my life in a positive way and to bring about the necessary modifications to bring my whole being into balance. To set myself free from the false standards of society.'[27]

Underpinning the overall attraction of converts to Islam, I would argue, are the spiritual values of the faith, or Sufism. Known in the West as Islamic mysticism, Sufism permeates the general Islamic principles that have found acceptance or attraction among British and other European people, especially women. The key issue to be stressed here is the ways in which Sufism – or the Sufi perspective on Islam – has contributed, through totality and integration, to the process by which Islam is transformed not just into an interesting approach to life but into an acceptable and, for some, irresistible way of life. This phenomenon is all the more important, given the increasingly grim picture of Islam that prevails in our time. In addition to the appeal of the spiritual values of Sufism to many British and other

Europeans, the Sufi gender paradigm in this context is also of particular relevance. Sufism offers a particular notion of feminine equality and dignity. To understand this concept, it is important to consider the Sufi approach to the feminine principle within Islam. The capacity of Sufism to incorporate and encourage feminine activities within its sphere in both spiritual and social terms attests to the importance attributed by the Sufis to the feminine element in the Divine nature itself. We shall look at each of these elements in turn.

Sufism and the Acceptance of Feminine Activities

Sufism continues to favour the development of feminine activities more than any other branch of Islam, reflecting the Quranic emphasis on the spiritual equality between the sexes: 'For Muslim men and women, for believing men and women; for devout men and women; for men and women who are patient; for men and women who humble themselves; for men and women who give charity; for men and women who fast; for men and women who guard their chastity; for men and women who remember Allah much – for them all has God prepared forgiveness and a great reward.'[28] 'And who so doeth good works, whether male or female, and is a believer, such will enter paradise, and will not be wronged the dint of a date-stone.'[29] Added to this is its constant reminder of women's ability to fulfil their spiritual needs, the respect of the Prophet for women in general, his ideal relationships with his wives and his kindness and care for his daughters, which 'excluded any feeling of dejection so often found in medieval Christian monasticism.'[30] Despite the fact that one can find what might be seen as anti-feminine sayings in the traditions and among some early Sufis, 'the Muslims scarcely reached the apogee of hatred displayed by medieval Christian writers in their condemnation of the feminine elements.'[31] For example, Eve was never regarded as the cause of the fall of Adam; nor was it ever considered that women did not have souls. On the contrary, the prophet declared that 'God has made dear to me from your world women and fragrance, and the joy of my eyes is in prayer'.[32] Such principles found in the Quran and the Prophet's example gave rise in Sufism to a particularly rich tradition of female spirituality. Hence, large numbers of women followed (and continue to follow) the spiritual path and in due time excelled in their virtues and piety; Chief among them was Rabia al-Adawiyya, considered to be the first woman saint in Islam (after the Prophet's wife, Khadija, and her daughter, Fatima). She is credited with introducing the concept of unconditional love of God into Sufism, thus transforming 'sombre asceticism into genuine love mysticism.' The following anecdote illustrates the notion of unconditional love: '[One day Rabia] ran through Basra with a bucket of water in one hand and a burning torch in the other, and when asked about the reason behind her actions, she replied: I want to pour water into hell and set paradise on fire, so that these two veils disappear and nobody shall any longer worship God out of a fear of hell or a hope of heaven, but solely for the sake of His eternal beauty.'[33] Her devotion and asceticism, as well as her contribution to the development of Islamic mysticism, earned her the respect and affection of all the Sufi masters of her time.[34]

Rabia was not the only such woman of her times. There were several other women at the forefront of the Sufi tradition who developed and articulated the Sufi way of life. Among these are Maryam of Basra, Rabia of Syria, Fatima of Nishapur, to name but a few; they attended Sufi meetings, consorted freely with Sufi masters, sponsored Sufi activities and organized circles in the pursuit of the mystical path. Some of them who had reached an advanced level in learning and mystical knowledge guided their husbands in religious and practical matters and contributed to the spiritual training of future Sufi masters, educating great mystical thinkers such as Ibn Arabi, who was taught for 2 years by the great Sufi saint Fatima of Cordova. His early encounter with her and other female mystics greatly influenced his positive attitude towards the feminine role in Sufism.

In general, these women played an important role in shaping the image of the ideal pious Muslim woman to be respected and venerated for her spiritual endeavours. These feminine activities continue to take place in modern times and can be found in some parts of the Muslim world[35] where Sufi women still teach and train souls who are longing for spiritual enlightenment, maintaining continuity with the early example of Rabia and her fellow Sufi women in following the spiritual path. The example of Rabia and other pious Muslim women like her serves as an inspiration and a model to be emulated in people's personal lives, especially at a time when there is widespread anti-spiritualism,[36] desacralization of knowledge, diminishment of feminine spiritual values and distortion of feminine dignity. For an ailing society, inner renewal and purification is the first step towards a more general cure for society as a whole. The following quotation illustrates this well: 'I knew that I yearned for more spiritual fulfilment in my life. But, as yet, nothing had seemed acceptable or accessible to me. I had been brought up essentially a secular humanist. Morals were emphasized, but never attributed to any spiritual or divine being. As I met more Muslims,

I was struck not only by their inner peace, but by the strength of their faith. In retrospect, I realize that I was attracted to these peaceful souls because I sensed my own lack of inner peace and conviction.'[37]

Sufism and Feminine Social Values

The emphasis placed by the Sufis upon the feminine values pertaining to the family while maintaining dignity and strength as worshippers before God has a special appeal for women who choose an orientation towards the family and the community. This comes at a time when feminine social values are diminishing and no longer held in esteem, indeed when there are constant efforts to undermine them in society. Ideals and concepts of womanhood and the family are no longer regarded as sacred but, on the contrary, as stigmatizing and stereotyping. These processes have resulted in confusion, leading to a void in the life of millions of women who want to live a life which is fulfilled by the capacity to nurture and strengthened by the independence of faith – aspects of life that are pejoratively referred to as 'traditional norms.' Sufism, with its strong affirmation of the sacred role of womanhood in society, presents an attractive alternative to fill the vacuum for those women who desire to live their lives as mothers, wives or daughters in a spiritual way. Sufis (and Muslims in general) respect mothers highly; for example, the exhortation in the Quran and by the Prophet to be respectful to mothers testifies to the honour bestowed upon the maternal role, especially in its spiritual aspect. There are many verses and Hadiths that stress that 'motherhood spent in accordance with the Shariah is one of the expressions of the spiritual role of a female.'[38]

The Quran and the Sunnah demand that mothers be venerated and cared for, especially in old age; the famous Hadith of the Prophet, 'heaven lies at the feet of mothers', provides much cause for reflection in the life of the pious Muslim, who then endeavours to ensure that mothers are always respected, treated kindly and gracefully obeyed. The very fact that the word for 'womb' in Arabic, *rahm*, derives from the word *rahma* (mercy), which itself stems from the Divine attributes of Ar-Rahman (the Compassionate) and Ar-Rahim (the Merciful), signifies the tremendously rich and deep understanding, in Islam, of the creation process as derived from the very unfolding of compassion and mercy, so that each and every dimension of motherhood precipitates and participates in that unfolding. For Sufis, this symbol and, in fact, the spiritual reality of the maternal facilitation of Divine Mercy was irresistible, as exemplified in one of the many Hadith Qudsi (the very words of God spoken on the tongue of the Prophet), such as that reported by Ghazzali: 'If My servant falls sick, I care for him as a loving mother tends her son.' Moreover, the great mystic, Rumi, is reported to have said, '[since] a mother's tenderness derives from God, it is a sacred duty and a worthy task to serve her.'[39] For the believers who benefit from the Sufi exegesis of the metaphysical understanding of the creation process, it is no wonder that they hold their mothers in awe and do their best to be good to them so that the blessings of God may descend upon them, for pious spiritual mothers possess *baraka* (the quality of the Sacred) by virtue of their proximity to God.

The role of spiritual mothers starts originally with Maryam (Mary), the mother of Jesus and the only woman after whom a chapter in the Quran is named. She is considered the 'Chosen amongst all women' and highly revered (among Muslims) for her piety, purity and submission. In this connection, the following Hadith is of great importance: 'Aisha (the wife of Muhammad) asked Fatima (the daughter of Muhammad): Did I see (you truly) when you leaned over the Messenger of God and cried; then you leaned over him and you laughed? She said: He informed me that he would die from his illness, so I cried; then he informed me that I would precede the other members of his family in being reunited with him, and he said, You are the chief lady (sayyida) of paradise, with the exception of Mary the daughter of Imran.'[40]

Amongst the women in the history of Islam, the first wife of the prophet Muhammad, Khadija, was the first to enter Islam; and while supporting her husband in his mission as messenger of God, she also looked after her children and ensured that peace and tranquillity prevailed in her home, thus becoming the 'embodiment of devotion and noble qualities' for Muslims, especially Muslim women. Her daughter, Fatima, mother of Hasan and Hossein, is regarded as the fountainhead of female spirituality in Islam; her extreme piety and devotion to her family elevated her to a high station. Both, Fatima and her mother 'stand at the beginning of Islamic piety and occupy a very distinguished rank.' Aisha, the youngest wife of the Prophet, is also highly honoured and respected; she served her husband as a devoted wife and guided Muslims with her Divine knowledge; her close relationship with the Prophet made her an authentic source of knowledge about his personal life[41] and so she ranks among the most reliable sources in the tradition of Hadith science. Other wives of the Prophet followed suit in their holiness and piety; all of them set examples for Muslim women by expressing their spirituality through their roles as mothers, wives or daughters.

Thus, from the Islamic spiritual (and therefore Sufi) perspective, the role of women within the family is highly valued and considered sacred since they are viewed as no less than the unfolding of God's mercy. Feminine qualities, as well as the homage paid to womanhood and their social and family roles, become vital for women who desire to live in and through God, although, due to the very fact that mercy is understood to have derived from the feminine attributes of God's nature, the example of women who bore no children but dedicated their lives to God was also a source of reverence and inspiration, as we shall discuss in the following section.

Sufism and the Feminine element in Spiritual Life

Conscious of the positive aspects of womanhood, the Sufis, more than others, highlighted the role of women in spiritual life, thereby ensuring that Sufism is permeated throughout with feminine traits. Here, the purely spiritual role of the female is fully accepted and elevated to the highest level. They bestowed upon women (in equality with men) the title of saint and accepted a woman (Rabia) as a leading figure in the early development of Islamic mysticism.[42] Ibn Arabi, in particular, played a major role in explaining the importance of the feminine element as a component of the Divine Reality;[43] his belief that the Divine Reality ultimately contains and transcends the polarity of the masculine, and the feminine continues to exert an influence on Sufis until the present day. He declared that 'there is no spiritual quality pertaining to men without women having access to it also' and 'men and women have their part in all degrees (of sanctity) including that of the function of [spiritual] pole [a designation attributed to the most formative and inspiring figure of any particular phase in the life of the religion].'[44] For Ibn Arabi, woman reveals the mystery of the compassionate God. Indeed, the feminine aspect is the form in which God can best be contemplated; he states: 'God cannot be seen apart from matter, and He is seen more perfectly in the human material than in any other, and more perfectly in woman than in man.'[45] In doing so, he elevates the image of the feminine to the highest level and paves the way for other Sufis to follow suit; for example, in the eighteenth century, Wali Muhammad Akbarabadi, the commentator on Rumi declared: 'Know that God cannot be contemplated independently of a concrete being and that He is more perfectly seen in a human being than in any other, and more perfectly in woman than in man.'[46]

Thus, from the spiritual perspective, women embody and express aspects of the Ultimate Reality, which comprises the masculine and the feminine principles as prefigured in the ninety-nine names of God. These names 'are traditionally classified according to Majesty (Jalal – the archetype of Masculinity) and Beauty (Jamal – the archetype of Femininity). God is conceived, for example, both as the Wrathful – an eminently masculine trait – and as the Merciful – identifiable as a feminine quality . . . moreover, if God is referred to as a He, the essence of God is referred to as a She'.[47] In their approach to Divine Reality, the Sufis have always stressed the feminine dimension of that Reality. As Murata explains, while the legalistic authorities emphasize the incomparability and distance of God, the Sufis insist on the similarity and nearness of God. Hence, for the dogmatic theologians, God is wrathful, distant, dominating and powerful. His rules must be obeyed; otherwise there is only punishment and hellfire. In other words, God's attributes 'are those of a strict and authoritarian father.'[48] In contrast, the Sufis see God as gentle, kind and near; they believe 'that mercy, love, and gentleness are the overriding reality and that these will win out in the end.' For them, 'God is not primarily a stern and forbidding father, but a warm and loving mother'.[49] Accordingly, they argue that the God of the theologians is a God whom nobody would ever love, essentially because He is too distant and difficult to comprehend, while the God of the spiritual authorities is a God who is compassionate and loveable because His prime concern is the care of His creatures. As a result, His creatures love Him in return, in part because this loving and caring God can easily be understood and approached.[50]

To sum up, while accepting the feminine characteristics of the Divine Reality, the dogmatic theologians lay strong emphasis on the masculine dimension of that Reality, relegating, in the process, the feminine aspect to second place. In contrast, the Sufis affirm the supremacy of the feminine dimension, primarily because the famous Hadith of the Prophet, according to which 'God's mercy precedes His wrath' (implying that God's feminine characteristics take priority over His masculine qualities), permeates their understanding and their approach to the Ultimate Reality.[51]

These spiritual ideals of femininity are not only derived from mystical interpretations; they comprise the very fabric of the authentic Islamic tradition. They are enshrined in the Arabic language, which is the vehicle of Islamic theology, and they are reflected in the intellectual and social manifestations of the overall Islamic heritage. These ideals 'permeated the ethos of traditional Islam. They may not have been articulated or even respected by all, but they were nonetheless implicit in the cultural ideals that defined gender relationships in societies that remained true to integral Islam. Ideals which continue to influence those who are trying to live according to the inner spirit of the tradition and not just outward prescriptions. This spirit leads to women being venerated and not incarcerated, held in awe and not treated with contempt.'[52]

The majority of converts, especially those who take a conscious decision to embrace the faith, undergo a lengthy process of educating themselves in Islam. Some learn Arabic to a high standard and go on to university to study Islam at degree level. In doing so, they become highly active and play prominent roles in Islamic organizations and institutions. The best among them even obtain certificates in Quran, Hadith, Fiqh (Islamic Jurisprudence) and Arabic Studies from recognized Islamic institutions in the Arab Islamic world, allowing them to teach these courses and thereby become authorities on these issues not only in their respective countries but also in the Islamic world. The steady increase in the numbers of European converts, together with the fact that these converts are highly committed members of their communities, means that they are actively taking part in the process of the indigenization of the Islamic faith and its practices. This has made it very difficult for non-Muslims in Europe and America to regard Islam as a foreign or alien religion any longer. Converts (together with immigrant Muslims) are also contributing to the popularization of the Islamic faith and discourse globally. However, this should not overshadow the fact that they are simultaneously leading the process of promoting what we can term as British Islam, French Islam, European Islam or American Islam through a process of integrating (consciously or unconsciously) Islamic ideals with various European values and precepts. Converts are in a good position to assess and challenge the religio-cultural principles of both sides of the divide: on the Western European side of the divide, they are challenging focal norms of modern Western societies such as individualism, consumerism, secularism and pop culture. On the Islamic side, they are questioning the validity of certain cultural practices and their relation to the faith, as well as the relationship between Islam and culture in general. In the same vein, converts are also playing an important role as bridge builders between the majority society and its Muslim population. In the current climate, characterized as it is by mutual fear and mistrust, converts are ideally placed to bridge the divide and restore trust, tolerance, mutual respect and understanding. For the wider society, they are working hard to present a positive and accurate view of Islam, while, for Muslims, they are endeavouring to help them better understand British and other European societies and their ideals and values[53].

Despite the fact that there is a good record of publications on the subject of conversion and religion in general, literature on conversion to Islam is limited, making the task of the researchers on the subject difficult. In the American/European context, there is the research undertaken by McGinty *Becoming Muslim: Western Women's Conversion to Islam* (2006), deals mainly with American and Swedish women converts. Anne Sofie Roald's *New Muslims in the European context, the Experience of Scandinavian Converts* published in 2004, which focuses on the Scandinavian converts. Also worthy of note is *Women Embracing Islam,* edited by Karin von Nieuwkerk and published in 2006; the study deals with the conversion of women in both Western Europe and America. In the British context, there is the initial work done by Ali Kose's book *Conversion to Islam: A Study of Native British Converts* (originally a PhD thesis), published in 1996. Then, there is the book written by Kate Zebiri on *British Muslim Converts Choosing Alternative Lives* (2007), and, very recently, the work of Ron Geaves on the life and times of Abdullah Quilliam (2010)[54]. All these works deal with one or other aspects of convert's lives and experiences after their conversion, but none deals exclusively with the theme of the present work. Hence, this study fills a gap in this field. The oversight or lack of interest in the subject by specialists is difficult to understand, given the importance of the subject of conversion to Islam in terms of the change it brings about and the impact it has on the lives and experience of the individuals concerned as well as the continuing vitality and the revival of the faith in today's world. In the European context, Britain has had its fair share of the existence of a good number of indigenous Muslims. British converts are a highly diverse group, coming from different social, economic and educational backgrounds. In recent years, this group, or community, has grown in confidence and become active in influencing Islamic discourse in Britain. New Muslims, especially those with a high profile in society, have brought skills and advantages to the Muslim community in Britain. They combine a good education and a common language and heritage with the rest of the society to attract interest in Islam and the Islamic tradition.

My approach in this study is textual and sociological, focusing on the intellectual and spiritual contributions of some of the prominent figures of this group and assessing their role in shaping Islam in British society, and presenting a more balanced picture of the faith than what is usually portrayed. Among those whom the study looks at are: Martin Lings, Gai Eaton, Tim Winter and Hamza Yusuf; the choice of these figures are based primarily on permissibility, spiritual and intellectual achievements, accessibility to their works (in terms of their works being available in the English Language) and respectability among both sides, that is the wider British society and the Muslim communities. The book does not deal with the contribution of Ian Dallas (Abdal Qadir) who has written a number of important texts on Islam and has supervised the translation of some of the classical texts, including the Quran, mainly because it was not easy to obtain interviews with members of the Murabitun (the group which he set up) and Abdal Qadir himself. Also, taking into consideration the long history of the movement, one could suggest that they have not had extensive impact on the wider Muslim community in Britain in comparison to the four case studies featured in this book. However, there is no doubt Abdal Qadir's contribution has had a significant influence on some people since the 1970s. There is perhaps a need for a comprehensive study of Abdal Qadir and his group to be undertaken to helpfully assess their impact on the Muslim community and wider British society over the last 40 years.

The research also investigates the positive role of these converts as cultural mediators between the wider society and the Muslim community as well as between the state and the Muslim citizens, thus helping in the process of building mutual trust, greater cooperation and positive understanding among all parties in Britain and, by extension, Europe. The work, more-over, will help readers to become aware of the evolution of a 'British Islam' that is more open, is rooted in British values and spiritual traditions and forms a part of the continually changing British religious landscape. The present study draws on academic literature, material written by prominent converts, interviews with converts, especially those who are case studies in the book, internet sources and discussions with friends and colleagues who are themselves converts but do not form case studies in the present book. Apart from this introduction, which sets the scene of the study, the book consists of seven chapters, notes, bibliography and an index. Chapter 1 focuses on Islam in Europe and European converts in Western Europe, their life stories, their contributions to the Islamic tradition and their impact on their particular society. Chapter 2 looks at the historical develop-ment of the convert group/community, especially that of early British converts, as well as its main features and characters. Chapter 3 continues the theme of British converts but looks at the post-World War II era and their roles, activities and impact, in particular in the last few decades. The remainder of the book focuses on the contribution to society of British converts at various levels, looks at the intellectual and academic contribu-tions of several respected scholars in British society and assesses their con-tributions towards presenting an accurate view of Islam and their efforts to form a British Islam. The case of the American scholar, Hamza Yusuf, is exceptional due to his positive impact on the possible evolution of British Islam. Chapter 4 contains the first case study, which deals with Martin Lings, while Chapter 5 focuses on Gai Eaton, the subject of the second case study. Tim Winter's work is examined in Chapter 6, and Chapter 7 investigates and highlights the works and efforts of Hamza Yusuf. Rounding off the study, the conclusion explains the positive steps taken by British converts to bridge the divide and pave the way for the formation of a 'British Islam'.

Chapter 1

Islam in Europe

A Historical Perspective

The presence of Islam in Europe is neither an 'alien'[1] nor a recent phenomenon.[2] Europeans have had encounters with Islam ever since its origins in the seventh century and the existence of Muslims in Europe can be traced back to historical Islam.[3] After their success in uniting the Arabian Peninsula and establishing their state in Medina, the Muslims burst outside the peninsula to spread the word of Islam. In the process, they succeeded in taking over Syria, Palestine, Egypt and North Africa, territories that had previously been part of the Byzantine Empire. From North Africa, they sailed to Europe, taking Sicily, the south of Italy[4] and the Iberian Peninsula, and reaching 'as close to England as Poitiers in France in 732.'[5] The conquest of these territories allowed them to establish a Muslim presence in Europe for many centuries, through settlements but also in due course through conversions on a large scale.[6] The advancement of Muslims into Europe created tension and was met with a swift reaction. The faith was vilified and branded as Christian heresy, and its founder, Muhammad, was accused of being an impostor and the anti-Christ.[7] His message was viewed as a potential threat – religiously, politically and strategically – to Europe's interests and hence needed to be contained or eradicated as quickly as possible; however, as long as Islam was united, it was victorious, and Christendom was unable to stop its advance.

The Crusades were aimed primarily at reclaiming lost territories and re-establishing earlier Christian glory, but they were not of sufficient strength and were unable to release Christendom from Islamic rule.[8] Europe had to wait several more centuries for its first chance of revenge when in 1492, Granada, the last major Muslim stronghold in Spain, was taken over by the successful alliances of Queen Isabel of Castile and her husband Ferdinand of Aragon. This victory cleared the way for the return of Catholicism and the expulsion of both Muslims and Jews from the Iberian Peninsula. But by the time the last Muslims had been expelled from Spain at the beginning of the seventeenth century, there was already a heavy presence of Muslims in another part of Europe, this time through the expansion of the Ottomans that started from the mid-fourteenth century and led to the fall of Constantinople in 1453. Victory over the Byzantines allowed the Ottomans to march through the Balkans with ease, in the process establishing Muslim communities as a result of many factors, chief among them being conversion to Islam on the part of some of the local population.[9] The Ottomans even besieged Vienna twice, in 1529 and 1683, although they failed to take the city.[10] In addition, 'Tatar soldiers from the Golden Horde, migrating westward settled in eastern Europe from the late fourteenth century; this led to the establishment of small Muslim communities in Poland and Lithuania.'[11] In contrast to Spain and Italy, Muslim expansion in the east of Europe left permanent Muslim communities.

In western Europe, initial Muslim contacts took place through visiting diplomatic missions from Turkey, Persia and India, but one can also notice ordinary Muslims there, such as Ottoman prisoners of war in Vienna who were left behind after the end of the siege of the city in 1683 and large numbers of merchants and seamen in the ports and trading centres, especially from the seventeenth century onwards.[12] Further interactions occurred during the imperial era when the balance of power shifted to Europe. A variety of well-known factors helped Europe to emerge as a collection of major modern powers in the late eighteenth and early nineteenth centuries. In contrast to Europe, the Muslim world was facing major crises, retreating and gradually giving way, allowing European states to pursue their own interests, which were becoming international in nature. And the Muslim world was at the heart of those interests; Napoleon's invasion of Egypt in 1798 heralded the beginning of the end of the Muslim empire as a major power in the international system and set the scene for European countries to compete with each other to establish spheres of influence in the region.

By 1881, Britain had become a dominant power in India, and soon afterwards it spread its influence over the Arabian Gulf region in order to protect its valuable possession, India. The opening of the Suez Canal in 1869 allowed Britain, after successful competition with other European countries, to take over Egypt in 1882. The occupation of Egypt led to the establishment of an Anglo-Egyptian Condominium over Sudan in 1898. In east Africa, it shared Zanzibar and Somaliland with other European countries and extended its influence as far as Yemen, taking over Aden, a key port on the Arabian Peninsula. France swept through most of north and west Africa, establishing firmly its dominion in countries as far afield as Algeria, Tunisia and Morocco. While Persia was already divided into spheres of influence between Russia and Britain, the Muslim central-Asian territories came under Russian occupation. The Sultanate of Sokoto with its Nigerian colony was absorbed by Britain. In southeast Asia, the Dutch assumed control over Indonesia, while Britain put the Malay states under its protection. By the late nineteenth century the only Muslim power that remained was the Ottoman Empire, which was coming to the end of its lifespan. It had already lost ground to European powers, especially in the Balkans, and, by the beginning of World War I, consisted only of Turkey proper and the Arab countries of the eastern Middle East. The defeat of the Ottomans during World War I led to the final demise of the Muslim power and the taking over by Britain and France of the remaining Arab territories in the Middle East. By 1919, only Afghanistan and Yemen (excluding the port of Aden), as well as Hejaz and Nejd on the Arabian Peninsula, managed to escape direct political subjugation and retained a semblance of independence.[13] The rise of European states as strong powers had major consequences for the Muslim world. It led to complete political and economic subjugation, with Muslims no longer having any control over their natural resources. The colonial relationship that ensued meant a loss of sovereignty and its replacement by political and economic dependence. A huge gap developed between Europe, which was progressing economically, politically and technologically, and the Muslim world, which was retreating in both the military and the political spheres.

During this period, however, other more subtle processes were occurring, the most significant of which was the movement of people from both sides, although somewhat limited at this early stage. From the Muslim world, sailors, traders, diplomats, exiles and students visited Europe for different reasons, although very few decided to stay there permanently. From the European countries, apart from military personnel and foreign diplomats, there were independent travellers who wrote extensively on the cultures of the Muslim world and on their own adventures in the lands of Islam; there were missionaries who were hoping to convert Muslims to Christianity; and there were those who wanted to make their fortunes, taking advantage of the fact that their respective governments were in charge of the political and economic affairs of those lands. Last but not least, there were visitors who wanted to know more of the world beyond the confines of European culture, and there were those who were searching for spiritual and religious fulfilment. Some of this latter group who travelled to the Muslim East converted to Islam; of these, a few stayed and married Muslim women while others returned home and set up their own religious groups to live according to Islamic principles and introduce Islam to non-Muslims.[14]

As mentioned, the movement of people, especially of Muslims migrating to western Europe, was of a limited extent in the first half of the twentieth century, but this pattern changed enormously after World War II, most markedly in industrial western European countries. The collapse of European economies at the end of World War II necessitated a period of reconstruction, which was initiated with the help of the so-called Marshall Plan to help Europe get back on its feet. This created a need for migrant labour to fill shortages in the indigenous European labour market; policies and supporting legislation were therefore created to encourage labourers (the majority of whom were Muslims) from former colonies to come and work in most western European countries, especially France, Germany, Britain, the Netherlands and Belgium. In due course, this legislation set the scene for a number of waves of international migration from the Muslim world; whereas earlier migrants came seeking economic better-ment, later on, especially from the 1970s and 1980s onwards, there were further waves of Muslim immigrants who came mainly for political reasons. The influx of Muslim immigrants in large numbers led to the establish-ment of considerable Muslim communities in various western European countries after they had decided to make these countries their permanent residence. This has altered the demographic composition of Europe and its religious landscape; Europe has become a multicultural society consist-ing of a variety of ethnic and religious groups, of which Muslims are among the most dominant.[15] Their presence on the continent is an inescapable fact, and their numbers are constantly increasing owing to several factors: first, the continuous international migration (both legal and illegal) from Muslim countries, which continues despite the stringent rules enforced in most western European countries in an attempt to reverse it; second, the birth rate among European Muslims, which is higher than among European natives; thirdly, and most importantly, the steady increase, especially in recent decades, in the number of western European natives who have converted to Islam, thus making it the fastest growing religion in Europe. Currently, Islam is the second religion in most western European countries after Christianity. The rest of this chapter will deal with the phenomenon of European converts to Islam.

Some Selected European Converts to Islam

There are no reliable figures as to the number of converts in western Europe,[16] either at the collective level or at the individual national level. As stated earlier, most European states do not usually inquire about religious affiliation in their national censuses, and mosques in most individual European countries do not keep formal records on the number of people who convert to Islam, making the prediction or estimation of numbers very difficult and haphazard, even at the provisional level. It may be added that, due to the current anti-Islamic feeling that has prevailed since the September 11 attacks of 2001, most European converts have decided not only to stop declaring their conversion publicly but have also stopped adopting new Muslim names, as often used to be the case. I know of at least two male friends who for years used Muslim names but after the September 11 attacks decided to revert to their Christian names for fear of discrimination. Like born Muslims, they feel under siege and suspected, but ironically this feeling of suspicion among converts sometimes comes from the Muslim community as well. By the same token, some female converts have also avoided donning the scarf or identifying themselves as Muslims; it is not clear how widespread this issue is, but it is certainly taking place among some female converts. Having said this, it is certainly possible to claim that the faith is attracting followers from among native Europeans – and at an increasing pace.

Conversion to Islam among western Europeans is neither new nor unheard of; the only difference is that in the past conversion took place among a few, mainly notable people who for one reason or another were attracted to Islam and accepted its tenets. In recent years, however, conversion has been taking place at an accelerating pace among people from a variety of social, political, educational and ethnic backgrounds, thus making the phenomenon highly important and significant for all parties concerned. There is now in each western European country a small but significant number of native converts who are highly active in their respective societies, some of them forming and establishing Islamic communities, though these have not yet been recognized as such. Scholars have differed in their explanations for this phenomenon: some have stated factors such as intermarriages, intellectual encounters, spiritual needs, curiosity (especially as a result of surfing the internet) and reaction to anti-Muslim feelings, while others have cited Islamic missionary activities as a driving force behind the increase in the number of converts in western Europe. In my view, this claim must be treated with caution as Muslim missionary work in reality is not well organized and is underfunded, especially after the September 11 attacks. Further, given the nature and contents of these missionary activities, it is very difficult to imagine their success and efficacy, especially among the elites of native European converts.

Despite the fact that European converts are small minorities in their respective countries, they are highly motivated and have taken active roles in mediating between the wider society and the Muslim community, as well as promoting the need for the Muslim communities. Some of them are also making an educational, intellectual/academic and spiritual contribution and hoping to form an expression of Islam that is at ease with the ideals of their respective societies. In tune with the overall theme of the book, the focus here will be on the life stories and intellectual/academic efforts of prominent European scholars who have converted to Islam and have contributed intellectually and spiritually to faith in general and Islam in western Europe in particular. The criteria for selecting these figures are based primarily on their prominence and seniority, popularity and accessibility (whether their works are available in English or not) and their impact on or the role they play through their writings in shaping the Islamic discourse in both their respective societies and the wider European context. It is important to stress that the list is by no means exhaustive and that, furthermore, my book deals neither comprehensively nor in depth with their intellectual achievements, for each one of these figures is a prominent scholar in his or her his own right, and to do them justice would require a separate and detailed work for each, which the scope of the current study does not permit. Hence, I will give a brief and concise account of their conversion and of their works on Islamic themes that have contributed immensely to the faith in their respective societies and beyond. The majority of the selected group have left us for the world of spirits but are still living with us as they have left an enduring legacy that continues to affect and influence so many people, both intellectually and spiritually. Moreover, several of them are little known in the English-speaking world; even though some good work has been done on them recently, this work is still confined to the privileged few. The average reader is still too unaware of their works to appreciate their contribution and impact. I still remember vividly (and still feel outraged by) a discussion I had recently with a prominent member of University's Philosophy department about the possibility of introducing a course on the writings of some of these scholars, about whom he was completely oblivious! But, first, let us get started.

René Guénon or Sheikh Abdul Wahed Yahia

Little is known about René Guénon in the English-speaking world despite the fact that he has left an enduring legacy that has had an important impact on that part of the world[17]. Born on 15 November 1886 in the city of Blois in west-central France, he had a conservative Catholic upbringing. As a child, he suffered from health problems that delayed his official education until the age of 12.[18] To compensate for this, his aunt taught him how to read and write until he was finally able to attend school. In 1906, he moved to Paris, where he was introduced to different spiritualist groups, with which he kept in continuous contact. He also joined Rollin College, where he gained a bachelor's degree in Philosophy and Mathematics. He spent the early years of his adulthood studying mathematics and philosophy, subjects that he both loved and excelled in later. In 1908, he became a member of the Grand Masonic Lodge and joined the Gnostic Church, which emphasizes the philosophical inquiries that lead to a deeper understanding of the Ultimate Reality. He likewise became interested in studying many traditional esoteric principles related to Hinduism, Islam, Christianity and Taoism. In 1909, he started publishing and editing a review journal called *La Gnose*, to which he contributed many works on the subjects of spirituality and esotericism.

In 1910, he met the famous French painter, Gustav Ageli, who was already a Muslim.[19] His relationship with Ageli strengthened, especially when the latter started to take an active role in *La Gnose* by publishing research works and French translations of Sufi texts. Ageli's influence on Guénon was crucial, especially on his eventual conversion to Islam. In 1912, he was initiated into Sufism, and, after an intense study of Islam, he embraced the faith and took the name Abdul al-Wahid Yahya. In 1915–16, Guénon managed to complete his degree in Philosophy from the prestigious Sorbonne University, after which he embarked on postgraduate studies, writing his PhD on the subject of Hindu doctrines. However, his thesis was rejected by the doctoral committee.[20]

This incident caused him to leave academia and focus on researching and writing. In 1924, he published one of his major works, entitled the *Orient and Occident* or *East and West*,[21] which deals primarily with comparative philosophy and spirituality. On the subject of Oriental Metaphysics, which was of keen interest to him, he explains the different approaches and views of Eastern and Western philosophies to the unseen world. He stresses the universality of metaphysics, pointing out that it belongs to all authentic religions. He warns that, in its pursuit of scientific materialism, Europe has lost most of its spiritual values; therefore, it is advisable to make use of Eastern traditions since their metaphysical principles are still intact. From this perspective, one may detect his disillusionment with the direction of Western civilization. In 1927, he published what became a highly acclaimed and widely read book, *The Crisis of the Modern World*,[22] followed by the *Reign of Quantity and the Signs of the Times*.[23] Earning him fame, publicity and respect, and reprinted many times, these books are still regarded today as essential reading for those interested in understanding the philosophical roots and development of Western culture and civilization.

One year after the publication of *The Crisis in the Modern World*, Guénon lost his wife. About this time he received an offer from a publishing house in Paris to travel to Egypt as part of a project involving the study and publication of some Sufi texts. He set off to Egypt in 1930 for 3 months' research leave and never returned, living in a house near Al-Azhar University and maintaining close and regular contact with Abdul Halim Mahmud, the rector of Al Azhar and a scholar of Sufism. In 1934, Guénon re-married and the marriage produced four children. During his permanent exile in Egypt, prominent Traditionalist scholars such as Titus Burckhardt, Frithjof Schuon and Martin Lings visited him, the latter even working with him while he was resident in Egypt. Nonetheless, Guénon generally preferred to stay out of the limelight and lived a secluded life, devoting his time to writing and publishing his major books and articles. In the end, the poor health that had accompanied him for most of his life worsened, and he died on 7 January 1951 at the age of 64. He was buried in Cairo[24].

Guénon left an enduring legacy of writings that demonstrate his ability as a competent mathematician, great philosopher, dedicated traditionalist and respected critic, especially of Western modern culture. His writings cover a wide range of subject areas, including metaphysics, symbolism, the failings of the modern world, spirituality and esotericism as well as the traditional sciences. He was the architect and founder of the Traditionalist school of thought that played, and continues to play, an important role in advocating and defending the traditional view based on the universality of Truth, or Perennialism. Perennialism holds the view that all authentic religions have the same perennial philosophy, or universal truth, and that this can only be realized through a return to an authentic religious form. Guénon was a prolific writer and, as stated above, his most influential writings are *Orient and Occident*, and *The Crisis of the Modern World*, a profound analysis and critique of the main characteristics and philosophical outlook of the modern way of life, as viewed from a traditional perspective.

His main theme in this regard was to shed light on the sharp differences or contradictions between the traditional worldview, as shared or accepted by all authentic world religions, and modernism. For him, modernism (to be equated with Westernism) was an oddity or anomaly in the history of humankind, a symptom of spiritual decadence, and the remedy for this inversion lay in the return to the wisdom of Eastern spirituality in order to help the West regain its lost spirit[25].

Other important books by Guénon are *Multiple States of Being*, and *Fundamental Symbols of Sacred Science*. These focus on the metaphysical and philosophical misconceptions prevailing in the modern West and the need to revive traditional sciences and doctrines that have been in decline in the West as a result of the rise of modern philosophy. His writings, moreover, include works that deal with certain concepts and specific religious traditions from the traditional perspective, for example, *The Symbolism of the Cross, Man and His Becoming according to the Vedanta, Introduction to the Study of Hindu Doctrines (his PhD thesis)* and *The Grand Triad*. Guénon's understanding of science is part and parcel of his efforts to revive the traditional worldview. His metaphysical views, in brief, lie at the heart of the Traditional School – namely the existence of the primordial and perennial Truth that is expressed in different religious traditions and metaphysical principles but has been lost in the modern world. Guénon believes that the illnesses of the modern world are caused by its refusal to accept and comprehend the metaphysical world, a world that is composed of both philosophy and spirituality. He sees everything in the physical world as an expression of the metaphysical principles that are contained in the primordial teaching of religions and applies these principles to every subject he deals with. Hence, he judges both the value of the traditional sciences of nature and the claims of modern secular science according to their distance or proximity to these principles[26]. Guénon was an ardent defender of traditional religions, chief among them Islam, and his writings clarified the misconceptions that many people had about the philosophical and spiritual principles of Islam and have had a great impact on many intellectuals, especially in the West. His legacy was, and continues to be, the point of entry for Europeans, especially among the elite and intellectuals, to spiritual Islam.

Leopold Weiss or Muhammad Asad

Leopold Weiss, one of the most prominent and highly respected thinkers of the twentieth century, was born in July 1900 in the city of Lwow, which was at that time part of the Austrian Empire but is now part of Poland. His Jewish parents descended from a long line of Rabbis and hoped that young Leopold would continue the line that had been broken only by his father, who had decided to become a barrister. Having this desire in mind, they decided to give him a solid Jewish education to prepare him for his future rabbinical career. Hence, he received rigorous instruction in the Hebrew religion from a private tutor who was hired specifically for this purpose, and the child was encouraged to spend long hours learning the sacred scriptures. By the time he was thirteen, he was fluent in reading and writing Hebrew, had an excellent knowledge of Aramaic, had completed the study of the Old Testament in the original and had become acquainted with the main source of Jewish Biblical exegesis, the Targum.[27] Despite these efforts, from an early age the boy had apparently showed no interest in the study of Judaism, later eloquently describing his feeling in the following way: 'In spite of all this budding religious wisdom, or may be because of it, I soon developed a supercilious feeling toward many of the premises of the Jewish faith. To be sure, I did not disagree with the teaching of moral righteousness so strongly emphasized throughout the Jewish scriptures, nor with the sublime God-consciousness of the Hebrew Prophets – but it seemed to me that the God of the Old Testament and the Talmud was unduly concerned with the ritual by means of which His worshippers were supposed to worship Him. It also occurred to me that this God was strangely preoccupied with the destinies of one particular nation, the Hebrews. The very build up of the Old Testament as a history of the descendants of Abraham tended to make God appear not as the creator and sustainer of all mankind but, rather, as a tribal deity adjusting all creation to the requirements of a "chosen people": rewarding them with conquests if they were righteous, and making them suffer at the hands of non-believers whenever they strayed from the prescribed path. Viewed against these fundamental shortcomings, even the ethical fervour of the later Prophets, like Isaiah and Jeremiah, seemed to be barren of a universal message.'[28]

Despite the fact that he did not pursue a religious career as his parents had desired, Weiss stressed that his early religious studies did help him to understand the essential aims of religion as such, whatever its form. According to him, his dissatisfaction with Judaism did not encourage him to seek spiritual truths in other religions. On the contrary, like much of the youth of his generation, he drifted away from all institutional religions; theological and philosophical issues did not matter to him – what mattered to him at that time was action, excitement and adventure. After World War I, Weiss started his study of art history and philosophy at the University of Vienna, but without great enthusiasm, and, as time went by, his interest in pursuing an academic career faded. In 1920, again disregarding his father's wishes, he left Vienna for Berlin to seek a career in journalism, for he was very interested in becoming a writer. As he struggled to build a new life for himself, his years in Berlin were initially difficult, but then he managed to join a newspaper as a reporter.

In 1922, he was invited by his uncle to visit Jerusalem, where he was exposed to the life and thought of the Arabs and became impressed by the way Islam infused their everyday lives with meaning, purpose, spiritual strength and inner peace. During this time he began writing articles for the *Frankfurter Zeitung*, the prestigious German newspaper. This was the beginning of his career as the newspaper's special correspondent for Middle Eastern affairs. In this capacity, he travelled extensively throughout the Middle East, mixing with ordinary people, debating Middle Eastern issues with Muslim thinkers and intellectuals and meeting heads of states in Palestine, Egypt, Iran, Afghanistan, Syria and Iraq. In the process, his interest in the Arab and Islamic way of life grew, and his knowledge of the Islamic scriptures, as well as of Islamic thought and history, intensified.[29] Islam and its followers had certainly made a good impression on him. On this issue, he wrote: 'I became increasingly aware of an absorbing desire to know what it was that lay at the root of this emotional security that made Arab life so different from the European: and that desire seemed to be mysteriously bound up with my own innermost problems. I began to look for openings that would give me a better insight into the character of the Arabs, into the ideas that had shaped them and made them spiritually so different from the Europeans. I began to read intensively about their history, culture and religion. And in the urge I felt to discover what it was that moved their hearts and filled their minds and gave them direction, I seemed to sense an urge to discover some hidden forces that moved myself, and filled me, and promised to give me direction.'[30]

In 1926, after concluding his travels, he returned to Frankfurt, where he continued to write for the *Frankfurter Zeitung* and married Elsa Schiemann, a widowed acquaintance who was 15 years older than himself. However, his work with the *Frankfurter Zeitung* did not last long, for he resigned his position and moved to Berlin again, where he worked for other, less famous newspapers. Soon after his move to Berlin (in September 1926), Weiss converted to Islam. The episode which prompted him to

take this decision was so moving that it may be worth quoting excerpts of
it from his book, *The Road to Mecca*, which he wrote 30 years later:

> One day . . . I found (myself) travelling in the Berlin subway. I began to
> look around at all the other faces . . . faces belonging without exception
> to well-dressed, well-fed people: and in almost every one of them I could
> discern an expression of hidden suffering . . . I wonder, do they know
> themselves what is going on in themselves? I knew that they did not – for
> otherwise they could not go on . . . without any hopes other than having
> more material amenities . . . . When (I) returned home, I picked the
> (Quran) up to put it away, but just as I was about to close it, my eyes fell
> on the open page before me, and I read: 'You are obsessed by greed for
> more and more until you go down to your graves. Nay, but you will come
> to know! And once again: Nay, but you will come to know! Nay, if you but
> knew it with the knowledge of certainty, you would indeed see the hell you
> are in. In time, indeed, you shall see it with the eye of certainty: And on
> that Day you will be asked what you have done with the boon of life.' For a
> moment I was speechless. I think that the book shook in my hands. Is it not
> an answer to what (I) saw in the subway? It was an answer so decisive that
> all doubt was suddenly at an end. I knew now, beyond all doubt, that it was
> a God-inspired book I was holding in my hand... At all times people had
> known greed: but at no time before had greed outgrown a mere eager-
> ness to acquire things and become an obsession that blurred the sight
> of everything else: an irresistible craving to get, to do, to contrive more
> and more – more today than yesterday, and more tomorrow than today
> . . . and then hunger, that insatiable hunger for ever new goals gnawing
> at man's soul: 'Nay, if you but knew if you would see the hell you are in.'
> This, I saw, was not the mere human wisdom of a man of a distant past in
> distant Arabia. However wise he may have been, such a man could not by
> himself have foreseen the torment so peculiar to this twentieth century.
> Out of the Koran a voice greater than the voice of Muhammad.[31]

His wife Elsa converted shortly after him. He then resigned his position at
the newspaper and set off on a pilgrimage with her to Mecca. Nine days after
their arrival, Elsa suddenly passed away as a result of a sudden, short illness.
Her sudden departure affected him tremendously, and it took him a while
to recover from the consequences of her loss. Weiss stayed in Saudi Arabia
for about 6 years, during which time he studied Arabic, the Quran, the
Hadith and Islamic history, besides becoming competent in Islamic law and
Islamic political theory. He also met prominent leaders, chief among them

being King Abdul Aziz, the founder of Saudi Arabia; King Faisal, son of King Abdul Aziz; and King Abdullah of Jordan. His extensive travels and contacts with Bedouins during his stay in Arabia gave him an insight into Arab culture and the Arab way of life that he fully enjoyed and appreciated.

To broaden his knowledge of Muslims living in other parts of the world, he went to India in 1932, where he met the poet and philosopher, Muhammad Iqbal, the spiritual founder of modern Pakistan. They soon formed a close relationship, and Weiss, under pressure and persuasion from Iqbal, decided to stay in India to help form the intellectual framework of the future Islamic state of Pakistan. His presence in India coincided with the outbreak of World War II, and this led him to being imprisoned as an Austrian citizen by the British governor of India of the day. He remained in prison for the full 6 years of the war from 1939 to 1945, the only Muslim among 3,000 European detainees in India, the majority of who were Nazi sympathizers. When Pakistan was created in 1947, the government entrusted him with the responsibility of building the intellectual foundations of the new state. He subsequently became head of the Middle East division of the Pakistan foreign ministry before being promoted to become Pakistan's Minister Plenipotentiary to the United Nations in New York, a post that he held until 1952, when he resigned to start working on his autobiography, *The Road to Mecca*, at the suggestion of an American friend. The book was completed in 1955, the year in which he left New York to settle finally in Spain with his wife Pola Asad, whom he had met and married in New York. Although his diplomatic career had come to an end, his writing never ceased. Indeed, he continued writing until his death in February 1992 at the age of 91.

Weiss was a prolific writer and his books, focusing mainly on Islam and Muslims, covered a wide range of topics. Among his most acclaimed publications are the following: *Unromantic East*, which is based on his travel experiences as a correspondent for the *Frankfurter Zeitung* and allows a deep insight into the Middle Eastern way of life and culture; *Islam at the Crossroads*,[32] the first book he published after he converted to Islam and an analysis of some of the problems facing the Muslim world at the time, besides containing a critique of some aspects of the Western way of life; and *The Road to Mecca*, a monumental and captivating work in which he vividly describes his 'Journey into Islam'. Although published in 1954, it still attracts interest among a wide readership in Britain and beyond. In 2009, Al-Mustaklah satellite channel, based in London, devoted almost two weeks to broadcasting daily programmes in Arabic as well as English on the importance of this book, encouraging both Muslims and non-Muslims to read and reflect on it.

Other important works are *Sahih al-Bukhari: the Early Years of Islam*, a translation and commentary on some of the Hadith recorded in Bukhari's collection; *The Principles of State and Government in Islam*, dealing with the legal and political framework of an Islamic state; *This Law of Ours and Other Essays*[33] on Islamic and Western civilizations, Islamic Law and the role of Ijtihad in facing modern challenges; and *The Message of the Quran*, a translation of the Quranic text into English and a commentary on it. This work is based on a rational approach and is consequently used for the most part by scholars of a modernist orientation. It is especially popular among Muslim feminists, as his liberal interpretations of some of the verses are related to women. A case in point is the verse that is related to women's dress, where, contrary to traditional commentaries which make female head covering obligatory, Weiss interprets the verse in a more secular way and renders it in a more specific rather than general fashion. He says,

> The specific, time-bound formulation of the above verse (evident in the reference to the wives and daughters of the Prophet), as well as the deliberate vagueness of the recommendation that women should draw upon themselves some of their garment (*min jalabibihinna*) when in public, makes it clear that this verse was not meant to be an injunction (*hukm*) in the general, timeless sense of this term but, rather, a moral guideline to be observed against the ever-changing background of time and social environment. This finding is reinforced by the concluding reference to God's forgiveness and grace.[34]

Weiss's contribution to Islam is immense in every respect. A man of integrity and humility, he found peace, security, sanctity and spiritual fulfilment in Islam. He firmly believed that Islam, despite all the problems that it faced as a result of the shortcomings of some of its followers, was still by far the greatest driving force humanity had ever witnessed. As such, he dedicated most of his life to defending his adopted faith in the face of Western onslaughts and criticism, frequently asserting that the dismal situation prevailing in the Muslim world was due primarily to the misinterpretation of Islam by Muslims rather than to Islam *per se*. For him, once Islam was interpreted properly, it would certainly provide its followers with the spiritual and ethical sustenance that both Judaism and Christianity were no longer in a position to provide or offer. His books, articles and speeches that focus on defending the cause of Islam and the Muslim faith represent his enduring legacy.

Titus Burckhardt or Sidi Ibrahim Izz al-Din

Titus Burckhardt, a widely acclaimed German-Swiss scholar, was born in 1908 in Florence, Italy, into a patrician protestant family which originally came from Basel, Switzerland. His father, Carl Burckhardt, was a sculptor, and his great uncle, Jacob Burckhardt, was a famous art historian. He was a school friend of Fritjhof Schuon's, one of the main advocates of the Perennial philosophy in the second half of the twentieth century, and their acquaintance was to develop into an enduring spiritual and intellectual friendship that lasted their whole lives. Initially, Burckhardt followed in his father's footsteps as a sculptor and illustrator, attending art schools in both Switzerland and Italy, but he later discovered that his interest lay more in oriental arts and traditions. Hence, he embarked on an intensive study of Eastern doctrines, the history of oriental art and oriental languages. This led him to travel to Morocco to learn more about traditional Islamic art, the Arabic language and spirituality. He described how he learned Arabic in Morocco as follows:

> From time to time Mulay Ali received me in a friend's orchard, in order to read Arabic texts with me. He chose these texts so that they might not only be useful to me linguistically, but would also demonstrate some aspect or other tradition. Often, when I arrived at the orchard, which lay within the city walls encircled by high hedges of bamboo, and crossed over a narrow dyke that facilitated the irrigation of the low-lying beds of mint and melons, he would already be sitting there, under an old fig tree, on a red mat that he always carried with him.[35]

His journey to Morocco was to change his life completely, both personally as well as intellectually. Apart from studying the Arabic language and Arabic literature, he also began an extensive study of Islamic jurisprudence and classical Sufism from the traditional masters of Islamic spirituality. He subsequently embraced Islam, adopting the name Ibrahim Izz al-Din, and followed the teachings of Sufi masters such as Sidi Muhammad Bouchara at Sale and Mulay Ali al-Darqawi in the famous traditional city of Fez. Burckhardt described his first encounter with Mulay Ali vividly.

> In the spring of 1933 I made up my mind to visit him in his house in Fez. He received me without too many questions, motioned me to sit down on a low cushion in his large bare room, took up an old Arabic book, and began to read to me about the second coming of Christ at the end

of time. Since I was not sitting directly in front of him, and since he had allowed the hood of his jellaba to slip backwards from his head, I could readily observe his noble and already aged face. It expressed two-fold nobility: his descent from the Prophet – and thus from the peak of Arab aristocracy – showed itself in the clear bold line of forehead and nose and in the fine contours of his temples and cheeks, which were sharply illumined by light from the inner courtyard; it made me think of the most noble of the faces in El Greco's 'Burial of Count Orgaz'. But in addition his features were marked by a spiritual discipline – the consciously assumed inheritance of his illustrious forefathers – which emphasized their simplicity and sobriety . . . Such was my first meeting with this venerable elder who, contrary to my expectation, declared himself ready to teach me the fundaments of traditional Arab science.[36]

Later he learnt that his old friend Schoun had also embraced Islam and had joined the *tariqah* of Sheikh Ahmed al-Alawi of Algeria, that is to say the Shadiliyyah Al-alwiyyah *tariqah*. Hence, he decided to join Schuon's *tariqah* when he returned to Europe.

Burckhardt gained a deep knowledge and developed a great appreciation of Islamic civilization, especially Islamic art and architecture. For him, 'The highest meaning of all Islamic art, its actual content, is always the unity, and light is unity, which manifests itself in a variety of graduations, and yet by its nature always remains indivisible . . . . There is no essential difference between spiritual and secular art in Islam. A living room can always be a room for prayer, too, in which the same rites may be performed as in a mosque . . . . its function is to provide man with a framework worthy of his dignity, to make him its centre, and at the same time to remind him that he himself is God's representative on earth.'[37] During the 1950s and 1960s, he became the artistic director of the Urs Graf Publishing House in Lausanne and Olten, Switzerland, where he managed to produce and publish a series of reproductions of important medieval illuminated manuscripts such as *The Book of Kells, The Book of Durrow* and *The Book of Lindisfarne.* The publication of these texts earned him wide acclaim among experts as well as the general public; while there he also edited a series of volumes entitled *Homesteads of the Spirit,* historical/spiritual studies of certain manifestations of sacred civilizations focusing on places such as Mount Athos, Celtic Ireland, Sinai, Constantinople and numerous others[38].

In the 1970s, Burckhardt was asked by the Moroccan government and UNESCO to work on a plan to safeguard the historical monuments of the city of Fez in Morocco. He responded to this request with great enthusiasm since he loved Morocco and knew Fez and its artistic heritage intimately, for he had already written his famous book on the city. The plan was completed at the end of 1977. In April 1980, he returned to Fez to take part in a UNESCO-organized campaign to save Fez, which had been placed on its world heritage list. It was to be his last earthly visit to the city which he loved and cared about so much.[39] After a highly productive life, Burckhardt died in the city of Lausanne in 1984 at the age of 75. He is regarded as one of the main expounders of the 'Traditionalist' or 'Perennialist' school of thought of the twentieth century, devoting most of his life to studying and writing on the Universal Truth, primarily in the areas of metaphysics, cosmology and traditional art, especially Islamic art. Although Burckhardt wrote exclusively in German and French, most of his excellent works have been translated into English, giving the English reader a chance to appreciate his contribution to Islamic art and civilization. The legacy he has left consists of precious works related to metaphysics, cosmology, the traditional sciences and traditional art and architecture. His great contributions to Islam lie in at least two major fields: Islamic art and Sufism. On the former, he wrote his impressive pieces such as *Sacred Art in East and West; Art of Islam;*[40] *Fez, the City of Islam*[41]; and *Moorish Culture in Spain.*[42] In all of these books, he has unveiled the symbols of Islamic art and their inner meaning and succeeded in highlighting the quintessence of Islamic art and its relevance and relation to the core teachings of the Islamic faith.[43]

Defending Islamic art against all criticism, Burckhardt states: 'The aniconism of Islamic art comprises fundamentally two aspects; on the one hand, it preserves the primordial dignity of man, whose form, "made in the image of God", is neither imitated nor usurped by a work of art that is inevitably limited and one-sided; on the other hand, nothing that could possibly be an idol, even in a relative and wholly provisional manner, may interpose itself between man and the invisible presence of God. What comes before all is the witnessing that there is 'No divinity but God': this dissolves every objectivization of the Divine even before it can occur.'[44] His monumental efforts, both theoretical and practical, led to a wide recognition, appreciation and finally acceptance of Islamic art in the West as a category of its own, namely qua Islamic art. Previously, Islamic art as such had gone largely unrecognized in the West; attention, if any, had focused on specific Islamic regions such as Arabian, Persian, Turkish or Indian art, ignoring the overall Islamic worldview integrated into it. Regional Islamic arts do exist, but all these artistic endeavours are informed by the sacred revelations and have derived their distinctive characteristics from the underlying Islamic perspective. In addition to his writings, his supervision of major exhibitions of Islamic art and his attendance at the two 'World of Islam' festivals in London in the 1970s paved the way for the introduction of graduate programmes in Islamic art as a distinct academic field in universities worldwide. Similarly, it heralded the establishment of Islamic art galleries in major museums throughout the world. For this, the Muslim world owes a great debt of gratitude to Titus Burckhardt.[45]

His second major contribution to Islam lies within the field of Islamic mysticism. Burckhardt did pioneering work in making Sufism known to the West, especially the work and teachings of Ibn Arabi, the Sufi master of Islamic gnosis. First, he translated Ibn Arabi's *Fusus al-Hikam*, or 'Wisdom of the Prophets', *Al-Insan al-Kamil* ('The Perfect Man') by Abd al-Karim al-Jili[46] and letters of Shaikh Al-Arabi Ad-Darqawi. He then wrote his own works on Sufism, such as an *Introduction to Sufi Doctrine*[47] and an *Introduction to Sufism*. His achievement in this regard manifested itself in the fact that he 'succeeded in reaching the heart of Akbarian metaphysics and making it known in contemporary language without divorcing it from the barakah of Sufism or the rest of the Sufi tradition.'[48] Nasr eloquently sums up his great contribution to Islam as follows: 'Burckhardt . . . left Western academic circles to embrace Islam both intellectually and "existentially". He was . . . a person of exceptional intellectual and spiritual gifts who went to the Islamic world as a young man to master the Islamic disciplines from within at the feet of masters of both the exoteric and esoteric sciences. He was providentially chosen to express the truths of the Islamic tradition, and in fact tradition in its universal sense, to the modern world and in a language comprehensible to contemporary man. His writings in fact represent one of the major formulations and statements of traditional Islam in the modern world.'[49]

Murad Wilfried Hofmann

A widely acclaimed and highly respected German diplomat, Wilfried Hofmann caused uproar among the German people by converting to Islam in 1980 while in the service of his country. The protest was based on the question of how such a high-ranking person could adopt Islam, given Western perceptions of the faith! His inclusion here is mainly based on his high-profile position as a former diplomat and ambassador, as well as on the impact his conversion has had on Germans, and by extension Europeans, especially their elites. Born into a Catholic family in 1931, Hofmann spent his school years in his home town of Aschaffenburg. In 1950, he went to study at Union College in New York state, where he majored in Sociology and Economics. After completing his first degree, he returned to Germany to start his PhD research on the 'Contempt of court by publications under the U.S. and German Law', completing it in 1957. In 1960, he gained a Master's degree in American Law from Harvard University. Soon afterwards, he embarked on a high-profile career: from 1961 to 1964, he worked in the German Foreign Service as an expert on issues of defence and nuclear deterrence; from 1979 to 1983 he served as the director of NATO and defence affairs in Bonn; and from 1983 to 1987 as the director of information for NATO in Brussels. He then represented Germany as an ambassador, first in Algeria from 1987 to 1990 and then in Morocco from 1990 to 1994. In 1995, he resigned his post in the German Foreign Service and went into retirement; for a while he lived with his Turkish wife in Istanbul, Turkey, but he currently lives in Bonn, where he lectures on Islam and Islamic issues.[50]

In his book, *Journey to Islam*, Hofmann stresses that his conversion to Islam was not sudden; rather, it was a long process spanning many years and culminating in his definitive decision to embrace the faith. Of this he says:

'For some time now, striving for ever more precision and brevity, I have tried to put on paper, in a systematic way, all philosophical truths which, in my view, can be ascertained beyond reasonable doubt. In the course of this effort, it dawned on me that the typical attitude of an atheist is not an intelligent one; that man simply cannot escape a decision to believe; that the createdness of what exists around us is obvious; that Islam undoubtedly finds itself in the greatest harmony with overall reality. Thus I realize, not without shock, that step by step, in spite of myself and almost unconsciously, in feeling and thinking, I have grown into being a Muslim. Only one last step remains to be taken: to formalize my conversion'[51].

In giving the account of his spiritual growth that led ultimately to his drastic decision, Hofmann stresses that he 'had felt Islam's magnetic attraction for many years, if not decades, because [he] felt intellectually and emotionally so much at home with Islam as if [he] had been there before'.[52] As stated above, Hofmann's conversion to Islam went through many stages and took a considerable time to mature. Many factors paved the way for him to enter into the fold of Islam, the first being in 1961/62 when he became an attaché to the German embassy in Algeria. There he saw at first hand the atrocities endured by the innocent Algerian people: 'Each day dozens of people were killed in the streets of Algiers, mostly from close range, execution style, simply for being an Arab, or for speaking up for Algeria's independence.'[53] The situation in Algeria at the time left him with bitter memories that have continued to haunt him even to the present day; one of those deplorable events he eloquently describes thus:

> On my way to the France V radio station . . . [a]n Arab who was crossing the street in front me was suddenly shot from the walkway by a European-looking gunman and collapsed right in front of my left front fender. With his gun, the assassin motioned me to drive on so that he could finish off his victim. But I would not and could not possibly do that. Finally, he condescended to walk around and give his victim the coup de grace. After that he slowly walked away, without the least sign of haste.[54]

These sad occurrences accompanied his first encounter with Islam as practised in real life:

> I witnessed the patience and resilience of the Algerian people in the face of extreme suffering . . . their confidence of victory, as well as their humanity amidst such misery . . . In order to find out what makes those incredible 'natives' tick, I began to read 'their book', the Quran . . . I have never stopped reading it to this very day.[55]

His second attraction to the world of Islam arose from his appreciation of Islamic art and architecture, especially their aesthetic characteristics and their spiritual roles in Muslim life. Early in life, Hofmann developed a great interest in art, beauty and ballet dancing, prompting him to read more about the history of art and attend ballet performances, where he met prominent dancers of the time. Thus, from 1955 to 1980, he worked as a ballet critic for *Das Tanzarchiv* in Cologne, *Ballet Today* in London and *Dance News* in New York and, also, from 1971 to 1973, as an instructor on the history of dance and ballet aesthetics at the Cologne Stage Dance Institute. All these positions he held while pursuing his main career as a lawyer and diplomat. When he had the opportunity to learn about Islamic art, it quickly became a powerful and exhilarating key experience for him; major Islamic architectural monuments such as the Alhambra in Granada and the great mosque in Cordoba convinced him that they were truly the products of a noble and sophisticated civilization. In this way, Islamic art has become his main priority and his 'new aesthetic home.'[56] For him, the appeal of Islamic art lies in its intimate and universal presence of Islam as a religion in all of its artistic manifestations: Calligraphy, space filling arabesque ornaments, carpet patterns, mosque and housing architecture, as well as urban planning. I am thinking of the brightness of the mosques, of the democratic spirit of their architectural layout; I am also thinking of the introspective quality of Muslim palaces, their anticipation of paradise in gardens full of shade, fountains and rivulets; of the intricate socially functional structure of old Islamic urban centres, which fosters community spirit and transparency of the market, tempers heat and wind, and assures the integration of the mosque and adjacent welfare centres for the poor, schools, and hostels into the market and living quarters . . . markets like the ones in [most Muslim countries] . . . are all well-integrated Islamic organisms functioning much along the same lines . . . everything . . . seems measured, solidly based on time-tested traditions. What I experienced as so blissfully Islamic in so many places . . . is the tangible effect which Islamic harmony, the Islamic way of life, and the Islamic treatment of space leave on both heart and mind.[57]

The third factor that hastened his religious transformation was the message of the Quran. As a young man, Hofmann was neither an atheist nor an agnostic but a religiously inclined person believing that there was not enough proof to deny the existence of God. He also considered that the intellectual denial or acceptance of God continued to be a matter of faith that was based on whatever seemed logical for the individual person. With this axiom in mind, he became a firm believer in the matter of faith. Nonetheless, in time he gradually became troubled by the notion that the Christian revelation had to be understood as *a priori* in conformity with the interpretation given by Paul. He felt especially uneasy with the concepts of the original sin, the divinity of Jesus, incarnation, sacrificial death and the Trinity and started to seek answers elsewhere. He described how the illumination came when he read Verse 38 of Chapter 53 of the Quran, which states that 'no bearer of burdens shall bear the burden of another.'[58] For him, this verse rejects the concept of original sin, the notion of intersession, the idolization of saints, church hierarchies and the role of sacrament; by implication, it also lays bare Christian teachings on salvation, incarnation, sacrificial death and the Trinity. In time, he began to see Islam as the pristine religion, based on the belief in the oneness of God, who has no partner, son or associate. He also saw Islam as the pure and original form of Abrahamic monotheism, which has succeeded in avoiding any subsequent process of deification.[59] In *Journey to Makkah* the effect that the Quran had on him is described in the following way:

'The Quran showed me the most lucid, most straightforward, the most abstract – thus historically most advanced – and least anthropomorphic concept of God. The Quran's ontological statements, as well as its ethical teachings, impressed me as profoundly plausible, "as good as gold", so there was no room for even the slightest doubt about the authenticity of Muhammad's prophetic mission. People who understand human nature cannot fail to appreciate the infinite wisdom of the "Dos and Don'ts" handed down from God to man in the form of the Quran'.[60]

Since his conversion in 1980 Hofmann has devoted most of his time to explaining the essence of Islam to both Muslims and non-Muslims. He believes that Islam as a faith can provide a cure to some of the current problems facing humanity in the contemporary world. His main focus is on the situation of Muslims in the West, but also on relations between Islam and the West, especially the issue of how to bridge the gap between the two and build bridges based on their common roots and heritage. A prolific author, he writes in both German and English. His main works are *Journey to Islam*, a record in which he reveals his encounters with Islam and the religious outlook of its people that ultimately led to his conversion and a work that aims to contribute to a better understanding and appreciation of Islam by non-Muslims, especially those in the West who still view the faith with suspicion;[61] *Journey to Makkah*,[62] a description of day-to-day life as a practising Muslim and an account of what happens when a Muslim attempts to live and practise Islam in the modern world and how others perceive and react to this way of life; *Islam and Quran*,[63] an introduction to all the main aspects of the religion of Islam, but also focusing on the Quran, especially its structure, formation, and teachings; and *Religion on the Rise, Islam in the Third Millennium*[64] and *Islam: the Alternative*,[65] both of which deal with issues relating to Muslims in the West, Islam and the West and the future of Islam in the modern world.

Throughout his writings, the underlying premise has been to stress the fallacy of the theories of the 'end of history' and the 'clash of civilisations'. He is an outspoken critic of some aspects of the Western way of life, for he thinks that the West, because of its excessive rationality, has lost its ideological moorings and Christian values. According to him, the West is 'the first region and culture in world history which has become agnostic or outright atheist both in theory and practice. The West has entirely lost its transcendental moorings. While still profiting from its Christian heritage, it is no longer Christian in the true sense of the word.'[66] The outcome of this has been drastic in terms of the spiritual, moral, social, environmental and economic consequences. Thus, he sees that Islam and Muslims have something to contribute to the future of the West to help overcome some of the problems that have beset it, asserting: 'I am thoroughly convinced that the West will either learn from Islam to honour again some of the most basic values only recently forgotten there, or that it will collapse in turmoil. You can live against the divine order of things some of the time, but not all of the time.' For him, Islam could help the West to eradicate racism and social prejudice, achieve social cohesion and a sense of community, improve its economy and restore its lost spirituality. His outspoken advocacy of Islam as a remedy for Western problems has exposed him to harsh criticisms in his own country, and his book *Islam: the Alternative* was hotly debated in the German parliament. Feminists and liberals in particular accused him of being an Islamic fundamentalist. Although Hofmann has been critical of Western culture, he emphasizes the fact that not everything in the West is bad. For him, the West is a mixed bag, and rejecting it totally or copying it blindly would be a mistake. Instead, Muslims ought to choose the good and leave the bad aside. He also advises Muslims, especially those living in the West, to try and integrate fully into the wider society so that Islam might become an integral part of Western heritage. For him, normalization and the integration of Islam in the West, especially in Europe, requires compromise on both sides: on the one hand, the West has to acknowledge and respect the Islamic contribution to Western civilization and must allow in their constitutions space for Muslims to practise the core principles of their religion; on the other hand, Muslims have to integrate into wider Western society, learn the language of the country they are in and emphasize Islam's respect for human rights, women's rights and democracy by making a distinction between Muslim culture (which is time bound and changeable) and Islam as a universal faith which transcends time and space.[67]

Frithjof Schuon or Isa Nur al-Din

Frithjof Schuon was one of the main representatives of the Perennial School in the twentieth century. This school of thought was originally founded by the French philosopher, René Guénon, but it was brought to full maturity by Frithjof Schuon. Its core concept stresses that 'Divine Truth is one, time-less, and universal, and that the different religions are but different languages expressing that one Truth'.[68] Hence, besides its formal legal meaning, every traditional religion has an inner aspect that is essential, primordial and universal. Schuon was a self-taught scholar interested in the principles of metaphysics. His grasp of these principles came at a very young age and, at a later stage, formed the basis of his metaphysical standpoint.

His biographers write that 'the notion of the transcendent unity of religions was evoked in him one day when, walking in the Zoological Gardens in Basel . . . he met an elderly Senegalese marabout, with whom he conversed for a moment. The marabout, in order to make himself better understood, drew in the sand a circle with radii and added, pointing to the centre, "God is the Centre, all paths lead to Him".'[69] Schuon was also a poet who wrote many collections of poems, especially towards the end of his life. In addition, he was a painter, the subjects of his paintings relating predominantly to the world of the Plains Indians, but also to the mystery of cosmic and human femininity. The former subject had its roots in his love and knowledge of the Red Indian world while the latter had its origins in metaphysics, cosmology and Schuon's affinity with Hinduism.[70]

Apart from doctrinal expositions, Schuon wrote extensively on the practices of spiritual life such as the prayer of the heart, meditation, contemplation, modes of spiritual realization, the spiritual virtues and stages of the spiritual path. He was born in Basel, Switzerland in 1907 to a German Catholic family. His father was a musician and poet who was also very interested in the Orient, and his private library contained books such as the *Bhagavad-Gita*, which greatly impressed Schuon when he read it at the age of twelve, the *Vedas* and the *Arabian Nights*, which his father used to read to the family every night. This was the family environment in which Schuon was brought up. He received his early education in Basel, but when his father passed away and his Alsatian mother decided to move to Mulhouse, France, he was educated in French schools. This resulted in his mastering both languages, which he later found useful in his writings. His formal education came to an abrupt end when he had to leave school at the age of sixteen to support himself as a textile designer. But this did not stop his quest for knowledge, which continued for the rest of his life, both at the practical as well as the theoretical level. While in Mulhouse, he came across the work of the French traditionalist, René Guénon, which influenced his thinking greatly and set him on the path towards the metaphysical principles that he had begun to explore earlier. His exposure to Guénon's works led to a long relationship with him (despite some disagreement at a later stage) that lasted until the death of the latter in 1951. At the age of twenty-one, he served in the French military for eighteen months before moving to Paris to work again as a textile designer. In Paris, he become interested in Islam, and started learning Arabic, first with a Syrian friend, then at the Paris Mosque.[71] In a letter dated 1931 to one of his friends he wrote: 'Islam is looking at me with its golden eyes; am I going to plunge into it without return, exhausted by my resistance to the vile atmosphere that gnaws at me like poison? Everything depends on the Will of God.'[72] Shortly afterwards, Schuon decided to become a Muslim and set out in 1932 for Algeria to see the celebrated Sufi scholar, Ahmed Al-Alawi. He stayed close to this scholar for 4 months, becoming one of his disciples and having the name Isa Nur al-Din conferred on him. Some have questioned the verity of this relationship, but in recent book, his biographers have asserted the authenticity of this affiliation and initiation.[73] To gain greater knowledge of the traditional Islamic way of life, in 1935, he visited both Algeria (for the second time) and Morocco. In 1938, he visited Egypt, where he met with Guénon for the first time. In 1939, he visited Egypt again on his way to India. Soon after he had arrived in India, World War II broke out, forcing him to go back to France to serve in the French army. He was captured by the Germans but managed to flee to Switzerland and settled there for almost 40 years. Between 1959 and 1963, he and his Swiss wife visited the U.S. mainly to experience the traditional way of life of the Native Americans, for whom he had had a special love since early childhood. In 1980, he moved permanently to Indiana and died there in 1998 at the age of 91.[74]

A prolific writer, Schuon wrote more than twenty books and a huge number of articles, mostly dealing with the realms of religion and spirituality. Not only do they reaffirm the traditional metaphysical principles and explain the inner dimensions of religion; they also offer a critique of the modern world and highlight the metaphysical unity of all orthodox religions. Among the most important books he wrote are *The Transcendent Unity of Religions*,[75] a classical work on comparative religion which stresses the metaphysical unity of traditional religions; *Understanding Islam*;[76] *Islam and the Perennial Philosophy*;[77] *Logic and Transcendence*; *Stations of Wisdom*; and *Christianity/Islam: Essays on Esoteric Ecumenicism*.[78] Schuon's intellectual contribution to Islam lies in his efforts to revive all traditional religions, including Islam. He stressed that Islam, like all major religions, has the capacity to solve the ills of the modern world and tackle its spiritual crisis. His presentation of Islam was fair, balanced and original; for when he dealt with the faith and its main principles, he presented them from within, thus demonstrating a solid understanding and affinity with the religion. In all his writings on Islam, his approach was firmly rooted in the spiritual and metaphysical principles of the faith. His contribution can also be seen and appreciated if we realize that he was writing at a time when all religions, especially Islam, were under attack in the West and beyond. The misrepresentation of the faith was at its peak when the attacks were aided by Orientalist scholars who set out to challenge Islam intellectually in order to serve political and economic ends. In all his writings on the faith, Schoun proved them wrong and challenged their academic credibility. However, his overall efforts in this respect proved to be limited: firstly, his writings on Islam, as on all orthodox religions, were highly spiritual in nature, thus limiting their access to specific (elite) audiences; secondly, his preference to remain secluded from the mainstream intellectual community, as well as his refusal to teach or lecture in public, limited his influence on the broader group of people who might be interested in his work on the transcendent unity of religions and comparative religion.

One might also add that his 'sovereign independence with regard to formalism,' to use the words of his biographers, caused him to be a controversial figure and to be misunderstood by Muslims and non-Muslims alike. For although he accepted Islam, became a member of a Sufi order and wrote beautifully about Islam, it is difficult to locate his standpoint in this context. For example, he did not follow the tenets of the Perennialist School in the same way as his fellow scholars, especially with regard to the issue of belonging to a specific religion. In essence, Perennialism believes in the transcendent unity of religions, but with a particular focus on treading one religious path. In this respect, he did not follow any particular tradition. These factors contributed to limiting the impact that his writings might have had on a wider audience. This is confirmed by Seyyed Hossein Nasr, the editor of *The Essential Writings of Frithjof Schuon*, in which he states: 'Considering the grandeur and depth of his metaphysical expositions and the fact that he is the premier living expositor of that Sophia Perennis which lies at the heart of all revelations, it might appear strange that so little is known about Schuon.'[79] Nonetheless, Schuon's writings still attract the interest of a number of scholars of different religious traditions in both East and West who respect his comparative approach to the study of religion. Among those who were influenced by his approach to Islam, especially in the West, are such important figures as Martin Lings Gai Eaton and, of course, his commentator and admirer, Professor Sayyed Hossein Nasr. In recent years, the latter has played an important role in explaining and disseminating Schoun's ideas and perspective, while the former have contributed immensely to the faith of Islam in Britain and beyond.

Chapter 2

Early British Convert Community
(or Native British Converts to Islam):
An Overview

Contact between Britain and Islam and the conversion of Britons to Islam is by no means a new phenomenon. Anecdotal information and stories inform us that, for example, the powerful Anglo-Saxon king Offa of Mercia (757–96) minted the first coin in Britain with an Arabic inscription that bears the Islamic declaration of faith. Historians and scholars ascribe this occurrence to either trade relations with the Muslim world (as the king at the time had diplomatic relations with the then powerful Caliph Haroon al-Rashid in Baghdad), tactical opposition to the Pope or his approval of the Islamic faith. The same can be said with regard to the Ballycottin Cross found on the southern coast of Ireland, which goes back to the ninth century. At the heart of the cross, there is an Arabic inscription that bears the word 'Bismillah' (or 'in the name of God'). By the time of the Crusades, we hear of news about the conversion of a number of Christians, the most notable among them being the English knight, Robert of St Albans, who, embarking on a crusade to Palestine, ended up embracing Islam in 1185.[1]

In the thirteenth century, we are told that King John of England expressed interest in becoming a Muslim. Excommunicated by the Pope and struggling to control his rebellious barons, he sent a secret mission to the ruler of Morocco, Muhammad al-Nasr, in 1213, asking him for military support. In return, he would not only help the ruler to conquer the rest of Spain from the King of Aragon but also embrace Islam. However, for unexplained reasons, the ruler of Morocco decided not to accept this invitation.[2] In 1588, Queen Elizabeth I had promising relations with the Ottoman Empire and even suggested a mutual alliance with Sultan Murad III against Spain.[3]

The Elizabethan era witnessed an increase in the numbers of English people converting to Islam and living in some parts of the Muslim world.

This was mainly due to their contact with the Muslim people. British travellers and adventurers brought the news that their fellow compatriots were turning Turks – meaning Muslims. Among them was the British consul in Egypt, Benjamin Bishop, who converted to Islam in 1606.[4]

Britain's increased involvement in the Muslim world in the second half of the eighteenth century intensified contact between their people. Many notable British citizens went to India and other parts of the Muslim world to serve with the Empire, gaining influence and wealth. By the same token, many Muslim seamen started to arrive in Britain through their employment with the East India Company; the opening of the Suez Canal in 1869 increased the recruitment of these men, especially in Yemen and Somalia, and many later settled in sea port cities such as Cardiff, Liverpool and South Shields. Parallel to this, a growing number of Muslim students came to Britain to study at the old universities of Oxford and Cambridge, including a good number of Indian aristocrats: for example, the post of personal physician to Queen Victoria was already held by an Indian Muslim.[5] The Muslim students who arrived in Britain at the time came from prominent and wealthy backgrounds; they were mainly sons of chiefs and notable persons who had connections in the British establishment. By the end of the nineteenth century more Muslim students arrived in Britain, especially from India. Their arrival was greatly influenced by British educational policy in India, which aimed at promoting English language, literature and culture among the middle and upper classes of the native Indians who were trained to work at the interface between the British Raj and the Indian people. To achieve this goal, British universities, especially Oxford and Cambridge, were encouraged to accept them. Hence, many came to prepare for the examinations of the Indian Civil Service while others came simply for reasons of prestige. Among those who achieved success in Britain were Muhammad Ali Jinnah, who later became the first prime minister of Pakistan, and Ameer Ali, who became the first Indian Privy Councillor and a member of the Judicial Committee. Many of these students and professionals returned home, but others decided to stay in Britain; living in and around London; they kept their Islamic roots and principles but mingled with the indigenous population, especially members of the middle and upper classes of British society. They also took part in setting up Islamic societies (see below); their stories, intellectual abilities and, generally, their arguments and discussions awakened the interest of some of the prominent members of the host society, who began to show a keen interest in the faith of Islam and in Muslim issues.[6]

Some Early Converts

This period also witnessed the emergence of a new phenomenon: an increasing number of indigenous British people who took the decision to adopt the faith of Islam. This may be attributed to the fact that British people were exposed to the teachings of Islam (as stated earlier) both in Britain as well as in the wider British empire, which spread to Muslim countries. Some of these early converts led ordinary lives while others played important roles in the establishment of Muslim societies or communities that left their imprint on Islam in Britain. Among the latter were statesmen, diplomats, aristocrats and writers; and at the time their conversion caused publicity and curiosity among the people and in the British press: 'Those who profess and call themselves Christians must face the fact that, within the last few years, several notable people have, apparently for genuine, conscientious reasons, accepted the religion of Muhammad. If Christ is not at fault in the matter then his followers must be.'[7] These converts practised their new faith in a genuine way and to the best of their abilities; some led ordinary lives, not leaving many written records on Islamic issues, and there is not much written about them beyond a few lines relating to their conversion, found mainly in the journals, *The Islamic Review* and *The Crescent*. Others lived an active life and played an important role in the history of the convert community in Britain. The following are a few examples of the first group and they are by no means a comprehensive representation of them: Henry Stanley, whose Muslim name was Abdul Rahman, was born in 1827 into a respected family. His father, John Edward Stanley, 2nd Baron of Alderley, was a politician and member of the House of Commons for the Whigs; he held many important possessions before he assumed the barony of Stanley. His mother, we are told, was descended directly from King Charles II, and was very active and influential in the social and political circles of her day. Later in life, she supported women's rights and helped to establish women's colleges and associations as well as a public school for girls. When his father passed away in 1869, Henry Stanley inherited his titles and became the 3rd Baron Stanley of Alderley. He was a historian who wrote and translated many books. He converted to Islam in 1862; no records exist on his post-conversion life except that he lived and practised the faith to the utmost.[8] *The Crescent* described him as a 'sincere and devout Muslim, [which] was known to very few men. His faith was not limited to a profession by word of mouth . . . [but] show how deeply Islam had entered his heart. [He was] not only regular in the five daily prayers, but also constant at tahajjud (midnight prayers); he was also very humble in his prayers . . . far above most born Muhammadans. When he talked of the holy Prophet, it was with profound love and deep respect . . . He was very well versed on the principles of Muslim Theology, and [had] comprehensive knowledge of the principles of Islam. Who could imagine that such a sincere and devout worshiper of the true God was living in the heart of Christendom?'[9] Henry died in 1903 at the age of 80 and was buried in his family estate in Alderley Park according to Islamic rites; his wife and two sons were present at his funeral, as well as the Secretary to the Ottoman Embassy in London. A Janaza service was also conducted in his memory at Liverpool mosque by his fellow countryman, Abdullah Quilliam,[10] (see below).

Another fellow convert of the same calibre was Lady Evelyn Cobbold, who in the same way as the famous convert to Islam, Muhammad Asad, fell in love with Islam, the Arabic language and the Arab world of the late nineteenth century. She was one of the important figures of her time: socialite, traveller, deerstalker, angler, as well as caring mother and grandmother. She was born in Edinburgh in 1867 to an aristocratic family; her mother, Lady Gertrude Coke, was the daughter of the 2nd Earl of Leicester and her father, Charles Adolphus Murray, was 7th Earl of Dunmore. He was a renowned traveller and explorer who travelled around the globe in the company of his family. One of the places which he and his family used to visit regularly was North Africa, especially Algeria and Egypt.[11] It was in such surroundings that Evelyn and her siblings were brought up, and the impact of this Arab/Islamic environment was so profound on young Evelyn that she became immersed in the language, culture and religion of the Arab world; she felt thoroughly at home in this environment, which she so ardently loved. Throughout her life, Lady Evelyn affirmed that there was no precise date for her decision to convert, that she had always felt Muslim at heart: 'I am often asked when and why I became a Moslem. I can only reply that I do not know the precise moment when the truth of Islam dawned on me. It seems that I have always been a Moslem. This is not so strange when one remembers that Islam is the natural religion that a child left to itself would develop. Indeed, as a Western critic once described it, "Islam is the religion of common sense".'[12] For her, then, there was no formal adoption of Islam; on the contrary, Islam was a natural part of her as a result of her childhood life in the Arab/Muslim world. She describes this early experience as follows: 'As a child, I spent the winter months in a Moorish villa on a hill outside Algiers, where my parents went in search of sunshine. There I learnt to speak Arabic, and my delight was to escape my governess and visit the Mosques with my Algerian friends, and unconsciously I was a little Moslem at heart. After 3 years' wintering at Mustapha Superieure we left the villa for good, much to my despair. . . . Some years went by and I happened to be in Rome staying with some Italian friends, when my host asked me if I would like to visit the Pope. Of course I was thrilled, and, clad all in black with a long veil, I was admitted into the august presence. . . . When his Holiness suddenly addressed me, asking if I was a Catholic, I was taken aback for a moment and then replied that I was a Moslem. What possessed me I do not pretend to know, as I had not given a thought to Islam for many years. A match was lit and I then and there determined to read up and study the faith. The more I read and the more I studied, the more convinced I became that Islam was the most practical religion, and the one most calculated to solve the world's many perplexing problems, and to bring to humanity, peace and happiness. Since then I have never wavered in my belief that there is but one God.'[13]

In 1891, while she was in Cairo and aged 24, she married John Dupuis Cobbold, a prominent man from a wealthy Suffolk brewing family. After the wedding, the couple returned to England to live in Suffolk and they had three children born between 1893 and 1900. During this period, Evelyn cared for her family, though her marital duties did not prevent her from travelling abroad. Her yearning for the Arab/Muslim world continued, and in 1911 she returned to the region with a female companion, the result of the trip being her first book, entitled *Wayfarer in the Libyan Desert* published in 1912. The book, we are told, is a sympathetic and detailed account of Islamic principles and the Muslim way of life, although she takes a critical stance towards the lives of women in some parts of the region. Facey states that from this time onwards her Muslim identity was clearly evident: she made regular trips to the Middle East, especially Egypt, befriended Arabs and corresponded with them, and became closer to Marmaduke Pickthall, a respected fellow British convert to Islam.[14]

It seems that her strong and vivid attachment to Islam caused her marriage to break down, and by 1922 her marriage had already ended with an amicable arrangement that secured her financial situation for the rest of her life. In 1929, her husband passed away, and his decease might have played an important role in her decision to declare her intention to go on a pilgrimage to Mecca, which she did in 1933 at the age of 65. Her journey to the holy places was facilitated by social connections rather than bureaucratic arrangements; a social contact in London put her in contact with a fellow British convert (Harry St John Philby) who was living with his wife in

Jeddah at the time. The couple did their best to ensure that she would complete the formalities without difficulty.[15] Interestingly, Lady Evelyn did not undergo faith scrutiny before she was allowed to undertake the pilgrimage – as her fellow countryman, Lord Hedley Churchward, had to when he decided to journey to Arabia for the same reason. She only went through papers and permission procedures. By the time she returned home, Lady Evelyn had decided to publish her diary impressions of her visit to Arabia in a book entitled *Pilgrimage to Mecca*, published in London by John Murray in 1934.[16] The book is a clear account of what she genuinely felt during this spiritual journey, an honest description of what she thought about the holy book of Muslims, the life of their Prophet, the history of Muslims, the position of women in Islam and Islam's attitude towards war and toleration. The book aroused the interest of British newspapers at the time and received favourable reviews: the Sunday Times stated that '[t]he pilgrimage to Mecca has often been written about, but never before from the point of view of a Western convert to Islam. Lady Evelyn has a fresh and original point of view which clarifies many things in the Moslem religion to Western minds'; *Country Life* magazine stressed: 'To her Islam is the religion of common sense, and it is that engaging quality that is the medium in which she presents her impressions of Mecca and Medina. To the historical significance of the holy places she brings knowledge and faith. One is left with as profound a respect for her determination as for her religion'; the *Manchester Guardian* declared that the 'book has a rare appeal of its own. If she may be thought to be a little prejudiced in favour of her adopted faith, we have been accustomed to hear in its disfavour so much which is based upon pure ignorance and antipathy that a little over praise, if such it be, comes as a welcome relief'; the *Belfast Newsletter* uneasily asserted that 'for the Christian her book must make sad reading, not because it is a sad story, but because she does appear to have found peace in such an unexpected quarter. It must be admitted that she has told her story with charm and ability and that her description of the Holy Land and Holy Cities of Islam deserves to rank with the classic narratives of earlier European adventures in the peninsula.'[17]

The book has recently been reprinted by Arabian Publishing Limited in May 2008 with an introduction by William Facey and Miranda Taylor, in which they claim that she was the first British Muslim woman on record to have undertaken the pilgrimage to Mecca. In her book, Cobbold presented herself as the first European woman to have participated in the Hajj.[18] It is very difficult to verify this claim, given the fact that other writers have mentioned other northern European women who participated in the Hajj with their husbands before her. Herman suggests that Cobbold might be the first woman to have undertaken the pilgrimage on her own and to write about it in diary form.[19] Facey and Taylor also claim that by re-editing her book, they have succeeded in rescuing her from obscurity and oblivion. This may be true for mainstream British publications, but it is certainly not the case for Muslim publications; for *The Islamic Review* allocated space to her personal life, her function on the occasion of the birthday of the Prophet Muhammad, her book and her burial.[20] Lady Evelyn survived her husband by more than 30 years, dying in 1963 at the age of ninety-five. Her burial instructions confirm an absolute commitment to the faith of Islam: she was laid in the grave with her face directed towards Mecca, the funeral prayer was conducted in Arabic and the Quranic verse 'Allah is the light of the heavens and the earth'[21] was inscribed in Arabic on her gravestone. Although Lady Evelyn did not leave much written work on Islamic issues, her book on the Hajj and even her *Wayfarer in the Libyan Desert* can be regarded as valuable contributions to the canon of Islamic literature in Britain. The way she presented the Islamic faith and the Muslim way of life during her visits must have had a considerable impact on those who read her works as well as on those who were very close to her, dispelling in the process any ignorance or misunderstanding about the faith and paving the way for mutual understanding between the two worlds she was very much part of. The re-publishing of her book is certainly timely; it will add a new dimension to the English literature on Islamic studies and will be of great value for courses on Islam and Islamic spirituality.

John Parkinson (or Yahya-En-Nasr Parkinson) was an author and gifted poet, born in the town of Kilwinning, Ayrshire, Scotland in 1874 to a respected family 'distinguished in the ancient history of Britain, and a branch of the Durham family, cadets of the North of England clan of the Featherstonehaugh'.[22] His mother passed away when he was in infancy, and therefore his grandparents took care of him and his education, later sending him to a Scottish boarding school where he exhibited a keen interest in learning and reading. But by the age of thirteen, he was compelled to leave school to work and support his elderly grandparents; 3 years later, at the age of sixteen, his grandparents died, leaving him alone to fend for himself. Though the circumstances were difficult, young John did not give up; on the contrary, his adversities gave him courage, determination and self-confidence. His aptitude for learning was rekindled and led him to study various subjects such as astronomy, mathematics, biology, science and philosophy. By the time he was twenty-six, he was already writing for local newspapers in Scotland on various topics of his many interests. The study of philosophy led him to the study of religion, and to joining the United Presbyterian Church in the process. This was followed by the study of other religions, including Islam. The simplicity and clarity of the teachings of Islam left such a deep impression on him that he soon decided to embrace the faith. His conversion to Islam aroused the wonder of the local newspapers in his town, and in 1907 one of these papers wrote the following about him: 'it may be news to a great many of my readers that Ayrshire has a Scotch Mussulman, a Moslem poet, the vice-sheikh of the British Muslims, in the person of Yahya-En-Nasr Parkinson of Kilwinning. [. . .] he finds his solace and refreshment in the Muhammedan faith which he embraced, in familiarising himself with the Chivalry of the Muslim warriors, and in the contemplation of the creeds of Islam.'[23] When he was asked by the writer what attracted him to Islam, he stated that it was because Islam laid down clear rules and regulations for guidance that were worthy of acceptance and that Islam was also suitable for people of different mental persuasions. Apparently, he thought that Christianity had doctrines that hindered human progress and affirmed that the progress of Europe was not due to Christianity. On the contrary, Europe civilized Christianity: 'the Renaissance and the Reformation were due not to Christianity but to Western contact with Saracen culture, through Cordova, Cairo, and the intermediary of the Crusaders.'[24] Parkinson did not live long; he was barely forty-four when he passed away. *The Islamic Review* described him as a man who had 'a supreme literary gift, his contributions [. . .] well known for their versatile character, display deep philosophy, sound logic, and vast information. He has got a facile pen, which he wields with clearness of expression and vigour.'[25] Apart from his writings in the local newspaper, Parkinson also published some short books, such as essays in Islamic philosophy, and *Al-Ghazali*; the former has recently been re-published, while the latter, an assessment of the fourteenth-century scholar, Abu Hamid Al-Ghazali, from a psychological perspective, can be found on the Woking website. In addition, he wrote some articles, including 'Cry on the Cross', in which he discusses the concept of God in Christianity and the various views among Christian scholars on the nature of Jesus (as human or divine).[26] It was in the field of poetry that he produced particularly fine work: 'his poetry . . . breathes a light and sublime philosophy, and indicates how pure, refined and cultured must be the person from whose soul emanates such grand and beautiful ideas.'[27] Among his finest poems is the collection *Lays of Love and War*', in which he declares: 'O, Allah, touch my lyre, With true poetic fire, That I in rhythmic swell, May Islam's glories tell.'[28] Others include 'Al-Mansur', 'Unity', 'Verses', 'Zengi', 'The Spirit of God', 'The Clarion of

Islam', 'The Dirge We Dirging Dree'[29], 'Woodnotes Wild', 'I love her', 'A Ballad of Chivalry' and 'Love-Dreams'.[30] Anecdotal information, moreover, tells us that he wrote thousands of lines of poems on historical Islamic figures. The main themes that permeate most of his published poems are chivalry and nobility, brotherhood and unity, courage and honesty from the traditional Islamic perspective or a traditional Islamic understanding of these values (*futuwwa*). It is in this particular side of his work that one can see his valuable contribution to Islam and Islamic literature in Britain; some of these poems have been re-published, while others are awaiting publication. Parkinson's poems have no doubt explained and vividly expressed some aspects of the beauty and integrity of the faith for Muslims and non-Muslims, especially for those with aesthetic tastes, such as for poetry.[31]

Three other important figures also need to be placed in this category. The first of these is Sir Abdullah Charles Edward Archibald Watkins Hamilton. Born in 1876 to a distinguished family, he was a baronet and relative of the British royal family. He was a lieutenant in the Royal Defence Corps and also worked as president of the Selsy Conservative Association. He embraced the faith in 1924 and declared that 'since arriving at an age of discretion, the beauty and the simple purity of Islam have always appealed to me . . . . As the time progressed, I wished to be at peace with my Creator . . . In becoming a Muslim I have merely observed the dictates of my conscience, and have since felt a better and a truer man'.[32] Three years later, he married Lady Hamilton (Lilian Maud Austen, born in 1912 and died in 1964), who also converted to Islam. Both lived according to the spirit of their newly adopted faith. Taking into consideration his aristocratic background and his prominent position, his conversion must have aroused the interest and curiosity not only of the local press but also of the inner aristocratic circle to which he belonged. Very little has been written about his post-conversion life, and we are not aware at this stage if he has left any written works. From the scattered information that is written about him in *The Islamic Review*, we are told that he was active, at least within his own circle, in defending the image of Islam and that he was a close friend of Lord Headley al-Farooq (see below). They both worked hard to create an environment conducive to a better understanding of Islam in Britain. Hamilton died in 1939 at the age of 62 and was buried in the Muslim Brookwood cemetery in London.

The second figure is Lord Hedley Churchward, or Mahmoud Mubarak Churchward, born in Aldershot to a respected English family which owned the second oldest house in Britain. His father ran a successful business in the town, which earned him respect, and he was well connected to the nobility of the time. Since Hedley was always in the company of his father, this allowed him to meet his father's friends and acquaintances, exposing him in the process to different kinds of people at an early age. Among the prominent people that young Hedley met were Queen Victoria and Empress Eugenie of France, whose house was close to the Churchwards' house. He was educated at Kilburn College, a place where he shared sweets with the sons of prominent figures from around the world. His aesthetic and artistic interests were discovered at an early age, and he was encouraged to develop them – which he did, eventually becoming a well-known scene-painter. His renown in this occupation opened the way for him to work at the Globe Theatre and finally in Drury Lane, where he met famous theatrical person-alities such as Lily Langtry, Genevieve Ward, Hermann Vezin and Henry Irving.[33] Hedley's initial contact with Islam came through sheer coinci-dence; a trip to Spain in early 1888 exposed him to the famous Moorish art and architecture in both Granada and Cordoba. He was so impressed that he decided to cross the straits to Morocco in order to acquire further know-ledge of this artistic Andalusian world. Once there, he instantly fell in love with the gentle and simple Islamic way of life that prevailed at that time. This trip led to repeated trips to Morocco, and in the process Hedley began to learn the language of the people as well as adopt their way of life, ultimately accepting Islam and declaring his conversion to Islam to his family when he returned home to Aldershot after one of his trips. His bio-grapher describes his solid conviction in the following words: 'No one who knew Churchward could doubt that he sincerely believed his religion was the best. At mosque and in private life, in Christian company or among his fellow-believers he always held to his creed, never aggressively, never with any wish to convert, but feeling a hearty anger about those who perverted or wrongly expressed the Koran's teaching.'[34] To further his knowledge of Islam, Hedley travelled to Egypt and studied for many years at Al-Azhar, one of the prominent religious institutions in the Muslim world. His knowledge of Islam improved to the extent that he managed to get a job as an imam in a mosque and later as a teacher of the life of the Prophet in an academy in Cairo. Looking for better work, he decided to go to South Africa, where his art work opened up opportunities for him. When he returned to Egypt, Churchward decided to start a family, marrying the daughter of one of the most prominent Egyptian jurists and living his life according to the spirit and letter of his adopted faith, 'saying the five prescribed daily prayers, wearing a golf cap so that his forehead could touch the ground as he bowed before Allah, giving to the poor, washing his forearms, fasting and regulating his whole life according to the usages of Islam'.[35] Despite this, Churchward felt that he was still not yet fulfilled, and in order for him to feel complete he needed to carry out what he had always dreamt of doing since he became a Muslim, that is to say to embark on a pilgrimage to Mecca. At the time, it was not at all easy to get permission to visit Mecca, especially for those of European backgrounds, due to bogus visitors and the difficult socio-political circumstances that then prevailed. But Churchward was determined to overcome those obstacles and achieve his dream of visiting the holy places of Mecca and Medina. Hence, he decided to use his position in Egypt and asked for a letter of recommendation from the Ulama of Al-Azhar, who subjected him to a three hours' faith examination before granting him the certificate that allowed him to travel to Mecca. In 1910, he set forth on his journey to Mecca to undertake his pilgrimage, which he did successfully. His biographer claims that Churchward was the first European[36] to genuinely complete the Hajj.[37] However, Herman disagrees, claiming that there was another European (an Englishman) who converted to Islam and undertook the Hajj in the early 1890s.[38] After his spiritual journey to Mecca and Medina, Churchward and his wife settled down in South Africa, where he suddenly died in 1929 and was buried in Johannesburg cemetery. Churchward's accomplishments within the context of his adopted faith are remarkable. For his determination to study at Al-Azhar and his ability to work after graduation as a teacher in Islamic studies display a sincere conviction of his new faith, which he followed both in spirit and letter for the rest of his life. His Hajj diary, published in 1931, was – and continues to be – regarded as a genuine and honest account of that trip; it is still a welcome and reliable source of Hajj literature and Islam in Britain.

The following are examples of early converts who were active and had high-profile roles both in Britain as well as in the wider Muslim world.

Abdullah Quilliam is one of the most charismatic and outspoken personalities among British converts in the late nineteenth and early twenty centuries. A scholar of religion and activist, he left an enduring legacy on Islam in Britain. He was born in Liverpool in 1856 to a respected and devout Christian family, his father being a watchmaker and his mother a Christian activist. His family came originally from the Isle of Man; hence, he used to spend his early childhood holidays there. He was educated at the Liverpool Institute, where he showed prominence, winning considerable numbers of prizes and certificates. During his teenage years he wrote articles for the press and various magazines and worked as a reporter for the Liverpool Albion. By the time he was twenty he was editor of both the Good Templar newspaper and the monthly satirical magazine,

The Porcupine. He went on to study law and in 1878, after passing his final
exam, was admitted as a solicitor, working mainly for himself but also
pursuing his press work until 1884. His career in law thrived and in due
time he managed to set up one of the most respected law practices in
Liverpool. Quilliam was articulate and a good public speaker, a man of
great aptitude for learning, renowned for his sound knowledge of the
history of the Isle of Man, his Biblical studies and his New Testament
scholarship. His library held more than two thousand books covering a
wide range of fields such as law, theology and science.[39] His busy and
active life finally took its toll on his health, forcing him to seek rest in the
south of France. While he was there, recuperating from the stress, he
decided to cross the Mediterranean and visit both Algeria and Morocco.
It was there that he first encountered Islam and ultimately fell in love with
the faith. In 1888, at the age of 31, he decided to embrace the faith and
commit the rest of his life to preaching it, especially in Britain. His conversion heralded the beginning of a long and difficult journey dominated
by his public association with Islam and strong defence of it. Initially he
started his mission by giving lectures on the faith of Islam, and soon after
he set up Liverpool Mosque and Institute in 1889. This mosque is regarded
as the first to be built in Britain, and now after years of neglect and disuse
it is receiving attention from the Muslim community in the city. The
Abdullah Quilliam Society, a private charity organization, decided to
refurbish the site and restore life to it: 'It's a heritage site for us. This truly
is the birthplace of Islam in Britain. We . . . want to make it into a heritage
centre for Islamic culture and interfaith dialogue.'[40] Quilliam's first converts were his sons and his mother, as well as several prominent scientists
and professionals. To expand his intellectual activities and disseminate
Islamic teachings to the British public, he set up a printing press in the
basement of the mosque, issuing a weekly newspaper called *The Crescent*
and a quarterly journal entitled *The Islamic World.* Both were dedicated to
publishing articles on Islam. He also wrote a book entitled *The Faith of
Islam,* which was published in 1899 and translated into many languages. It
is stated that the book was widely read and that among its readers were
famous dignitaries such as Queen Victoria and the ruler of Egypt. In due
time, these printings attracted local, national and international interest
and made Quilliam a prominent figure, especially in the Muslim world.
He also set up a Muslim college to educate both boys and girls, and
a weekly debating society to discuss Islamic issues and current affairs
that concerned Muslims in Britain and worldwide. Geaves claims that
70 per cent of his articles in *The Crescent* focused on foreign affairs,

relating especially to his concern over the impact of colonialism and the loss of Muslim lands.[41] In addition, Quilliam was very much concerned about the social problems in his surroundings and the ethical issues of his time, especially the suffering of the poor. Hence, he established a nursery, which he called the Medina Home, to cater for the illegitimate children in his city.[42] His works attracted Muslims and non-Muslims, his followers increased in record time and his reputation soared, thus bringing fame and success for Quilliam and his community in Britain, the Muslim world and further afield. In Britain Quilliam was rarely out of the sight of local and national newspapers; his public lectures were widely attended up and down the country and his scholarship was fully acknowledged: for example, in 1907 the Geological Society of London made him a fellow due to his dedication to the subject. In the Muslim world he was acclaimed as the champion of Islam in the West. This appreciation was illustrated in various forms: for example, the then Sultan of Turkey granted him the title of Sheikh al-Islam of the British Isles, the Sultan of Morocco conferred upon him the title of Alim (religious scholar – a title that can only be conferred on those who are well versed in the Quran, Hadith and Islamic science), the Shah of Persia appointed him as his Counsel in Britain and the Sultan of Afghanistan rewarded him with financial gifts to support his efforts in Britain. Beyond that, he received two honorary doctorates in law from Barrett College, North Carolina, and the University of Liberia for his contribution to Oriental and Islamic literature.[43] Quilliam's contribution to Islam in Britain is immense; it consisted not only of his writings but also of his prolific public lectures that attracted wide public interest. Both in his writings and his lectures he lost no opportunity to explain the main principles of Islam on the nature of God, the concept of oneness (*tawhid*), brotherhood and unity, the life of the Prophet, Islam and science (which he passionately stressed throughout his argumentation and emphasized that this formed one of the main reasons for his conversion to the faith), Islam and other religions, Islamic law, the position of women in Islam, especially polygamy, which he vigorously defended, accusing Christians of being hypocrites on this issue, Muslim history, in particular, Muslim Spain and its tolerant attitude towards people of the book, and multiculturalism. Like Headley's (see below), his approach to all these issues was a comparative one, attempting to illustrate the superiority of Islam over Christianity in these areas. This was expressed by Geaves as follows: '[Quilliam] firmly believed that Islam and Islamic ethical systems – the egalitarian laws of marriage and divorce, matters of sexual morality, family life, views on alcohol consumption, doctrinal positions on the unity of God, the understanding of revelation and the modes of worship – were all superior to Christianity, a religion which he believed to be in decline, morally defunct and unable to deal with reason.'[44] At the practical level, he played an impressive pastoral role that no other convert has played until the present time, and, in this regard, he is to be commended. He looked after orphans, visited sick people, especially lonely migrants, helped the poor and destitute, performed Muslim funerals, signed marriage certificates, provided shelters for those who had nowhere to stay and defended the legal rights of those early immigrants, especially Muslim sailors. This pastoral care, in all its forms, became in time the main pattern of his activities not only in Liverpool but also in other parts of the country. He became the point of contact for the police, hospitals and workhouse authorities on these issues. Geaves believes that his pastoral role in Liverpool and beyond indicates that he was formally regarded as the main representative of Islam in the UK.[45] The uniqueness of Quilliam lies in his profound sensitivity towards issues related to justice and fairness, which for him transcend concepts such as patriotism, nationalism, ethnicity and religious identity. This sense of egalitarian spirit was evident in his attitude and judgement even before his conversion to Islam, for example, in his opposition to capital punishment and the mistreatment of blacks in America: 'Indeed, it can be argued that he converted to Islam because he believed that it was the religion in which he could find the justice that he felt the world deserved.'[46] Against this backdrop, it would be difficult to imagine that he would be able to separate his religious and moral convictions from social and political affairs both nationally and internationally. This was particularly the case with regard to British foreign policy in the Muslim world, which violated his sense of political justice and forced him to condemn it publicly. Both, *The Crescent* and the *Islamic world*, were employed as vehicles to convey his views and his frustration with the British role in the Muslim world, especially in Sudan. He issued religious rulings condemning British military forces and urged Muslims to unite and refrain from fighting against each other. He also launched attacks on the media coverage of Islam and Islamic issues, as well as on the Church, especially with regard to its missionary activities in Muslim countries.

The success of Quilliam's efforts to attract converts to his faith, his outspoken criticism of British expansion policies in the Muslim world, his loyalty to the Ottoman Caliph and his struggle with the media, all combined to make life difficult for him and to make it difficult for him to continue his mission. In 1908, he left Britain for Istanbul, and with his departure the mosque and the institute gradually declined until they were finally closed down. Nielsen states that Quilliam left Britain 'for good',[47] but we know that this was not the case, for after a period of time spent in Turkey he returned to Britain under a new name (he was now Henri de Leon), became a member of the Woking Institute in South London and continued to serve his adopted faith until his death in 1932. Quilliam left an enduring legacy that provides a role model for contemporary British Muslims. As a scholar, he was a man of letters, with a sound knowledge of both Western and Islamic thought; he engaged actively with the intellectual climate of his time, defended the principles of Islam on professional terms without resorting to either apologetics or confrontational discourse, and as such he gained the respect and admiration of both friends and foes. As an activist and leader (and like Headley in this context – see below), he set up a community which transcended ethnic and sectarian divisions and was united by religious beliefs – an ideal model that contemporary British Muslims clearly need to bear in mind in view of the current segmentation among them. Finally, he provided roots, history and a sense of belonging not only for 'indigenous' converts but also second- and third-generation British Muslims: 'it is extremely important especially for the [converts and] younger generation who are searching for roots in this [country]. We can say your roots are here.'[48]

Lord Headley was a prominent peer, statesman and writer. Born in London in 1855, he was educated first at Westminster school (London), then at Trinity College, Cambridge, where he was also an amateur boxer, winning both the heavy and middleweight championships for his College. After graduation he worked in education, but later became editor of the Salisbury Journal. He became a peer in 1877 and served in the army, reaching the rank of Colonel. He was a sportsperson keen on fishing, rowing, swimming and playing golf. In 1892, he decided to take up civil engineering as a profession, working mainly on the problems of coast erosion and the protection of foreshores. His dedication to this work won him the Bessemer Permian award of the Society of Engineers and the Silver Medals of both the Royal Scottish Society of Arts and the Institute of Civil Engineers of Ireland. This culminated in the presidency of the Society of Engineers in London. His work took him to India in 1896, during which trip he supervised the construction of road works.[49] His stay in India brought him in direct contact with Islam that left an impact on him. In 1913, he succeeded to the barony, and shortly afterwards he decided to publicly embrace Islam. Lord Headley was brought up a Protestant but also studied Catholicism; he described his conversion to Islam as a long-contemplated process rather than a sudden break with Christianity: 'It is possible some of my friends may imagine that I have been influenced by Mahomedans; but this is not the case cause, for my present convictions are solely the outcome of many years of thought'.[50] Lord Headley also asserted in a public speech in Cairo that he had been a Muslim at heart for over 50 years, but he was unable to declare his true convictions for reasons beyond his control.[51] Soon after his conversion he decided to go Mecca on a pilgrimage, but the looming First World War and then its outbreak prevented him from going ahead with his plan to visit the holy lands. It was not until 1923 that he was able to fulfil his dream and undertake his pilgrimage together with his long-standing friend Khwaja Kamal-ud-Din. In an issue of 1923, *The Islamic Review* states that Lord Headley was the first British Muslim to go on the pilgrimage,[52] but we now know that this is not correct as there were other British people who undertook the Hajj before him (see above). Perhaps one could argue that he was the first British peer (in terms of seniority) to have participated in the Hajj. Although he was an engineer by profession, he was a man of literary tastes and of great writing ability, and he utilized these skills to express his views and convictions clearly. Headley's contribution to Islam was considerable, both at the theoretical as well as the practical level; at the theoretical level he wrote many booklets and articles on Islamic issues, especially using either a comparative approach, comparing Christianity with Islam, or defending some key Islamic principles that had been misrepresented or misunderstood in Britain or, furthermore, explaining the Islamic belief system and cultural achievements to both non-Muslims and potential converts. Among his booklets is *A Western Awakening to Islam*, published in 1914; it deals with several issues such as the inner peace of Islam, which, according to him, emanates from a clear and simple view of God, as well as easy and direct access to Him: 'Islam is the religion of grand simplicity; it satisfies the noblest longings of the souls, and in no way contravenes the teaching of Moses or Christ.'[53] The booklet also deals with the position of women in Islam; Lord Headley defends the teachings of Islam regarding women and criticizes Western misrepresentations of it, at least theoretically speaking. However, his approach to the subject, at least in real terms, tends to be superficial and sometimes smacks of apologetics. Apostasy is another issue which Lord Headley treats in this booklet. He refutes the accusation that Islam sanctions the killing of a person for changing religions; instead he affirms that the Quran makes it clear that there is no compulsion or violence in religion and that true Muslims would not cross this line, which is clearly demarcated in the Quran. The attack on the integrity of the founder of Islam by several Christian missionaries is another important subject that Lord Headley deals with extensively in the book. He criticizes the writings of these missionaries for not being truthful to their faith in giving the true facts about the teachings of Islam: 'I am sorry to have to confess to a feeling of deep humiliation and shame at finding that any of my countrymen could stoop to duplicity and misrepresentation in order to advance their views on the subject of religion. It is that very religion which should teach scrupulous fairness and love of truth.'[54] Other issues such as the expansion of Islam 'by the sword', the loyalty of Muslim citizens and the methods of preaching Islam are all dealt with in a mature and orderly way.

The affinity between the original Church of Jesus Christ and Islam is another small book written by Lord Headley; this one focuses partly on the historical development of Christianity and partly on some of the diverse views regarding its tenets among Christian scholars. Basing his assumptions on some of these views, he stresses that there is an affinity between the early message of Jesus and the teachings of Islam: 'a study of the Quran will reveal the fact that there is nothing antagonistic to previous revelations – Muhammad's instructions, as laid down in the book, completely back up the Bible teachings, extending them to suit the requirements of the time.'[55] He laments the fact that most British people are unaware of the teachings of Islam and that their ignorance of the essential principles of the faith have led to great misconceptions and antagonism between the two sister religions. He affirms that if British people genuinely understood the message of Islam, there would be no more tensions and conflicts: 'I feel certain that, if the people of England fully grasped what Islam really means – common sense, and the natural desire we all possess to have appeals made to our reasoning side, as well as to our feelings – would help to put away the shameful misunderstandings which at present exist.'[56] A further important topic which Lord Headley tackles is the issue very often mentioned by some orientalists that Islam did not encourage its followers to excel in science, technology and culture whereas in Christendom this has occurred, as we can see in current achievements in most of the Western world. He refutes this view and stresses the Muslim contribution to human civilization. He reminds those who subscribe to such a view of Muslim success and achievements in various fields of science and knowledge, especially in cities like Cordoba, Baghdad, Istanbul, Cairo, Delhi, Isfahan and Damascus. The influence of Muslim civilization on modern European thought and knowledge is also highlighted: 'our present civilization is very largely due to the benefits and results of Islamic culture in Spain, Sicily and the Near East, which permeated European life after the Reformation and during the

Renaissance.'[57] The final part of the booklet deals with issues related to slavery, aggression and intolerance from both historical and comparative perspectives between Islam and Christianity. '*The three great prophets of the world, Moses, Jesus, and Muhammad*' is his third booklet, published in 1923, and deals mainly with the lives and teachings of these great Semitic Prophets, the setting in which they appeared, their personal and moral influences on their communities, their successes and pitfalls, and the nature and condition of the world they left behind. All these issues are investigated from a comparative perspective; in this context, Headley believes that Muhammad left a far better world behind him after his departure than did either Moses or Jesus.[58] Lord Headley also wrote many articles on various Islamic issues that appeared in local journals and newspapers, especially in *The Islamic Review*. In all his intellectual engagements, his prime motive was to dispel the misconceptions relating to key Islamic principles in Britain. He was an outspoken and even daring critic (more than other converts of his time with the exception, of course, of Abdullah Quilliam) of those he suspected of misleading the British public by spreading false information on the Islamic faith.

At the practical level, Lord Headley was extremely active and influential, joining the newly established Islamic Society in Woking soon after his conversion and becoming one of the prime movers behind its missionary activities. His leadership and commitment to the Woking mission drew together prominent convert personalities, chief among them being Yehya Nasr Parkinson, Stanley Musgrave, Khalid Sheldrake and M. Leon, who we know now was the famous Abdullah Quilliam. They worked successfully to promote the objectives of the Woking mission, for although there were prominent Muslim personalities in Woking, converts generally seem to have been running its affairs. Through Headly's unwavering efforts, the Woking mission developed under the auspices of an autonomous body called the British Muslim Society, which was inaugurated in December 1914 and of which Headly was the first president [59]. The main object was to introduce Islam to the British people: 'our first object should be to show all those we come in contact with that our religion is not exactly antagonistic or hostile to . . . Christianity; it is rather a religion possessing 600 years of additional enlightenment, but based, like Christianity, on duty to God and our neighbour.'[60] The majority of those who joined the Society were members of the upper and middle classes of British society, some of whom had been officers in India and other Muslim countries, and their families. The Society regularly met for the Friday prayers in London and for Sunday service at the Woking mosque; the Sunday meetings were mainly held in the form of ceremonies for those who desired to declare their conversion to Islam. Both the Society and the Woking mission also used to hold regular public meetings for people who were interested in learning about the faith, as well as for potential converts; during these meetings lectures were delivered, followed by questions and answers, and literature on Islam was distributed. On special religious occasions like the birthday of the Prophet Muhammad the Society would hold a meeting in one of the London hotels and invite a prominent speaker to deliver a lecture on the life of the Prophet. During all these meetings, Lord Headley would use the occasion to explain Islam and its tenets to those who were present.[61] As a member of the upper class, Lord Headley capitalized on his connections in aristocratic circles and explained Islam to the nobility, wishing either to win over potential converts or to promote an enlightened view of the faith among its members: 'Europeans very commonly look upon Mahomedanism as barbarism, but when they have learnt all that Mahomad did to mitigate the savagery and barbarism he met with in Arabia and elsewhere, they will not be slow to put aside their present opinions.'[62] *The Islamic Review*, the mouthpiece of the Woking mission, was also a vehicle for him to explain and propagate his view of the Islamic message, as mentioned earlier. To secure larger numbers of potential converts and sympathizers, especially among the general public, the Society and its first president decided to present Islam in a rather peculiar way. For example, he believed that prayers were ceremonial and not an essential part of the Islamic faith, and therefore not to be insisted upon, especially for English converts: 'It is quite impossible for the busy city man to pray Muslim fashion five times a day at the appointed times . . . He probably sends up the silent prayer.'[63] In this context, it is important to stress that prayer, from the Islamic perspective, is a vital mode of communication between humankind and the Ultimate Reality; it is also regarded as spiritual nourishment and therefore essential to the spiritual well-being of people who are very much immersed in worldly affairs. Thus, to view it as a minor and not essential pillar of faith is rather strange.

To avoid any controversy that might hinder his efforts to propagate Islam, he chose not to become involved in politics, as Abdullah Quilliam had done before him, for example: 'As first President of the Society, I shall . . . say that we must not enter into the field of politics, for if we do so we shall be certain to come to grief, either through internal dissensions or through collision with some outside authority . . . to succeed we must not allow any political considerations to in any way interfere with the propagation of Islam.'[64] What is more, he declared that his mission to spread Islam would not be achieved by attacking other religions but rather by showing the beauty of the faith: 'my chief object is not so much to attack any particular branch of the Christian religion as to point out the beauty and simplicity of the Muslim faith.'[65] To achieve his goals, he pressed ahead, using all avenues such as recruiting the press, holding public meetings, cooperating with other Muslim societies, especially the Muslim Literary Society, and disseminating Islamic literature for the public in Britain. The latter goal was achieved by setting up a trust called the Trust for the Encouragement and Circulation of Muslim Religious Literature under his leadership.[66] What was unique about his approach (and indeed the overall approach of the Woking mission) was the form of Islam he advocated. It was a universal Islam that had no sectarian or divisive inclinations and was based on the pristine nature of the faith, characterized by mutual respect and tolerance. This approach was certainly the main reason for the success of the mission under his leadership and even beyond. Apart from the above, Lord Headley is credited with laying the foundations for the famous London mosque. He was the first person to urge the British government to give its permission for the mosque's erection. Headley's efforts to disseminate the faith were not confined to Britain but extended as far as other Muslim countries. He played high-profile roles in India, Turkey, Egypt and South Africa, managing to create an environment in which he was able to make many contacts; and these were certainly made use of for the purpose of his mission in Britain.[67] There is no doubt that Lord Headley's contribution to Islam in Britain is immense, and impossible to cover comprehensively or give it due recognition in this brief overview. A more detailed study on the work of this dynamic and energetic figure would certainly fill the gap and would surely be a welcoming addition to Islamic literature in Britain.

Muhammad Marmaduke Pickthall

One of the most prolific and respected writers among his generation, Marmaduke Pickthall was novelist, linguist and above all a gifted translator of the Quran. He was born in London in 1875 to a devout Christian family. His father, Charles Grayson Pickthall, was a clergyman; and his mother, Mary O'Brien of Irish descent and the daughter of Admiral Donat Henry O'Brien, was a strong, responsible and independent-minded woman. Marmaduke had a younger brother, Rudolph, or Bob, whom he adored and of whom he never felt jealous despite the fact that Rudolph was his mother's favourite. On the contrary, he 'was no trouble to her (and) was ever content to play alone, quiet and self-absorbed'.[68] The first few years of his childhood were spent in Chillesford, which he liked so much that he later wrote three novels and many short stories that were all placed in East Suffolk. When he was 5 years old, his father died and his mother moved to London to look after her two sons almost single-handedly. Initially he attended a day school in Kensington, where he displayed a remarkably retentive memory and an interest in mental arithmetic; but these promising signs were ruined, especially his aptitude for mathematics, at the age of nine when he fell ill with brain fever. His mother then sent him to Chillesford where his father's successor as parish vicar, a kind and warm person, taught him Latin and some Greek, and inspired in him an interest in astronomy and nature, especially flowers. It was a happy time for him, but he had to move again when his mother moved house to Harrow, and Marmaduke was admitted to Harrow School, one of the most prestigious public schools in the country. Among his contemporaries was Winston Churchill. But he was not happy there; the bullying, the fagging system and the overall atmosphere proved too much for him, and in 1890 he left Harrow after only six terms. His recollections of the unhappy time at the school were later eloquently portrayed in his English novel, *Sir Limpidus*.[69] Marmaduke had earlier shown a remarkable gift for languages; realizing this, his mother decided to take him to Europe to further his aptitude for foreign languages. He perfected his French and learned Italian, and later when in Wales and Ireland, he mastered both Welsh and Gaelic. However, this did not yet win him a place in the Foreign Service, which gave him a sense of total failure: 'having failed in one or two adventures, I considered myself an all-round failure, and was much depressed. I dreamed of Eastern sunshine, palm trees, camels, desert sand, as of a paradise which I had lost by my shortcoming.'[70] At this juncture, and hoping to learn Arabic to secure a post in the Consular Service, he was presented with the opportunity of going to Palestine by way of Cairo; he duly accepted it and sailed to the East in 1894, when he was not yet 18 years old. The journey to the Middle East heralded the beginning of a momentous change in his life; like Muhammad Asad, he instantly fell in love with that part of the world for reasons he later explained in the following way: 'When I read Alf Leylah wa Leyla (*the Arabian Nights*) I see the daily life of Damascus, Jerusalem, Aleppo, Cairo and other cities as I found it in the early nineties of the last century. What struck me, even in its decay and poverty, was the joyousness of that life compared with anything that I had seen in Europe. The people seemed quite independent of our cares of life, our anxious clutching after wealth, our fear of death . . . They undoubtedly had something which was lacking in the life of Western Europe . . . that inward happiness which I so envied.'[71] Once there, he lost no time in learning Arabic, mixing with the people of the land, travelling into the depths of the Palestinian hinterland and Syria and donning their traditional clothes. Perfecting his Arabic, which he was able 'to speak like a native', young Marmaduke found himself at home in the Middle East and was impressed by the traditional Muslim way of life prevailing at the time. He saw a world of unlimited freedom, where Islamic rules and regulations were respected and implemented in time-honoured fashion; a place free of sectarian bigotry, narrow patriotism and blind fanaticism; a place where the theme of brotherhood was expressed in mutual respect, where ethical disagreement between the different schools of thought was discussed and where there were no class divisions in places of worship and, finally, where faith was deep and fervent due to the fact that it was upheld and sustained by sincerity, honesty and inner happiness.[72] All these issues ultimately prompted him to adopt Islam. It must be stressed that the Muslim world he saw and lived in was not the one we see today: 'He saw the Muslim world before Westernization had contaminated the lives of the masses, and long before it had infected Muslim political thought and produced the modern vision of the Islamic state, with its ideology, centralized bureaucracy, secret police, Pasdaran and Basij. That totalitarian nightmare he would not have recognized as Muslim. The deep faith of the Levantine peasantry so amazed him was sustained by the sincerity that can only come when men are free, not forced, in the practice of religion. For the state to compel compliance is to spread vice and disbelief; as the Arab proverb which he well knew says: if camel-dung were to be prohibited, people would seek it out.'[73] Absorbed by what he saw and felt in the Orient, Pickthall, at that tender age, decided to become a Muslim but was discouraged from doing so by 'his Muslim teacher, the Sheykh-ul-Ulema of the great mosque at Damascus. When he one day mentioned to this noble and benign old man his desire to become a Muslim, Sheykh-ul-Ulema reminded him of his duty to his mother and forbade him to profess Islam until he had consulted her. "No, my son," were his words, "wait until you are older, and have seen again your native land. You are alone among us as our boys are alone among the Christians. God knows how I should feel if any Christian teacher dealt with a son of mine otherwise than as I now deal with you" .'[74] He heeded his advice, left for home and did not convert until 20 years later, when he publicly declared his conversion to Islam in 1917 at the age of fifty-two. Once back home, he married Muriel Smith, who converted to Islam a few years after his conversion and settled down to lead ordinary life. During this time, he worked on his writing skills and began to write short stories, the first two of which were published in 1898 and 1899, going on to publish almost a novel per year on either British or Near Eastern subjects.[75] Pickthall was also content with his religious life, attending Church and practising his Anglican faith. However, Tim Winter believes that beneath the surface he was wrestling with doubts and cynicism and that it was this agonizing over faith that really fired his ability to write.[76] And what a remarkable ability he proved to have; within record time (for he died fairly young at the age of sixty-one) he produced twenty-four books: his magnificent *The Meaning of the Glorious Quran* in addition to his major writings on various subjects in journals such as *The New Age* (London), *Islamic Culture* (Hyderabad), *The Islamic Review* and *The Islamic Review* and *Modern India* (both Woking). His first novel, *All Fools*, published in 1900, did not display his potential literary abilities, and since it was later viewed as one of his worst novels, he decided to buy the unsold copies and destroy them. However, his second novel, *Said the Fisherman*, published in 1903, proved to be one of the most successful of his novels and earned him a name in the literary world. E. M. Forster wrote: 'Pickthall was the only contemporary English novelist who understands the nearer East', while H. G. Wells declared: 'I wish I could feel as certain about my own work as I do of yours, that it will be alive and interesting people 50 years from now.'[77] This was followed by another four novels: *Enid* (1904), *Brendle* (1905), *The House of Islam* (1906), and *The Myopes* (1907). In 1907, after a period of productive writing and a break of around 10 years, Pickthall returned to the Middle East; this time he went to Egypt, but also visited his beloved Damascus. The result was that he wrote more novels, chief among them being *The Children of the Nile*, *The Valley of the Kings*, and *Veiled Women*, published in 1908, 1909 and 1913 respectively. During this time, he also became involved in politics and was actively opposed to British foreign policy in the Muslim region. When the coup of 1908 brought the Young Turks to power, he supported their cause and saw their reform as an opportunity to improve the situation of the empire under Ottoman rule: The years 1912/13 were difficult years for the empire, especially with regard to its European provinces. When Pickthall visited Turkey for 4 months in 1913, he observed the political situation, managed to learn Turkish, mixed with the people and donned their dress. While there, he developed a special affection for the Turks, believing that their system guaranteed autonomy and measures of respect and freedom for the various provinces of the empire: 'Turkey is the present head of a progressive movement extending throughout Asia and North Africa. She is also the one hope of the Islamic world.'[78] When he returned to England, he wrote many articles in *The New Age* on the reform of the Young Turks and the need for the British government to support them in their endeavours. With a few friends, he set up an

Anglo-Ottoman society 'to advocate a political and commercial understanding between Great Britain and Turkey and firmly to oppose encroachment on the Ottoman Empire'.[79] But his campaign to save the 'sick man of Europe' did not fall on sympathetic ears; on the contrary, the situation continued to worsen rapidly, and the outbreak of hostilities in November 1914 shattered his dream of saving the empire. After publicly supporting the empire and calling for a separate peace treaty with Turkey, his pro-Ottoman stance brought him into conflict with the British authorities, who regarded him as security risk and denied him a prominent position at the Arab Bureau in Cairo. Pickthall was also outraged by the upsurge of enmity towards Islam and the Ottoman Empire, as well as by the triumphant mood expressed by politicians and religious leaders alike; in 1917, he announced his conversion to Islam and began to play an important role in the activities of the British Muslim community, especially in London and Woking.[80] Among other functions, he became the imam of the Notting Hill mosque in London, leading prayers and preaching in Arabic and English; he lectured at meetings of the Muslim Literary Society; he then became the imam of the Woking mosque (after Khwaja Kamaluddin, the founder and imam of the Woking mosque, left for India), leading Friday prayers and delivering sermons; and he conducted the *Taraweh* prayer during Ramadan and led the *Eid al-fitr* prayer at the mosque. Describing his sermons at Friday prayer, *The Islamic Review* wrote that 'his sermons have been characterized as much by his great scholarship and erudition as by his skilful and masterly elucidation of the popular Quranic themes. His recitations of the Arabic texts have been most inspiring. Our English friends will, we trust, have rejoiced to see one of their own race lead in prayers in Arabic a congregation of mixed races.'[81] In addition, he took over the editorship of *The Islamic Review*, published by the mosque, and for one year ran the Islamic Information Bureau in London, which issued a weekly paper called *The Muslim Outlook*.[82] The turbulent war years and his active involvement in the politics of the time did not prevent him from writing. Between 1913 and 1920, he wrote an impressive eleven novels: *The Black Crusade, Veiled Women* (mentioned above), *With the Turk in Wartime, Tales from Five Chimneys, The House of War, Knight of Araby, Oriental Encounters, War and Religion* and *Sir Limpidus*. Again, all these novels incorporate either British or Middle Eastern themes, and as usual they reflect clearly, as through a mirror, the characters and events they portray. Bitterly alienated by British foreign policy during the war and after, Pickthall gladly accepted a job in India in 1920. Peter Clark believes that the period in India 'was tantamount to self-exile from Britain', for he was out of favour (on account of his 'unpatriotic' position), a loner with no followers or sympathizers, and the issues he supported were unwanted and unpopular.[83] He stayed in India for 15 years and, according to his biographer, they were the happiest and most fruitful years. For although 'Syria, Egypt, Turkey – he had known and loved and served them all, and his first love and loyalty were always to these . . . yet his best service was given to India and India most fully rewarded that service.'[84] Initially, he worked for 4 years as the editor of the *Bombay Chronicle*, a major Indian newspaper, which he managed to bring back to its original standard within 6 months and increase its circulation to double what it was when he assumed its editorship: 'I have now put all the staff upon their dignity, making them realize that the "national" paper must not stoop to littleness of any kind, must even compliment a decent adversary every now and then.'[85] While he was busy attending to the paper, he became involved in Indian political and religious activities, backing the Caliphate movement, encouraging its supporters to adopt non-violent resistance, befriending Gandhi and cooperating with him on drawing up strategies for the overall future of India. He also preached at the mosque at Bijapur, lectured at the University of Aligarh and began to learn Urdu. In 1924, he moved to Hyderabad, a prosperous and cultural centre at the time under the governorship of the Nizam. With the latter's encouragement and support, Pickthal launched the journal *Islamic Culture* and became its editor for 10 years. Under his editorship, it became – and continues to be – one of the Muslim world's leading academic journals. He was also given the headmastership of one of the leading schools in the city and the directorship of the Hyderabad civil service. In the midst of these major responsibilities, Pickthall found time to write, authoring and publishing another five books between 1920 and 1930: *Islam and Progress* (1920), *The Early Hours* (1921), *As Others See Us* (1922), *The Cultural Side of Islam* (1927) and *The Meaning of the Quran* (1935). At the start of 1935, Pickthall retired and returned to England. He and his wife settled in Cornwall but kept in contact with Muslims both in London and India. In May 1936, he died of coronary thrombosis at the age of 61 and was buried at Brookwood Cemetery, not far from Woking. There is no doubt that Pickthall was a committed Muslim and sincere in his religious life; he loved and observed his faith, practising his religious obligations meticulously (praying regularly, fasting at Ramadan and abiding by the Islamic prohibitions, though unfortunately a plan to undertake the Hajj did not materialize); he preached his adopted faith enthusiastically and urged Muslims to be upright and put Islamic notions of morality into practice, as he himself lived and practised the faith. But Pickthall was above all a gifted linguist, Orientalist, novelist, prolific writer, translator of the Quran and a sincere and respected Islamic

scholar. As a novelist, he produced some of the best stories sincerely depict-
ing human characters, behaviours and attitudes; he was a keen observer,
able to understand and eloquently portray the subjects he wrote about. His
enchantment with the Near East, and his profound knowledge of the indigenous cultures and languages allowed him to fully understand their identity
and consequently portray them clearly and accurately. His style of writing is
lucid and enjoyable; it ties you up in the story and allows you to live the
events. As a scholar and authority on Islam, which is where our concern lies,
he wrote on various aspects of the faith and made extensive contributions
to it. This change of perspective started in 1917, when he converted to
Islam, and his writings gradually started to take on more Islamic themes
than ever. His first Islamic writing was a prose hymn in praise of the Prophet
Muhammad, published in January 1917 in *The Islamic Review* and Modern
India.[86] This was followed by a set of lectures that were later published in
book form, entitled *Islam and Progress* (1920). In this book (and like Quilliam
before him), he declared that 'Islam alone was a progressive religion. Other
religions were unfit to claim that their tenets countenanced progress.'[87] His
main work on Islamic culture and civilization appeared in 1927 under the
title *The Cultural Side of Islam*. Reprinted many times and still widely read on
the Indian subcontinent, the book discusses critical issues for Muslims, the
most significant among them being the rise and decline of Muslim culture.
He attributed the success of Islamic culture to the conduct of the early
Muslims: their adherence to the moral principles of Islam, their tolerance
and acceptance of others, their willingness to learn and benefit from other
cultures and civilizational achievements, their good will and benevolence
towards others and, above all, their universal outlook, for they applied one
standard and one law for both Muslims and non-Muslims; there was no
partiality. A non-Muslim whose conduct was good and who conformed to
the law was respected and favoured over a professed Muslim whose conduct
was bad and who did not conform. When Muslims, both as individuals and
as nations, gave up all the above principles, they declined and weakened,
not so much because of external factors, but, above all, because of their
own shortcomings.[88] This is a standard Sacred Universal law or, as he calls
it, Shariah law: 'The test is Conduct. The result of good conduct is good,
and the result of evil conduct is evil, for the nation as for the individual.
That is the teaching of Islam, and never has its virtue been more plainly
illustrated than in the history of the rise and decline of Muslim civilization.'[89]
A further theme that he discusses in the book is the concept of brotherhood in Islam, which he regards as 'an ideal and an institution' that distin-
guishes Muslims from other religious communities in the sense that Islam,

through the Quran and Hadith, legalized it and succeeded in turning it into reality. The Prophet, Picthall says, 'not only proclaimed the fact of universal human brotherhood, but for the first time in the history of the world, made of it a principle and fact of common law. All the ordinances of Islam tend towards it, and it is shown to be the only ground of genuine human progress.'[90] First, there are the moral injunctions, which not only stress brotherly relationships between individuals and nations, irrespective of wealth, birth, colour, race, rank and power, but also strictly prohibit bigotry, narrow patriotism and aggressive nationalism. Second, there are the religious rules and obligations, the adherence to which would strengthen and broaden this Islamic universal fraternity; 'for it has bond together black and white and brown and yellow people in complete agreement and equality, has reconciled the claim of rich and poor, the governor and the governed, slave and free'.[91] These are the weekly congregation prayers, the annual pilgrimage to Mecca, the yearly fasting month of Ramadan and the annual collection of *Zakat* to be paid to the poor and needy. This bond of brotherhood was, and continues to be, strong and an important element of Muslim identity despite wars and differences of opinion between Muslims. However, in recent times this institution has been weakened due to the neglect by Muslims of some of their religious duties.[92] It must be noted that for him this Muslim brotherhood is a stepping stone towards universal human brotherhood under the guardianship of one God. A further two important issues dealt with in the book need to be highlighted: tolerance and the position of Muslim women. On the subject of tolerance he states that the West falsely accused Islam both historically and as a religion of being intolerant. To argue against this assumption, he adopts historical and theological approaches; historically, he compares the situation of non-Muslims, especially Jews and Christians, under Muslim rule in Damascus, Baghdad, Spain, Cairo and Istanbul and then contrasts it with that of Muslims and Jews under Christian rule, especially in Spain, Sicily, Apulia and Greece. For him, although Christians and Jews under Muslim rule occupied an inferior position compared to that of Muslims, they were certainly better than those of Muslims and Jews who were under Christian rule. Muslims protected Christians and Jews and gave them security, autonomy and the liberty of conscience. They were never prosecuted or massacred until Muslims disregarded their religious injunctions in later times; by contrast, Muslims and Jews suffered greatly when they came under Christian governorship. Theologically, Pickthall stresses that there is nothing in the Islamic texts that leads to intolerance, especially towards Jews and Christians and that, if Europeans knew the scriptures well, they would not have launched the Crusades against Muslims or persecuted them when they came under their rule. Pickthall believes that the teachings of their priests and the information that the people were fed in those days by their religious leaders caused Europeans to become extremely bigoted and intolerant towards non-Christians, especially Muslims. Thus, while Islam, as a religion, encouraged tolerance and peaceful co-existence among non-Muslims, Christianity, as taught by the Church, missionaries and priests, promoted fanaticism, bigotry and non-acceptance of non-Christians. In fact, tolerance, if it exists, was considered irreligious: 'Of old, tolerance had existed here and there in the world, among enlightened individuals; but those individuals had always been against the prevalent religion. Tolerance was regarded as un-religious, if not irreligious. Before the coming of Islam it had never been preached as an essential part of religion.'[93] Ironically for him, when Christians abandoned their religious law, they became more tolerant, while Muslims, when they disregarded their religious law, grew less tolerant! He puts this in the following way: 'It was not until the Western nations broke away from their religious law that they became more tolerant; and it was only when the Muslims fell away from their religious law that they declined in tolerance and other evidences of the highest culture.'[94] In doing so, Muslims, according to Pickthall, have lost the vision of mercy, openness, majesty and freedom from bigotry and prejudices that their scriptures offer to them, and unless they reclaim that vision, they are doomed to condemnation. Pickthall was very concerned about the situation of Muslim women at the time, especially the pitiful position of Muslim women in India, which he witnessed and condemned. Despite the fact that it was a delicate subject, he did not hesitate to air his views in the hope that his efforts in this regard would improve their overall conditions. So he wrote and spoke of it frankly and in an honest spirit. Pickthall declared that the situation of women did not reflect the real vision of Islam but rather the un-Islamic perception of false pride; as such it constituted a crime for which the whole of the Muslim community must pay. Pickthall stressed that he judged women's position by the Shariah and not by any foreign paradigm. The law, for him, gives women social, economic, political and educational rights, but women are denied these rights by men of limited knowledge and dogmatic interpretations, thus misleading people about the true representation of women in Islam: 'Women', he said, 'have equal rights with men before the Shariah and (the) Quran proclaims that they are equal with men in the sight of God.'[95] Instead, women are subordinated, confined to their dwellings, denied education and opportunities to develop their minds and their society and stripped of their economic and political rights; worse than that, they are forced to don un-Islamic veiling. Pickthall was an outspoken critic of veiling the face, which was widely practised at that time in India. He urged Muslims in India to do away with it; of its theological basis he says: 'The veiling of the face by women was not, originally, an Islamic custom. It was prevalent in the cities of the East before the coming of Islam, but not in the cities of Arabia . . . it has never been a universal custom for Muslim women, the great majority of whom have never used it; for the majority of the Muslim women in the world are peasants who work with their husbands and brothers in the fields. For them the face veil would be an absurd encumbrance.'[96] To enhance the overall position of women, he stresses the gradual improvement through the medium of education, which he believes to be the only way forward for women's emancipation. Pickthall also takes up the question of polygamy (not widely practised in India due to the economic circumstances); like Quilliam before him, he supports the practice not as an institution but as a necessity for special cases, although he does not elaborate on the way to prevent abuses if it is allowed.[97] In addition, he deals with art, science and literature, the question of free will and fatalism, as well as the meaning and application of *Jihad*. His main intellectual contribution to Islam in my opinion is his monumental translation of the Quran, a task that is not easy to accomplish by virtue of the fact that he was a convert and that his first language was not Arabic. Moreover, his attempt came at a time when the view among religious scholars was that the Quran could not be translated and that to do so was tantamount to committing a grave sin. Nonetheless, he embarked on the project that took him more than 2 years to accomplish. Pickthall had contemplated the idea long before he started the project; for he was not satisfied with other translations due to their emphasis on words rather than on the overall meaning. His translation is the first English translation by an English Muslim, and it aimed to serve the needs of English readers, especially English-speaking Muslims. 'The Koran cannot be translated', he said. 'The Book is here rendered almost literally and every effort has been made to choose befitting language . . . the result is only an attempt to present the meaning of the Koran . . . in English. It can never take the place of the Koran in Arabic, nor it is it meant to do so.'[98] The work was scrutinized and approved by a committee of learned scholars, and when it appeared in 1930, it was regarded as one of the best translations into a foreign language. *The Times Literary Supplement* declared that it was 'a great literary achievement'; Sir Denison Ross congratulated Pickthall on 'a really great achievement'; and Muhammad Ali exalted: 'At last, thank God, we have a real translation.'[99] The translation made his name, for he is still remembered and known all over the world as the translator of the Quran.

It was, and continues to be, the most popular and widely used translation in the English-speaking world and the Indian subcontinent, having been reprinted many times in the UK, the US, India and some Arab countries. It has also withstood the test of time: more than 50 years since it first appeared, it continues to offer guidance and meaning on the great Islamic religious text.

It can be clearly seen from the above that the intellectual contributions of the early converts to Islam are immense in every respect. Their efforts in highlighting accurately and professionally the teachings and principles of Islam from within and on their own terms is highly appreciated by Muslims, and also by non-Muslims who are drawn to the sacred and the reality of religion. They have evidently left a great intellectual Islamic legacy with regard to the history of Islam in Britain that will surely exert an influence on those British Muslims and non-Muslims who are interested in the role and impact of the faith in Britain. Having said that, however, judging by their huge intellectual endeavours in this context, one would have thought that the view of the faith in Britain was more balanced and accurate, but unfortunately this was not the case. The study, representation and view of Islam in general continued to be tainted by bias and prejudice 'through the absolution of . . . Western concepts and methodologies that were applied to Islam with the sense of superiority and hubris going back to the Renaissance definition of the European man'.[100] Unfortunately, their voices and the voices of some exceptional Western scholars who studied Islam impartially and even-handedly were overshadowed not only by people who were pursuing a particular agenda but also by people who had no interest in religion at all, be it Christianity, Islam or any other religion.

Chapter 3

Native British Converts:
Post-World War II Era Onward

The subject of post-World War II converts is to be looked at against the backdrop of the process of modernization and secularization that Europe, including Britain, had undergone since the Renaissance. During this period, Europe witnessed drastic social, economic and political upheavals, as well as major intellectual and religious changes as a result of the Reformation, the Industrial Revolution, the emergence of capitalism and the rise of modern science and technology. These developments paved the way for the emergence of a new Europe mainly based on and anthropocentric rather than theocentric worldview in which human being became the centre of everything, or, to use Nasr's phrase, the new Europe replaced the kingdom of God with the kingdom of man. He explains this process very eloquently in the following way: 'the freedom of reason from revelation and intellectual intuition, combined with an emphasis upon humanism, rationalism, empiricism, and naturalism, led to many new developments, including a new science based on power rather than wisdom, and made it possible for Europe to expand over the globe and become dominant over other civilizations. It led to the Industrial Revolution, modern technology, and modern science.' [1] Although these modern developments have brought benefits to humankind (in terms of eradicating disease and bringing about various material comforts), they have been achieved at a very high cost. For they have led to the emergence of the following problems: the population explosion, destruction of the natural environment, death of millions of people (due to modern means of warfare), emergence of the heavy consumer and material attitudes combined with extreme poverty, break-up of the social fabric of society and, most of all, loss of the real meaning of life combined with spiritual poverty.[2] The last two issues are of great concern to us here for they have led, and continue to lead, many people in the West, including Britain, to turn away from Christianity and seek guidance, direction and spiritual fulfilment in Eastern religions. The following statement illustrates the point well: 'from the beginning of the twentieth century and especially since the Second World War, many Westerners who have had the thirst for spiritual experience and religious knowledge but who have not been able to find what they have been seeking in the context of the existing religious institutions in the West have turned to Eastern religions. Some have turned to Hinduism, others to Buddhism and a number to Islam and especially to Sufi teachings within Islam.'[3] The teachings of Sufism were, and continue to be, the main point of entry to Islam for British people, especially the elites. It must be stressed here that Sufism in the Muslim world is a powerful opponent to religious extremism, as well as a significant source, both spiritually and intellectually, of credible answers to the challenges presented to Islam by modernism. In the West, it is an important means of comprehending Islam in its totality and essential reality and is 'a central link between the spiritual traditions of Islam and the West'.[4] For these reasons, Sufism has become extremely popular not only in Britain but also throughout Europe and North America. Hence, it is important to dwell, albeit briefly, on the meaning of Sufism, its role in strengthening the individual and society and its continuous success in attracting converts to Islam not only historically but also today. Sufism, or the spiritual values of the faith, is the core, or the essence, of the religion of Islam; for Sufism is Islamic spirituality, even if Islamic spirituality is not confined to the phenomenon of Sufism. The spiritual values of the religion of Islam are brought into sharp focus by the Sufis and are implemented practically by them in various ways. But the Sufis do not claim that these values and the doctrines and practices emerging therefrom are anything other than those of quintessential Islam. Their 'esotericism' is but the complement of the exotericism of the formal religion, and both are rooted in the sources of the Islamic revelation – the Quran and the Sunnah of the Prophet. To understand the inner, spiritual values of the revelation, one can turn to the Sufis, who have incorporated these values organically into a dynamic way of life. Insofar as most Sufis integrate these inner values with outer Shariah practice, the result of their presence in Islamic society is a strengthening of the religion as a whole; it was not simply that the Sufis promoted these inner values at the expense of the outer forms of Islam.

'Sufism . . . became the framework within which all popular piety flowed together; its saints, dead and living, became the guarantors of the gentle and co-operative sides of social life. Guilds commonly came to have Sufi affiliations. Men's clubs claimed the patronage of Sufi saints. And the tombs of local saints became shrines which almost all factions united in revering. It is probable that without the subtle leaven of the Sufi orders, giving to

Islam an inward personal thrust and to the Muslim community a sense of participation in a common spiritual venture quite apart from anyone's outward power, the mechanical arrangements of the Shariah would not have maintained the loyalty essential to their effectiveness.'[5]

Sufism, as Martin Lings says, 'is necessary because it is to Islam what the heart is to the body. Like the bodily heart it must be secluded and protected and must remain firm-fixed in the centre; but at the same time it cannot refuse to feed the arteries with life.'[6] If one wishes to appreciate the deeper motives for conversion to Islam, one cannot afford to ignore this inner aspect of the religion. The following quotation illustrates this well: 'I knew that I yearned for more spiritual fulfilment in my life. But, as yet, nothing had seemed acceptable or accessible to me. I had been brought up essentially a secular humanist. Morals were emphasized, but never attributed to any spiritual or divine being. As I met more Muslims, I was struck not only by their inner peace, but by the strength of their faith. In retrospect, I realize that I was attracted to these peaceful souls because I sensed my own lack of inner peace and conviction.'[7] Men and women – in particular, those belonging to the higher classes or the elite, who have no social, economic, or racial motives for conversion – are drawn to Islam by the spiritual values which Sufism has espoused, even if this is not always made explicit. But before elaborating this claim, it is necessary to give a brief account of the role of Sufism as a vehicle for conversion to Islam. Historically, Sufism has played a major role in spreading Islam and recruiting non-Muslims to the faith. It has been asserted that the spread of Islam beyond the frontiers of the Muslim states, and thus the Islamization of such areas as Anatolia, Bosnia, Kashmir, Indonesia, India and West Africa is attributable in large part to the efforts of Sufi saints. This is the conclusion reached by Thomas Arnold in his classic and still unsurpassed study of the spread of Islam.[8] Arnold shows that, far from being 'spread by the sword', as the common stereotype would have us believe, Islam was in fact spread by peaceful means: by the preaching of the Sufis on the one hand and by the impact of traders on the other. Indeed, the two often went hand in hand, as traders were themselves often members of a Sufi order, from the thirteenth century onwards.

The appeal of the Sufis continues to this day, providing one of the main points of entry to Islam, especially for contemporary Europeans, including the British and Americans.[9] Nasr describes it as 'the flower of the tree of Islam . . . .or the jewel in the crown of the Islamic tradition'.[10] The emphasis of Sufism on a universal supra-intellectual but very real tawhid (or science of God's unity), its focus on inner practices as a force for the transformation of individuals, its insistence on the detachment of the individual from the world rather than abandonment of it, its care for the welfare of the community and its aim to bring about justice through injecting moral and ethical values into human lives has made it one of the most attractive forces of the religion of Islam, especially in Western society.[11]

In addition, its ability to fill the spiritual vacuum created by such ideologies as secularism, socialism and modernism has made it particularly important as an avenue to converting to Islam.

The men and women, especially from the elite, who showed interest in or entered into Islam, did so by virtue of the fact that they were challenged by what one might call the 'spiritual intellectuality' of the inner dimension of the religion. Having read literature on Sufi spirituality written by both practising Muslims/Sufis and objective Western academics, they became aware of the link between the inner, universal spirit of the faith and its outer, particular form, known increasingly, and more accurately, as the form taken by Islamic mysticism. Many intellectuals came to see such values as secular cleverness, wealth, relativism and pragmatism in the light of Sufi ideals of wisdom, sacrifice, a sense of the absolute and idealism. These characteristics ultimately lent a sense of balance and completeness, primarily through the power of integration proper to Sufism. Integration means tawhid, the verbal noun stemming from the verb *Wahhada*, literally 'to make one'. Whereas, theologically, this means declaring or affirming God's oneness, in Sufism it comes to mean realizing oneness – the oneness of God – but also the oneness of being, and thus the necessity of 'being one', or being 'integrated' as a personality in order to properly affirm and realize the oneness of God. Thus, tawhid is fully realized when God is worshipped by the 'whole' human being: to be 'whole' is to be 'holy' (the words being etymologically related). This state of integration stands at the very antipodes of the dissipation and agitation that so many feel is generated by modern life: 'For to be dissipated and compartmentalized, to be lost in the never ending play of mental images and concepts, or psychic tensions and forces, (means) to be removed from that state of wholeness which our inner state demands from us.'[12] Sufism strives towards the attainment of the state of purity and wholeness 'not through negation of intelligence, as is often the case in the kind of piety fostered by certain modern religious movements, but through the integration of each element of one's being into its own proper centre'.[13] As such, the spiritual method is crucial for the integration of the person, for it brings the dispersed elements in the human being back together and ensures that the outwards shifting tendency is controlled and reversed so that the person can live inwardly with his/her emotions, reactions and tendencies, aiming primarily at the centre rather than the rim[14] 'for at the centre reside the One, the Pure and ineffable being which is the source of all beatitude and goodness, whereas at the periphery is non-existence, which only appears to be real because of illusory perception and lack of discrimination'.[15]

To achieve such a transformation of the human mind, body and spirit, normative Sufism does not go beyond the framework of the law but seeks to base its practices on the injunctions of the Shariah. Sufism integrates the outward (*zahir*) and the inward (*batin*) aspects of the faith and integrates male and female on the basis of the integration within God of *jalal* (majesty) and *jamal* (beauty), ultimately resulting in a totality on the metaphysical plane, which implies complementarity at the human level within and between man and woman. This is very much a part of the traditional Islamic conception of the nature of things. Therefore, when men lack beauty (*jamal*) of the soul, they tend to oppress those weaker than themselves through lack of compassion, thus disobeying God in the process through lack of wisdom and submission. When women lack strength (*jalal*) of the soul on the other hand they are unable to assert their true strength, whereas Sufi women have always been able to summon their reserves of strength and remain impassively independent. Sufi women throughout the ages have been an inspiration to other women and have taken on male disciples.[16] This affirms the necessity of the feminine/spiritual dimension as a balancing factor; for when men (and women) lose the balance between the two sides of their nature, then *ihsan* – that is virtue or beauty of soul – loses its meaning. Where there is no perception of or conformity to beauty – *ihsan* in the deepest sense – there is no virtue; and where men (and women) have no virtue, society collapses into the kind of chauvinism and abuse that characterize male-female relations in so many parts of the Muslim world. As a consequence, a considerable number of Westerners are attracted to Sufism and then to Islam. Currently, there are many Sufi groups in Europe and America which are able to attract converts to Islam.[17] Moreover, there are centres that are dedicated to the study of Sufism in the West, chief among them being the Muhyiddin ibn al-Arabi centre in Oxford. The number of people who have adopted Sufism and then Islam both in Europe, including Britain, and in the United States is considerable; they include 'ordinary' people who once sought inner peace, such as now middle-aged people who lived through the 'hippie' periods in the 1960s and 1970s[18] and those who were disillusioned with the Western material way of life and decided to embrace Islam to fulfil their spiritual needs. Further, a significant number of Western intellectuals found consolation in the wisdom of Sufism. These include the French philosopher, René Guénon, whose teachings on Sufism have become a model for Europeans interested in the spiritual dimension of Islam[19] such as the Swiss intellectuals, Schuon and Burckhardt, the English mystic, Martin Lings, and the former diplomat and writer, Gai Eaton. More recently, we can refer to Tim Winter (although from a different Sufi perspective) of Cambridge University. These three latter scholars will be dealt with separately as specific case studies at a later stage.

The Contemporary British Convert Community

It is difficult to ascertain whether there is a cohesive British convert community as such. There might be some groups or pockets dotted around the country and there might be prominent individuals here and there, but there is certainly no single 'community' in the literal sense of the word. Having said this, one may surmise that among these groups and individuals there are various forms of networking and collaboration and that they are also actively involved with the Muslim community on matters of common interest.[20] Statistically, there is no precise figure to put on the number of this 'community'. Tim Winter of Cambridge University, for example, puts it at fifty thousand members while Yahya Birt of Kube publishing believes that the number is no more than ten to twenty thousand. It is a highly diverse community in terms of age, socio-economic and educational background, which makes it difficult to make any meaningful generalizations, except that a large number of them come from Catholic rather than Protestant or Jewish backgrounds. In the past (as we have seen above), conversion to Islam was sporadic and took place predominantly among notable persons who had encountered Islam either by working in the Muslim world or by meeting some prominent Muslims in Britain; they had been so impressed by the Muslim way of lives or by the nature of their religion that they decided to embrace their faith. In recent years, especially after the 11th September attacks in the United States, the phenomenon has gained significance as the rate of conversions increased and became frequent particularly among members of the affluent British middle class. This generated interest, and even some unease, among certain sections of the British media, which found it difficult to comprehend that a number of rich and educated British people should choose Islam as an alternative way of life. For example, in January 2002, the Daily Mail newspaper concluded an interview with Joe Dobson, a convert and son of former health minister, Frank Dobson, by stating: 'He is certainly a beguiling advertisement for his faith . . . it is still impossible not to feel a sense of unease that the bright young son of a Government minister was forced to turn to Islam to find what he was look-ing for – because the world around him could not provide it.'[21] These people do not embrace Islam through missionary efforts; rather, they come to Islam for spiritual and intellectual reasons, as previously mentioned. Once they have converted, the majority stay loyal and uphold their new religious beliefs and practices. In the last 15–20 years, British converts have grown confident enough to become active in influencing Islamic discourses in Britain. New Muslims, especially the educated ones, are very active in society and work hard to present Islam in a more balanced way. Their aims are to bridge the gap between Muslim Communities and the wider society; help the main Muslim community to integrate; and shape an Islam that is not only based on universal Islamic principles but also rooted in some of the celebrated British values such as mutual respect, openness, tolerance, fairness and justice. Their approach is based on cooperation with govern-ment and society on the one hand and Muslim communities on the other with a view to combating extremism, alienation and Islam phobia. A large number of them offer advice to the government on policy issues relating to Islam, Muslim communities and wider society. Their contributions can be observed at various levels and are beginning to affect and shape the future of British Islam: intellectually and academically,[22] a good number of convert scholars are working either privately or in various British higher education institutions who through their writings have contributed tremendously to the presentation and teaching of Islam. Among these[23] are Tim Winter[24], who has translated the work of the fourteenth-century scholar Abu Hamid Al-Ghazali the revival of Islamic sciences, Martin Lings (who has predomi-nantly worked on Sufism), Gai Eaton[25] (traditional Islam), Neal Robinson (Quranic studies), Yasin Dutton (Islamic law, especially Maliki law), Jeremy Henzell-Thomas of The Book Foundation and David Waines, former head of Religious Studies at Lancaster University.[26] The intellectual contributions of especially the first three of these scholars to Islam in general and British Islam in particular are immense. Their writings portray Islam in a more coherent and balanced way, rather than marked by distortions or apologet-ics. Most importantly, they have managed to present Islam not only phenomenologically, but also as a living reality. For a long time Islam in Britain, unlike Christianity and Judaism, was (and continues to be) taught by non-Muslims purely as an academic subject and from outside the faith. These scholars have the advantage of knowing both worlds; in other words, they are insiders as well as outsiders and are thus able to present (and teach) Islam not only academically but also spiritually, a subject area and a living

reality that trains both mind and soul. This enriches and adds a new perspective to the overall educational process. In addition to the above veteran
scholars, one can refer to a new generation of scholars whose writings and
works will have a positive impact on the shape of British Islam. These are
Muhammad Seddon, of Chester University, Sophie Gilliat-Ray from Cardiff
University, Ian Draper and Laura MacDonald[27], both from Birmingham
University. At the social level there are some well-known converts who work
with Muslim youth to tackle issues such as anger, frustration, alienation and
extremism. Among those who have played a role in this area is Yahya Birt,
whose PhD thesis is on Muslim youth and who advised the government on
youth issues. Batool Al Toma (or Mary Geraghty), a further important figure
in this regard, has a degree from the University of Wales and currently
works as Research and Education Officer at the Islamic Foundation in
Leicester. Born in 1955 in Ireland into a practising Catholic family, she
practised Catholicism until her late teens when, according to her own
reports, she began to question theological issues related to her faith. She
was introduced to Islam through a Muslim friend and subsequently began
her journey to the faith: 'I think it was the fact that I could actually argue
out, in a rational manner, all the beliefs and understandings and religious
concepts – rituals and everything to do with the faith itself. And of course I
was able to accept Jesus, as a prophet of God and was able to come to a
(more) rational understanding of his role.'[28] Batool is very active within the
'convert community', heading the New Muslims Project which she found
in 1993. This project caters for the specific needs of new Muslims and
'provides support for those interested in and new to Islam'.[29] One of the
vehicles for such help is the journal 'Meeting Point', a quarterly publication
that she edits;, it gives advice to converts on Islamic issues, and the topics it
discusses range from education to current issues, with questions by converts
answered by Muslim scholars. It also gives information on conferences and
events throughout the country. It is hugely popular among the converts and
highly admired and appreciated by them, as the following statement by a
convert indicates: 'Meeting point is exactly what converts need in that it
shows the continuing processes of conversion, the similarities in the
problems and hurdles we all experience whether they be social, food, cloth-
ing, Charismas . . . your magazine covers it all.'[30] In my opinion, this journal
acts as a link between all indigenous converts in the country, giving them a
sense of belonging and a sense of identity, making them feel part of a
cohesive community that shares the good and the bad of this world. Apart
from her role in this project, Batool is also involved in media consultation
on British converts and very often acts as a government advisor on Muslim

issues. British converts are also greatly involved in education; among those who devote their energies to this important sector are Ibrahim Hewitt and former pop star, Cat Stevens or Yusuf Islam. The former was born into a Christian family in Tynemouth; having embraced Islam in 1981, he has since been active in Muslim-related issues both in Britain and beyond. An ardent advocate of faith-based schools, he worked for a time as the chairman of the Islamia Schools Trust and is currently the head teacher of the Al-Aqsa primary school in Leicester, an independent faith-based school. He believes that faith schools produce loyal and law-abiding citizens as well as people of faith for believing families. Hewitt is also involved in charity work, especially for those in dire need around the world. In this context, he acts as the chairman of the Board of Trustees of the Charity 'Interpal,' which is a 'non-political, non-profit making British charity that focuses on the provision of relief and development aid to the poor and needy of Palestine.'[31] Yusuf Islam's support of education, especially faith-based education, is immense. Born in London in 1948 to a Swedish mother and Greek Cypriot father, he was the youngest of three children. Although a Greek Orthodox, he was sent to a Catholic school by his father, but when he discovered that his interest lay in art, especially music, he decided to become a singer. Islam succeeded in his chosen profession, becoming a celebrity star in not only Britain but the United States. A Los Angeles newspaper wrote about him as 'an exceptional singer and artist, able to combine strength, and fragility and sometimes mystery in his highly personal composition'.[32] But the more he succeeded, the more he withdrew; his spiritual need led him to study Eastern religions, but he was still not satisfied. Islam states that despite the fact that he indulged in the life of a rock star, he nevertheless managed to protect his soul; this was very important when he later converted to Islam. His encounter with Islam came when his brother, after a visit to Jerusalem, brought him a copy of the Quran; it proved a revelation for him. Speaking of the holy book, he said: 'it was the timeless nature of the message . . . the words all seemed strangely familiar yet so unlike anything I had ever read before.'[33] In 1977, he embraced Islam and changed his name to Yusuf (from the Quran chapter on the Prophet Joseph) Islam, dedicating his time and wealth to education. He opened and funded Islamia Primary School, which became the first Muslim school in the country to be funded by the government. This was followed by another three schools. On the importance of education he stresses: 'I earnestly believe there is a need for strengthening the moral base of education . . . the horrors which are happening more and more in schools: murders, teenage pregnancies, drugs, the lack of respect, violence, bullying, racism. Surely kids deserve a better start and chance in life?'[34] His work in this field prompted the Prince of Wales to praise his efforts to establish peace, cohesion and mutual understanding through education; and both Exeter and Gloucestershire universities conferred on him honorary doctorates for his service to education, as well as his dedication to promoting peace and understanding between Muslim and Western cultures. After a long absence from music, Islam decided to use his skills as a musician to teach the basic principles of Islam through his songs, mainly written for children, and he has since released many albums. His educational albums finally led him to return to music and to stage performances, but this time with the intention of imparting the true message of his faith; for he believes that the language of song is the most effective means of communication and, whereas politics separates people, music has the power to unite them.[35] Apart from his role in education, he is also a humanitarian activist working for many charities to help alleviate the suffering of orphans and the needy in many countries around the world. He truly is a spokesperson for both his faith and the British Muslim community, not only in Britain but worldwide. The contribution of converts to Islam can also be observed in the media; among the names worthy of mention are Yvonne Ridley and Sarah Joseph. The former was a high-profile journalist, born in 1959 in Stanley, County Durham, to a devout Christian family who sent her to Sunday school. As a young girl, she wanted to work in the media, especially reporting; after attending a course at the College of Communication, she started writing for newspapers such as the *Sunday Times*, the *Independent*, the *Observer* and the *Sunday Express*. Her conversion to Islam came as a result of her captivity by the Taliban when she entered the country illegally with an undercover assignment after the September 11 attacks.[36] While in captivity, she was asked if she would convert to Islam; she refused, but promised that if she were to be freed, she would read the Quran and study Islam.[37] After her return to England, she decided to fulfil her pledge and read the Quran; she approached the text with preconceived ideas, especially the sections on women 'because I wanted to know what is in this religion that makes men subjugate women [. . .] the more I read the more I realized that far from subjugating women the Quran elevates women and makes this quite clear.' She continues: 'The women's liberation movement began in the pages of the Quran [. . .] some of the ideas promoted by the Taliban could not possibly have come from the Quran [. . .] It is culture over faith.'[38] As a feminist, she is certainly impressed by the egalitarian approach of the Quran towards gender issues, especially women's issues. When women read the text through feminine lenses, they see justice and equality and conclude that the Quran is not to blame for some of the current abuses endured by women; it is, rather, the patriarchal interpretations that obscure the authentic message of the text. After a period of two and a half years of studying the faith, Ridley publicly embraced Islam in 2003; she has since been very active in promoting a balanced view of the faith, using her high-profile profession as a journalist to remove misconceptions about Islam, Muslims and Muslim women. Her writings and public speeches demonstrate a clear determination to speak her mind, even in the face of criticism because of her rather challenging style. The most notable figure in this context is Sarah Joseph, editor of *Emel* magazine, a high-quality Muslim publication that targets both Muslims and non-Muslims. The magazine focuses on Muslim life in Britain and highlights its positive aspects as well as the achievements of Muslims in Britain. It also looks at the difficulties facing them and attempts to diffuse false notions about Islam and Muslims. Converting to Islam at the age of 16 and gaining a degree in Religious Studies from King's College London, Joseph has had considerable experience in the media. She became the first female editor of *Trends* magazine in 1994 and worked as a specialist researcher for the BBC's Learning Zone and the BBC's 2001 Islam series.[39] In July 2005, she was awarded an OBE for services to interfaith and women's rights. Commenting on the award, she stated, 'I feel my husband and children, my family, the emel team, the Islamic society of Britain, the Islamic awareness week project, the community groups and universities where I have spoken – this OBE belongs to the all,' adding: 'It is a great signal to the wider society that a hijabed woman is fully participating in society and can win such an award.'[40] Joseph speaks highly of her adopted faith but also stresses the positive values of British society and the need for Muslims to be proactive within the wider society through good deeds: 'We must engage with our neighbours, help them; allow them to feel the generosity of Islam through our actions and deeds. Through our dignity and concern for them they should feel that Islam is something at home in this country, and good for the society. All the talks and all the events we hold will amount to dust if our neighbours are not touched by good and righteous conduct.'[41] As a bridge builder, Joseph strongly encourages the Muslim community to integrate into the wider society in order to achieve the change required; otherwise the consequences will be dire: 'Change will not be effected and the people of this island will not see the goodness of Islam if we choose to live . . . in isolation, it might be very convenient, but it is short-term thinking with potentially disastrous consequences. We have to live amongst the people and engage with them. We have to teach and learn, and empathize with their day-to-day realities. We must share our joys and experience their sorrow. And we must do all this out of sincere love and conscientiousness.'[42] In her view, British Muslims have to offer their help to solve the difficulties facing British society: 'we need to see ourselves and our faith as part of the solution'[43] to issues such as social deprivation, unemployment, alienation, extremism and racism. As a member of the task group, she is very often consulted by the Foreign Office and mainstream media on Islamic issues and Muslims in Britain.

Chapter 4

Post-Second World War Case Studies: Case Study I: Martin Lings or Abu Bakr Siraj al-Din

The post-Second World War era is important in the sense that it consolidated the movement that took root two decades earlier and was led by a number of distinguished Western thinkers and writers who were dissatisfied with the atheism, materialism and consumerism that were taking hold of the western society and sought the solution to these problems not on the plane of ideology or politics, but on the spiritual plane. That is, they searched for the spiritual realization granted by divine revelation and made accessible through fidelity to traditional orthodoxy. Prominent among them was the French Muslim thinker, René Guénon, who wrote his masterpiece *The Crisis of the Modern World*,[1] criticizing the secular foundations and values of modern Western culture since the Renaissance and highlighting the spiritual vacuum of modern life[2]. Instead, he and others emphasized the need to return to the universal traditional principles and values that lie at the heart of every revealed religion. This movement is now a full-fledged school called the Traditionalist School, which includes respected scholars who are outspoken critics of the atheistic tendencies of the modern age and upholders of the sacred principles of all authentic religious traditions. Hence, they are also known as 'perennialists', adhering to what they term the 'perennial philosophy' or *sophia perennis*, which regards all religions as authentic pathways to salvation in the hereafter and sanctification in the here below. Within this movement, such authors as Seyyed Hossein Nasr, Martin Lings and Gai Eaton were known to have, in addition to their perennialist worldview, a particular attachment to Islam. Their practice and their presentation of Islam was not based on any kind of polemical rejection of Christianity or Judaism; rather, their stress was on the esoteric and universal dimensions of Islam; and on the fact that these dimensions were still accessible in the modern world through the phenomenon of Sufism.

Martin Lings

Martin Lings is regarded as one of the foremost expositors of the principles of the Traditionalist School of thought, founded by the French Muslim scholar, René Guénon, in the first half of the twentieth century. Lings was a renowned scholar and writer, a great Sufi master, a gifted linguist, an accomplished metaphysician, a translator, an artist (especially sacred art) and a poet, and, above all, a 'gentle soul,' to use Shaykh Hamaz Yusuf's phrase.[3] Born in Burnage, Lancashire, England in 1909 to a Protestant family, his parents offered him the best public-school education available at the time. His early childhood and schooldays were spent in the United States due to his father's work. When he returned home, he was sent to Clifton College in Bristol, where he became headboy.[4] As a child, Lings was always conscious that there was something wrong with the world in which we live, and he wished that he had been born in earlier times, when he could have known or met great prophets, saints or sages: 'From my childhood I had seen that something was very wrong with the world and I was conscious of a nostalgia for past times. What struck me above all was the extreme ugliness of the modern civilization. Why had I not been born into an earlier age?'[5] After Clifton College, young Lings went to Magdalen College, Oxford, to study, gaining a BA (1935) and an MA (1937) in English literature. His university years seem to have been marked by religious disillusionment, for in his book, *A Return to the Spirit*, he writes that during those years he decided to abandon all forms of worship except individual prayer and instead focus on 'a religion of beauty (that) centred on nature and on art'.[6] For him, religion was no longer in a position to offer him any intellectual satisfaction and for that reason he no longer knew what to think of it.[7] At Oxford, he became a friend of C.S. Lewis, who was his tutor and one of the leading figures in the English department of the university. Lewis recognized his great potential, but his hopes were dashed when young Martin exhibited a thirst for universal truth as expressed in the writings of René Guénon, of which Lewis was very dismissive. Despite this, their friendship continued until Lewis's death in 1963 at the age of 65.[8] After graduation, Lings worked as an English teacher in Poland, which was followed by an appointment as lecturer in Anglo-Saxon and Middle English at the University of Kaunas in Lithuania, in which position he remained until 1939. In 1940, he journeyed to Egypt to see a friend, but the tragic death of his friend soon after his arrival led him to stay there and take up a post as lecturer in English with a focus on Shakespeare at the University of Cairo. His temporary visit to this country thus became a permanent stay, for in 1944 Lings married his childhood friend, Lesley Smalley, and the couple lived in a village near the pyramids. The house was a traditional dwelling formed as a sanctuary and shield from the hustle and bustle of the modern centre of Cairo. Lesley had also converted to Islam and became his life-long spiritual companion until his death in 2005; she survives him and currently lives in their Westerham home in the county of Kent, just south of London. In addition to his work at the University of Cairo, Lings wrote plays on Shakespeare, learned Arabic and worked as the personal assistant of his first 'spiritual guide,' René Guénon, who was living in Egypt. Lings's plan to stay in Egypt for the rest of his life came to an abrupt end in 1952 when the 'free officers' assumed power and dismissed the King. Anti-British demonstrations took place in which three of Lings's friends were killed and the British staff at the University of Cairo was promptly dismissed without proper compensation. These events – and one might add the death of his intellectual mentor, René Guénon, in Cairo in 1951 – forced Lings to reconsider his plan, and he returned home. Out of work in London, he decided to study Arabic and pursue his PhD studies at the School of Oriental and African Studies on the twentieth-century Algeria Sufi scholar, Ahmed Al-Alawi, which he completed in 1959. His thesis, which was later published in the form of a book, was described by the *Journal of Near Eastern Studies* as 'one of the most thorough and intimately engaging [work] on Sufism to be produced by a Western scholar.'[9] The distinguished Cambridge University professor, A. J. Arberry, praised the lucid style and compelling exposition of Ibn Arabi's 'Pantheistic' philosophy and welcomed the work as a new and original contribution to the field of Islamic mysticism.[10] In 1955, Lings joined the staff of the British Library and was appointed Keeper of the Arabic Library and later Keeper of Oriental Books and Manuscripts at the British Museum and the British Library, positions he occupied for almost two decades until his retirement in 1973. As Keeper of these rare manuscripts and books, he was able to publish two catalogues of printed Arabic books in both the British Library and the British Museum. His position also helped him to focus his attention on the aesthetic side of the holy Islamic texts, especially the Quran, publishing two classic works on this subject: *Islamic Calligraphy and Illumination* (1971) and *The Quranic Art of Calligraphy and Illumination* (1976). Lings's retirement in 1973 did not put a stop to his intellectual and spiritual endeavours; on the contrary, he pursued these activities vigorously, writing, lecturing, travelling around the world (especially in the Muslim world) and spiritually guiding people around him until his death in May 2005.

The Road to Islam

Martin Lings's spiritual journey to Islam came as a result of divine providence rather than personal choice, for he stresses that Sufism, the esoteric dimension of Islam, was the path he favoured least among traditional spiritual paths. Convinced that an 'initiatic' path or process was no longer available within Christianity, his heart was set on Hinduism or even Taoism, but certainly not Sufism. Lings's return to religion after a period of disillusionment came as a result of his discovery of the works of the French Muslim scholar, René Guénon,[11] whose writings sparked off a life-long spiritual transformation in him; for he remarked that, when he read his books, he felt as if he was finally confronted with the truth. It also caused rapport in the higher reaches of his intelligence and awakened his thirst for spiritual fulfilment: 'My new-found knowledge of esotericism caused vibrations in the higher reaches of my intelligence, reaches that had previously been in a semi-dormant state for want of a truly metaphysical object; and that awakening meant that the deeper reaches of my will were impelled to vibrate with spiritual aspirations.'[12] Lings enthusiastically shared and accepted Guénon's view of the transcendent unity of world religions; he attributes his readiness to embrace such views to the fact that his intelligence was never in a position to entertain the belief that there was only one valid path to the Divine. He eloquently explains the whole process of his spiritual transformation in the following statement: 'My intelligence had never been able to accept the exclusivist idea that there is only one valid religion. But now it had learned and most readily accepted the truth that the great religions of the world, all of them equally Heaven-sent in accordance with the various needs of different sectors of humanity, can be graphically represented by points on the circumference of a circle, each point being connected with the centre, that is, with God, by a radius. The points stand for the outward aspects of the religions, whereas each radius is the esoteric path which the religion in question offers to those who seek a direct way to God in this life, and who are capable of compliance with the demands of that way of sanctification, demands far more rigorous and exacting than those of the exoteric way of salvation. I knew immediately that my place was on one of these radii that lead from the circumference to the Centre. Which radius it was to be had yet to be decided.'[13] Although Guénon's writings had a strong spiritual influence on Lings, his practical role or function was never meant to be a spiritual master for spiritual seekers, perhaps because he did not have the chance to be initiated into an esoteric way that would qualify him at a certain stage to guide willing disciples. Guénon had advised Lings that if he was to tread the spiritual path, he would require a spiritual master who would accept him and initiate him into the way. For a while, Lings oscillated between Christianity, especially Catholicism, and Hinduism, hoping to find the answer to what he was looking for. As he puts it: 'My supplication was always one and the same, that I should find a truly great spiritual Master who would take me as his disciple, initiate me into the way, and guide me to its End.'[14] Desperate for that spiritual master, he learned of the Sufi group (*zawiyah*) in Switzerland, headed by Frithjof Schuon; Frithjof was one of the disciples of the great Algerian Sufi Shaykh Ahmed al-Alawi, who died in 1934, soon after Schuon was declared to be the Shyaykh's successor in Europe, offering spiritual guidance to those who were longing to tread the Sufi path. Initially, as stated earlier, Sufism was his least favoured path, and so his choice was unexpected. But after giving it some thought, he set off for Basel to meet the Shaykh (Frithjof Schuon), of whom he says, 'I knew when I was in his (Schuon's) presence that I was in the presence of a true saint and also the spiritual master that I was seeking. When I say 'true saint', I don't mean just a saintly man but a true saint of the first magnitude, such as one cannot expect to meet in the twentieth century . . . I knew this with a certainty.'[15] Within a few weeks, Lings had accepted Islam; he took the Muslim name Abu Bark Siraj al-Din and was initiated into the Shadhiliyyah Darqawiyyah Sufi order. He was 29 years old. Being one of Schuon's disciples meant a complete change in Lings's life, which he cherished and privileged for the rest of his days: '[my] certitude never wavered during the 66 wonderful years that I have been privileged to be his disciple. I am still acutely conscious of that privilege despite his death in 1998.'[16] One might speculate about the reasons for his certainty about this, in addition to what he says about his prayers for a master being answered. First, Guénon's initial positive recommendation of Schuon came when the latter was contributing to his French Journal *Etudes Traditionnelles*. (We say 'initial' because the relationship between Guénon and Shuon later soured due to a serious disagreement between them over the nature of the esoteric aspect of Christianity as a path that would lead to the Ultimate Reality.[17]) Secondly, another positive recommendation in favour of Schuon came from the Moroccan spiritual master, who was Titus Burckhardt master, Mawlay Ali ad-Darqawi in Fez, the grandson of the great Mawlay al-Arabi ad-Darqawi. According to Lings, Burckhardt, after a period of 1 year spent under the guidance of Mawlay Ali, he encouraged him to become a disciple of Schuon; this was later on confirmed by a letter from the Moroccan Shaykh to Burckhardt, informing him that he counted Schuon and his disciples among those of the brethrens of the Prophet Muhammad: 'Ye are among the brethren referred to by the Prophet in his Tradition,'[18] he wrote, citing one of the famous Hadith.[19] A third favourable mention of Schuon came from the former rector of Al-Azhar in Cairo, Shaykh Abd al-Halim Mahmud, who was also a well-known Sufi scholar with several disciples around him. This referral came in the context of his book on Sufism entitled 'Qadiyyatu't-Tasawwuf', published in three editions, the last of which appeared in 1999. Lings points out that in this book Mahmud describes Schuon as an authoritative scholar (a great achievement for someone who was a convert!). Lings also mentions the story of an American couple who had approached Shaykh Mahmud in 1969 and solicited his approval to become his disciples; he declined, advising them to join Schuon's Sufi group: 'Your place is not here, but there is a branch of the order to which I belong, the Shadhili tariqah . . . in Switzerland . . . it is there that you should go for spiritual guidance.'[20] They followed his advice and joined the group, and it is from them personally that Lings heard their story. The most important factor in his loyalty and unshaken fidelity to Schuon, Lings states, was his belief that Schuon was needed by providence to complete what Guénon had started, especially at the practical level; for, although Guénon had prepared the ground for the esoteric path, it was Schuon who bridged the gap and developed it further, stressing its functional/operative aspect. Nasr stresses that Schuon's 'message brought more than the writings of Guénon . . . the central significance of religion and the truth that esotericism and traditional metaphysics can only be realized within the framework of revealed religion.'[21] We assume that the underlying reason for Lings to have written in detail on the importance of Schuon in his conversion and spiritual journey to Islam just before he died is twofold: firstly, to give due credit to his life-long spiritual master, who had had an immense influence on him; and, secondly and most importantly, to stress the integrity of his master, who was very often misread, misjudged and isolated[22]. It is important to note that although Lings is known to be one of the main expositors of the Perennialist School, which is based on the esoteric truths found in all authentic religions, it is clear that he firmly located himself in the authentic Islamic tradition, not only esoterically but also exoterically. Here, he was clear and specific with regard to his path within the framework of the School – in contrast to his spiritual master, who 'cannot be identified as belonging to any given religion since his perspective is fundamentally supra-confessional, esoteric, and universalist.'[23] His dedication to the religion which he adopted found expression both in his writings (as the main exponent of the Islamic tradition, especially Sufism) and in his actions, or 'lived life' (as the spiritual master of the famous Shadhili tariqah).

Contribution to Islam

Martin Lings's contribution to Islam in general and British Islam in particular is immense and can be divided into two aspects: on the one hand, intellectual/academic and, on the other, spiritual. However, it must be emphasized that it is very difficult to separate the two aspects since most of his spiritual gifts overlap with his literary works; nonetheless, we will use this division for our purpose here.

Intellectually/academically, Lings was a very productive scholar, his works spanning nearly six decades and covering a large variety of topics, for he was not only a gifted linguist and poet who translated several books[24] and wrote many poems but also a genuine author and a respected producer of Shakespeare's plays. Hence, it would be unjust, within the limited space of this chapter, to pretend that we are in a position to cover his entire works; our aim, rather, is to examine some of them in general terms and focus on those that are specifically Islamic, which is certainly our main concern in this book. First of all, however, let us take a brief look at the style and character of his writings, as well as their general impact on Lings's readers. Anyone who has read his books is struck by the eloquence and poetic style of his works, the accuracy and authority of his arguments, the faithful application of the spiritual principles which he so strongly believed in and the creative utilization of these principles. Shah-Kazemi, one of Lings's disciples and main commentators on his works, describes his writings as follows: 'we sense, in the books of Martin Lings, the imprint of his own unmistakable, elegant style, a certain flavour or taste (*dhawq*), bespeaking a particular spirit or inspiration. Reading his books, one is struck both by the unshakable certitude that pervades them, and by the almost tangible sense of the author's own effacement in the truths he so eloquently articulates. In the writings of Martin Lings one feels an intellectual power delivered with a certain lightness of touch; the books therefore express in their own way that combination of spiritual authority and profound humility that so distinctly marks his personality, and so deeply impresses itself upon all those who have had the privilege of coming within the sphere of his guidance.'[25] Lings's works can be divided into three categories. The first deals with the main principles of Perennial philosophy, especially the philosophical perspective that is rooted in the inner truths contained in every revealed world religion. Among these books may be mentioned *Ancient Beliefs and Modern Superstitions*, first published in 1964,[26] this book discusses the general loss of interest in religion in modern times and the inability of the modern mentality to appreciate the Sacred and real things as they are. *The Eleventh*

Hour, The Spiritual Crisis of the Modern World in the Light of Tradition and Prophecy deals mainly with the current decline of the human condition, with eschatological questions and the signs of the end of time.[27] Lings regarded the current age we live in as one of decadence and degeneration and believed that this decline would continue to worsen until the end of this (final) cycle of human history. Despite this dim prediction, Lings sends out a message of hope amidst the darkness engulfing humanity: the decadence of our age would be offset by an increase in divine mercy and divine grace at the end of time. This is a familiar theme in Islamic theology and eschatology,[28] claiming as it does that there is abundant divine mercy to make up for the prevailing degeneration, and thus spreading hope and determination rather than gloom and despair. His emphasis, therefore, 'on the darkness of our times, of the imminence of the end of the cycle, was . . . not in order to inculcate a senses of doom and gloom; rather, in order to precipitate our awareness of the need to take advantage of the immense compensations of divine grace: every moment . . . .is to be transformed into a moment of mercy. One should avail oneself, in every single moment, of all the "available" mercy, and thus galvanize one's soul for "the one thing needful."'[29] *Symbol and Archetype, A Study of the Meaning of Existence* examines the traditional doctrine of symbolism, as well as the importance of symbolism in our existence and its role as the only explanation of our existence. Its main aim, as stated in the preface, 'is to enable the reader to dwell on certain basic aspects of symbolism in relation to the Divinity, the hierarchy of the universe, the function of man, his faculties and his qualities, the conditions to which he is subject, the natural objects which surrounded him, his works of art, and his final ends, all with reference to the great living religions of the world, and in particular to Christianity and Islam'.[30] The book is dense and compact, but profound and lucid in conveying its central message.[31] There are two more books within this category. *A Return to the Sprit: Questions and Answers*[32] was his final academic work, completed only a few days before he passed away. Its title is captivating in the sense that it reveals how a resting soul, born of the Spirit and having dedicated its entire life to the Spirit, declared itself ready towards the end to return to the Spirit[33] – in the same way as the Quran says in Chapter 89: 'O, (you) soul, with (complete) rest and satisfaction! Come back you to your Lord – well pleased (yourself), and well-pleasing to Him! Enter you, among My devotees! Yes enter you My heaven!' The book in part describes Lings's spiritual journey to Islam, which culminated in his final adoption of the faith at the relatively young age of 29, and the spiritual influence that Schuon exerted on him throughout this journey. The other part of the book contains some important answers to questions related to such issues as: Do the Religions Contradict One Another? What is the Spiritual Significance of Tears and Laughter? What is the Spiritual Significance of Civilization? Why 'With All Thy Mind'? And what is the Quranic Doctrine of the Afterlife and how is it Related to Sufism? In his answers to these questions Lings did his best to stress the transcendent unity of the revealed religions and to bridge the gap between them, especially between Christianity and Islam. He also provided simple but profound answers[34] to those longing for spiritual direction, as well as for those troubled by contemporary confusion. Hence, we agree with Gai Eaton's judgement that the book is a 'remarkable summation of a body of work extending over half a century dealing with some of the most difficult questions dividing Christians and Muslims (and as such) is essential reading for anyone who seeks answers to the really important questions that trouble the contemporary (Western) mind.'[35] *The Underlying Religion, An Introduction to the Perennial Philosophy*, co-edited with Minnaar,[36] consists of twenty-five essays, four of which were written by Lings and the remainder by some of the main exponents of the Perennial Philosophy such as René Guénon, Ananda Coomaraswamy, Frithjof Schuon, Titus Burckhardt and Seyyed Hossein Nasr. The collection was not original in the sense that all the essays had been previously published, but they were carefully selected and presented to provide a clear and balanced approach to the foundations of this school. In my opinion, the book aims to introduce the main principles of the school in an accessible and comprehensible way, especially for the average reader. For one of the main criticisms that have been levelled at this school is the complexity of the writings of its main exponents, especially the writings of Frithjof Schuon, the main figure in the overall development of the essential themes of the school. His writings tend to be profound, extremely spiritual and creative and not easy for the standard reader to grasp the main points he discusses. This also accounts, in my view, for the relatively limited influence this school has had in the overall current academic environment[37] despite the fact that some of its members, such as Burckhardt, Lings, Stoddart and Nasr,[38] are highly respected intellectual and spiritual figures. In this respect, the book can be regarded as a welcoming step towards disseminating more widely the teachings of the Perennial School. The second category of his writings comprises his literary works, for Lings was also a gifted man of letters, both in poetry and drama, his acclaimed works in this domain being *The Secret of Shakespeare*[39] and *Collected Poems*.[40] In the former, Lings looks at the esoteric and spiritual messages of Shakespeare's plays, asserting that his plays are indeed a form of Sacred non-liturgical art predominantly 'concerned with the esoteric theme of the purification of the human soul, and the restoration of (the) primordial state of beatific union with God.' For Lings, '[i]f a play is about the soul's journey toward perfection, which it reaches at the end, and if the play draws us into it – then watching the play becomes a spiritual experience for the audience.'[41] Here, Lings introduces a new meaning and understanding of the works of this famous playwright and actor, for in his interpretation of the inner meaning of Shakespeare's works, Lings 'is evidently inspired by a vision of the beauty and harmony, the "holiness" and "wholeness", of the ultimate nature of things, a vision which, far from being simply an aesthetic perception, is essentially contemplative and thus has ramifications on all planes of the soul'.[42] Thus, if the works of Shakespeare are taught and presented from this inner perspective, their impact on the souls of learners and viewers will be highly positive and spiritually rewarding. With regard to verse, Lings was a gifted poet, well versed in the oratory of classical English poetry and capable of writing inspiring poems himself. A gentle soul so strongly committed to the Sacred could not but produce moving and refined verse, full of wisdom and spiritual insight. The following verses on his feelings about *bay'at ar-ridwan*, the pact of allegiance between the Prophet and his helpers, illustrate the point.

> *When half a thousand years and more*
> *Had passed, and men allegiance swore*
> *To the Arab Prophet, beneath the tree*
> *My willing hand was still not free*
> *From bonds of time and space to be*
> *Between his hands in fealty.*
> *Such blessings missed, time was when I*
> *Within myself would wonder why*
> *Half quarrelling with the book of fate*
> *For having writ me down so late.*
> *But now I no longer my lot*
> *Can question, and of what was not.*
> *No more I say: Would it had been*
> *For I have seen what I have seen*
> *And I have heard what I have heard.*
> *So if to tears ye see me stirred*
> *Presume not that they spring from woe:*
> *In thankful wonderment they flow.*
> *Praise be to Him, the Lord, the King,*
> *Who gives beyond all reckoning.*[43]

His writings on specifically Islamic issues form the third and final category, and it is in this domain that his works excelled all other works that he wrote, demonstrating in particular his genius and his affinity and love for the Islamic tradition, as well as his impact and contribution to Islam in general and British Islam in particular. The first work to be mentioned in this context is his impressive book on the life of the Arabian Prophet Muhammad[44]. This book is internationally acclaimed as a classic masterpiece on the life of the Prophet in the English language and also regarded as equal to the classical Arabic text on which it is partly based in terms of authenticity, reliability and academic integrity. It has been translated into a dozen languages, has gained a number of prizes in the Muslim world and has had the utmost impact on not only Muslim but also non-Muslim readers. Many individuals have benefited both academically and spiritually from reading this book. It is now widely used in classes of Religious/Islamic Studies in British universities and, by extension, Western universities, thus filling a gap in those institutions and replacing sources that very often presented either a biased or apologetic account of the Prophet. Hence, we endorse the Religious Studies Review's appraisal that '[b]efore the appearance of this book, Western languages lacked almost entirely a comprehensive and authentic account of the life of the Prophet Muhammad . . . Now Lings . . . has produced a superb narrative that, in its sobriety and dignity of style and its scrupulous and exhaustive fidelity to authentic and reliable sources, constitutes a major addition to Islamic literature in English. While remaining close to the Arabic sources he cites, Lings shows himself able to render Arabic speech in comprehensible and idiomatic English that is neither markedly archaic nor jarringly contemporary, thus conveying what is, for Muslims, the essential timelessness of the events related.'[45] The book's uniqueness stems from the fact that Lings translated previously unpublished material for his research; but most importantly, as a spiritual master, he was able to impart the spiritual elements woven into the narrated events 'to the reader with an existential force that at once overwhelms, inspires and transforms.'[46] In his overall approach, he appeals to both mind and soul, and this explains why individuals who have read his book attest to the fact that their lives have been transformed or their piety and humility have been restored. The following statements illustrate this: 'Lings was among the early lights of my life . . . I read his gripping narrative on the life of the Prophet . . . almost in one sitting . . . and when I put the book down I finally understood what it meant to "taste the sweetness" in having love of the Prophet and of the Prophethood in general. It would be but the first book of Mr Lings that would be transforming . . . The "tyranny of quantity" once again shows its cracks: one man inspiring so many to reclaim the esoteric and also to love the last Prophet . . . The "Sabiqun" (the "foremost" in faith and certitude) are few in our times . . . It seems that they're even fewer now.'[47] It is now well over two decades since the book was first published; nonetheless its value and import, both academically and spiritually, are as great as ever before. In fact, its relevance has increased remarkably in the light of the recent attacks in some parts of Europe and America on the integrity of the Prophet of Islam. Under these unfavourable circumstances, the book (as well as his other books on Islam) is a breath of fresh air for those Muslims and non-Muslims who are interested in stressing the common word between people of all faiths. Equal in distinction to his work on the life of Muhammad are two other important books: *A Muslim Saint of the Twenty Century*[48] and *What is Sufism?*[49] Based on his PhD thesis from the University of London, the former is regarded as an authoritative and original work on the writings and legacy of one of the most important Algerian Sufi scholars in the early twentieth century. It is, as our author says, 'a self-sufficient book which can be read without any special knowledge of the subject, and even without any general knowledge of Islam. It only presupposes one quality in reading, and that is – for want of a better expression – a sincere interest in the things of the Spirits.'[50] It has been translated into many languages, including French, Spanish and Arabic, and has been used at universities in Britain as a definitive work on Islamic spirituality, thus consolidating his stature as a specialist in Islamic mysticism and the history of Sufism. Its academic value lies in the fact that it gives an insider's depth to the analysis of the most subtle aspects of Sufism, providing a fresh approach to this oft-misunderstood aspect of the Islamic faith in the West. One of the important chapters of this book is *wahdat al-wujud*, the 'Oneness of Being' attributed to the Sufi mystic Ibn-Arabi; in his argumentation on this doctrine, he gives a precise understanding of it and then presents a logical critique of the Western academic approach to it. For him Oneness of Being 'is the Supreme Truth and therefore the ultimate goal of all mysticism.'[51] To illustrate this, he cites various Sufi traditions that affirm the universality of this doctrine, underpinning, of course, his approach and avowing his belief in the transcendent unity of all religions.[52] Shah-Kazemi points to Lings' distinction in this chapter between union and oneness; very often stress is (wrongly) laid on giving the impression that *tawhid*, or oneness, is equal to union, but Lings makes a clear difference 'between union and oneness, the first pertaining to a lower ontological degree and, in the final analysis, entailing a metaphysical contradiction, while oneness (tawhid) is the expression, not just of the indivisible oneness of the transcendent

Divinity, but the immutable oneness of Reality.'[53] Here, Lings cites a Hadith *qudsi* which states: 'My slave seeketh unremittingly to draw nigh unto Me with devotions of his free will until I love him; and when I love him, I am the Hearing wherewith he heareth, the Sight wherewith he seeth and the Hand wherewith he smiteth and the Foot whereon he walketh.' He then comments: 'It cannot be concluded from this Tradition that this identity was not already there, for the Divinity is not subject to change. The "change" in question is simply that what was not perceived has now been perceived.' He thereafter cites two verses from the Quran: 'We are nearer to him than his jugular vein' and 'God cometh in between a man and his own heart' to stress that 'He is nearer to him than he is to his inmost self. The Oneness here expressed exceeds the oneness of union.'[54] These few paragraphs, according to Shah-Kazemi, clearly stress 'the whole difference between a mystical experience in which 'union' is a momentary state whereby two separate entities are seemingly united, and metaphysical realization, wherein the One-and-only is grasped, permanently and beyond the realm of experience, as ultimate Reality, transcending all things and immanent in all things, whence the possibility, for the mystic, of attaining Supreme Identity, or Self-realization in God.'[55] The book also deals with some of the key Sufi principles such the ritual purification, symbolism, the spiritual master, gnosis and prayer from the perspective of the Al-Alawi's understanding, all presented in a lucid and captivating way. The book, in my view, presents both Muslims and non-Muslims with valuable, previously inaccessible material on the writings of one of the main Sufi scholars in the modern era, without which his legacy would have remained obscure and unknown to us.

In his *What is Sufism?* Lings presents a compelling exposition of Islam in general and Islamic mysticism in particular, explaining the main doctrine, history and practices of Sufi spirituality. But before he does this, he sets the scene for two important issues that mark his distinct contribution to, or imprint on, them: the Islamic roots of Sufism and its crystal-clear Universality. In Chapter 1, entitled the 'Originality of Sufism', Lings criticizes those in the West who claim that Sufism has no religious basis and that it has always existed as such, independent of any religious form. Instead, he affirms the Islamic origins of Sufism as part and parcel of the Islamic faith since its emergence in the seventh century. In this connection, he offers this breathtaking statement to assert his point: 'Sufism is nothing other than Islamic mysticism, which means that it is the central and most powerful current of that tidal wave which constitutes the Revelation of Islam . . . Sufism is both authentic and effectual. As to the thousands of men and women in the modern Western world who, while claiming to be "Sufis", maintain that Sufism is independent of any particular religion and that it has always existed, they unwittingly reduce it – if we may use the same elemental image – to a network of artificial inland waterways. They fail to notice that by robbing it of its particularity and therefore of its originality, they also deprive it of all impetus. Needless to say, the waterways exist. For example, ever since Islam established itself in the subcontinent of India, there have been intellectual exchanges between Sufis and Brahmins; and Sufism eventually came to adopt certain terms and notions from Neo-Platonism. But the foundations of Sufism were laid and its subsequent course irrevocably fixed long before it would have been possible for extraneous and parallel mystical influences to have introduced non-Islamic elements, and when such influences were finally felt, they touched only the surface. In other words, by being totally dependent upon one particular (Islamic) Revelation, Sufism is totally independent of everything else. But while being self-sufficient it can, if time and place concur, pluck flowers from gardens other than its own. The Prophet of Islam said: "Seek knowledge even if it be in China."'[56] After affirming its Islamic origins, he then proceeds in Chapter 2 to confirm its Universality and, by extension, the Universality of the Islamic message. Being part of the Perennial tradition, Lings stresses that all esoteric paths are equally universal for they all lead to the Absolute. However, Islam, and therefore Sufism, has an added universal dimension. This is due to two factors: firstly, Islam is the final revelation for humankind in this cycle of time, thus making it 'something of a summing up . . . The Islamic credo is expressed by the Quran as belief in God and His Angels, and His Books, and His Messengers.'[57] Then there is the important verse in the Quran (V: 48),[58] which recognizes and accepts all previously revealed religions and makes the Islamic scripture the most universal of all texts. There is nothing comparable to this in any other religion. The second factor that adds a further aspect of Universality to Islam is its primordiality, for Islam has always claimed to be nothing but a return to the primordial religion. He stresses: 'there is a certain coincidence between the last and the first. With Islam, "the wheel has come full circle", or almost; and that is why it claims to be a return to the primordial religion, which gives it yet another aspect of universality. One of the characteristics of the Quran as the last Revelation is that at times it becomes, as it were, transparent in order that the first Revelation may shine through its verses; and this first Revelation, namely the Book of Nature, belongs to everyone.'[59] It is thus to Lings's credit that he succeeded in correcting the view of the originality and universality of Sufism as part and parcel of the Islamic faith at a time when

Sufism was regarded in the West as part of new spiritual movements that had no religious basis. This was something that even his spiritual master, Schuon, who also believed this, could not express as strongly and as eloquently as Lings did. One final book[60] which we may refer to is his masterpiece *The Quranic Art of Calligraphy and Illumination*,[61] a splendid work that came out of his deep love of Islam, the religion which he had adopted, and also his fondness of both the Arabic language, which he had perfected, and traditional Arab culture. Seyyed Hossein Nasr describes him in this way: 'He was at once very English and deeply Arabized.'[62] Lings adored the Arab world, especially Egypt, which he considered his second home, and he was always at home with the Arabic language. Hence, it was obvious that his artistic genius would be attracted by Quranic lettering. The book illustrates the uniqueness of Quranic calligraphy, which developed as a result of the spiritual impact of the revelation on the souls of the Arabs who pioneered and excelled in this form of sacred art.[63] Its importance lies in the fact that it fills a major gap in this particular field of study, for while Islamic architecture is relatively well known throughout the world, Islamic calligraphy and illumination had remained obscure and neglected. Commenting on the spiritual transformation that had led pre-Islamic Arabs, who showed disdain for the art of writing, to practise and ultimately excel in this art form, he says: 'The analogy we are drawing is based on the change from almost nothing to almost everything; and in the case of calligraphy the change is, perhaps, even more striking than in that of architecture . . . the Arabs have never been surpassed as calligraphers . . . (their) innate aversion to writing had no doubt a very positive part to play in the genesis of Arabic calligraphy. These people were in love with beauty of their language and with the beauty of the human voice . . . Their disdain for writing showed a sense of values; and in the light of final results it is legitimate to suppose that it was the reverse side of an openness to calligraphic inspiration, as much as to say: since we have no choice but to write down the Revelation, then let that written record be as powerful an experience for the eye as the memorized record is for the ear when the verses are spoken or chanted.'[64] The book is still peerless in terms of its originality, academic authority and, above all, its spiritual impact and aesthetic sensibility.

Spiritually, Ling is regarded by many people, Muslims and non-Muslims alike, as the first English Sufi saint, or *wali Allah* (friend of God) in Islamic terms, and this is sufficient to illustrate his deep spiritual influence. His thorough knowledge of the Quran, the Traditions of Muhammad and the Sufi doctrine made him one of the most respected Sufi masters in the contemporary West. He devoted his entire life (after conversion) to the

Ultimate Reality, first as a disciple and member of the Shadhiliyyah order and then as a master of the same order with many disciples and followers around him. As a spiritual guide, he was a man with great qualities such as humility, sanctity, discipline, intelligence, wisdom, sincerity and, above all, kindness and compassion. He brought many Muslims back to their faith and also recruited many spiritual seekers to Islam. His influence during his lifetime, and even after his departure, on friends, students and followers alike was immense, which is illustrated in the following statements: 'I couldn't begin to describe the immense influence he had on my life. He is someone who would constantly remind us of what we should strive to become'; 'as a spiritual master he saw in you what you needed most and he gave you that. There was a certain luminance to Shaykh Abu Bakr.'[65] Probably the most eloquent statement on Lings's character and influence came from Reza Shah-Kazemi, who states: 'his gentle, kind disposition was but the surface expression of a strong character implacably rooted in the Absolute, a character which radiated through great subtlety of intelligence and a flawless aesthetic sensibility. To encounter this combination of radiant generosity and adamantine discipline, penetrating intelligence and purity of soul, was to experience nothing less than the attraction of divine grace, of *Lutf,* gentle and sweet, yet of immense power. This same quality can be sensed in his writings – unshakable certitude and intellectual authority are expressed with a lightness of touch, an elegant simplicity; his style of writing was as attractive as its content was convincing.'[66] Martin Lings's legacy, both intellectually and spiritually, is an enduring one and will endure for generations, especially in Britain, where his books continue to benefit both Muslims and non-Muslim and his spiritual order continues, now as before, to attract seekers of the Truth.

Chapter 5

Post-Second World War Case Studies: Case Study II: Gai Eaton or Hasan Abdal Hakim

Charles Le Gai Eaton (or Hasan Abdal Hakim) was one of the most prominent and highly respected Muslim converts in Britain. After his recent death early this year, he was described as 'a towering patriarch of British Islam.'[1] His departure was also viewed as the 'end of an era for Britain.'[2] These comments may sound glossy or emotional, but they certainly reflect sincere and deep appreciation for the comfort that this man and his books have offered people in the confused world in which we live today. Kind, articulate and straight to the point, Eaton was a man of integrity and intellectual sincerity and a seeker of the Truth. He was born in Switzerland to British parents on 1 January 1921; his father, Francis Errington, was a prominent lawyer while his mother, Ruth, was, according to him, 'a feminist, an Ibsenite, a Wagnerian and an admirer of the German philosopher Nietzsche'.[3] His mother was the dominant figure in his upbringing, and he was much closer to her than his father, sharing her bed until the age of six. Eaton was sent to various schools in both Britain and Switzerland before the age of 14 he was sent to Charterhouse, one of the original nine public schools in England. When he finished school, he went to King's College, Cambridge, to study history. After graduating shortly after the outbreak of the Second World War, Eaton was commissioned into the British Army in 1941. Leaving the army in 1943, he worked as a stage manager and actor. In 1944, he married the famous actress, Kay Clayton, but their marriage was short-lived although it produced his first son, named Leo. From 1945 until his retirement in 1977, he worked in many professions: actor, journalist, university lecturer and finally diplomat in many countries such as Jamaica, Egypt, India and Ghana. From 1977 to1999, he worked part-time in the Islamic Centre in London as a consultant on Islamic issues and also as the editor of the journal, *The Islamic Quarterly*. In 1956, he married again; his second wife, the Jamaican artist, Corah Hamilton, stayed Christian until her death in 1986. The marriage was stable and produced three children: Judy, Maurice and Corah Ann, who along with Leo became the centre of his life, especially after Corah's death.[4] Eaton did not stop working until he left this world; despite his old age he kept very busy writing, delivering public lectures as well as broadcasting and commenting on various Islamic and Muslim issues in the West. This was in addition to counselling and advising born Muslims and Muslim converts who needed spiritual help and guidance. This was the outer course of the late Gai Eaton's life, which is comparable to those of so many ordinary people in Britain today. But, it was his inner journey that led him to embrace Islam and the way he expressed that journey that captivated anyone who read his books, especially *Remembering God, Reflections on Islam* and *A Bad Beginning and the Path to Islam*.

The Road to Islam

Eaton was brought up in an agnostic home; his father never mentioned religion, while his mother, although raised in a religious milieu, disliked religion, especially organized religions. The outcome was that young Eaton did not have a religious understanding in his childhood. The first time he encountered religion was at Charterhouse when he was 14. There, the school introduced him to the world of Christianity through the school chapel and classes in Christian texts. But this experience did not leave any real impact on him; he attributes this to the modern Western understanding of the role of religion in human life, observing: 'Religion cannot survive whole and effective when it is confined to one single compartment of life and education. Religion is either all or it is nothing; either it dwarfs all profane studies or it is dwarfed by them . . . Religion had nothing to do with the more important studies which formed the backbone of our education. God did not interfere in historical events, He did not determine the phenomena we studied in science classes, He played no part in current events, and the world, governed entirely by chance, and by material forces, was to be understood without reference to anything that might – or might not – exist beyond its horizons. God was surplus to requirements . . . (we were told) human evolution was a journey from the darkness of superstition into the light of reason . . . knowledge had advanced only through a constant battle against the obscurantism of religion (that caused) senseless wars of religion.'[5] Despite this, young Eaton was still burning with the desire to know the true meaning of his existence, where he came from and where he was going to. Hence, he turned to philosophy in an attempt to find the answers; he read the works of Descartes, Kant, Hume, Spinoza, Schopenhauer and Bertrand Russell, or works that explained their ideas; but soon he was disappointed and 'depressed by their mental gymnastics, their arid speculations and their unfounded faith in logic and reason. These were not sages. They knew nothing and were simply spinning ideas out of their own poor heads. Even a schoolboy could do that. (He) was seeking men who could see far beyond the horizon which limited his own vision, men who knew.'[6] It is astonishing for a boy aged only 15 to speak with such confidence about the whole of Western secular thought that had been taken for granted until the present time! Eaton's unabated search for true knowledge led him to discover the *Primordial Ocean* by W. J. Perry which stresses that 'behind the tapestry of forms and images, there were certain universal truths regarding the nature of reality, the creation of the world, and of mankind, and the meaning of the human existence; truths which were as much a part as our blood and our bones'.[7] This book provided him with the key metaphysical elements that he was longing for; this was followed by the introduction and then friendship with the philosopher-novelist, Leo Myers, whose works were influenced by the study of Hindu Vedanta.[8] This metaphysical doctrine was finally to lead Eaton to the works of the French Muslim scholar, René Guénon, who was the founder of the Traditionalist School of thought. After reading Guénon's works, Eaton was no longer the same person. He states: 'No one who read him and understood him could ever be quite the same again. Like others whose outlook had been transformed by reading Guénon, I was now a stranger in the world of the twentieth century.'[9] After a period of extensive reading on Islam, Eaton became interested in the Sufi path of Islam in preference to other mystical paths; of Sufism he says: 'Assuming that one was unable, for personal or temperamental reasons, to follow a Christian monastic path, then what was the alternative? Buddhism (is) too alien for most westerners. Hindu Vedanta offered many keys to spiritual understanding, but one had to be born a Hindu – born into a particular caste – to belong. Sufism, on the other hand, offered all that could be found in the other traditions (including Christian mysticism) and, at the same time, belonged to the Semitics stream of revelation. A westerner could feel at home in it. (But) one could not follow a Sufi path without being a Muslim in the full senses. The inner dimension could be approached only through the outer one.'[10] After a short period of reflection, Eaton decided to embrace Islam in Egypt in 1951 under the guidance of the Sufi mystic Martin, whom he described as a man with 'a quality he could only identify as holiness and a faith that was neither intellectual theory nor passionate emotion, but simply a state of being'.[11] Despite his longing for the inner

Truth, Eaton lived a free and uncontrolled life; therefore, his adoption of Islam did not entail a sudden and complete rupture with his previous 'unrestrained' life. On the contrary, it took him a great deal of time to fashion his life according to the requirements of the faith, a faith that succeeded over time in tempering his rebellious and defiant bent, especially towards things worldly. This is understandable, given the fact that human nature cannot easily adapt itself to the rules of faith. For a long time after his conversion to Islam, Eaton lived a life full of contradictions between what his intellectual intuition allowed him to discover and believe in on the one hand and his ordinary life as an individual at the practical level on the other. While the faith to which he belonged now stressed balance in all aspects of life in order to achieve harmony, Eaton had no balance and was living a double life: preaching but not practising! Of this life he says: 'I faced and have done on many occasions . . . the extraordinary contradictions in human nature and, above all the gulf that often separate the writer setting down his ideas on paper from the same man in his personal life. Whereas the aim in Islam is to achieve a perfect balance between different elements in the personality so that they work harmoniously together, point in the same direction and follow the same path, it is common enough in the West to find people who are completely unbalanced, having developed one side of themselves at the expense of all others. I have sometimes wondered whether writing or speaking about wisdom may not be a substitute for achieving it. This is not exactly a case of hypocrisy . . . since such people are entirely sincere in what they write or say, indeed this may express what is best in them; but they cannot live up to it.'[12] Having said this, once he had decided to commit himself to the code of conduct of the religion – or, as he used to say, 'put myself in prison'[13] – he sincerely upheld the integrity of the faith and contributed immensely to it both practically and intellectually.

Main Contribution

Eaton's contribution to Islam in general and British Islam in particular is remarkable at both the practical and intellectual/spiritual levels. At the practical level, Eaton served the growing British Muslim community for about 22 years tirelessly and with dedication. From 1977 to 1999, he worked as a consultant on Islamic affairs in the Islamic Cultural Centre in London, where he was also entrusted with editing *The Islamic Quarterly*. During these years, he became closely involved in Muslim affairs and worked not only in his capacity as consultant and editor but also as advisor and counsellor to those Muslim and non-Muslim citizens who wanted his help and advice on questions of Islam, especially Sufism, as well as on family issues: 'visitors who came to the Reception desk saying they wanted to learn about Sufism were simply told: "Room 7. Mr Eaton." Here I had a comfortable office overlooking the courtyard of the Mosque and here also people who found it easier to talk to me than to some of the imams came after Friday prayers seeking advice, usually on family problems, occasionally on Sufism.'[14] In addition, he used to give talks at the Centre to Muslim groups on certain occasions, especially in the month of Ramadan, during which he would speak his mind on Muslim issues even if some of his views ran contrary to their wishes and their understanding; for, while he would defend the faith and its egalitarian principles, he would most strongly reject Muslim self-indulgence and bitterly criticize the attitudes and actions of complacent Muslims. For Eaton, Islam was a spiritual path for the cultivation of *adab*, or good manners, kindness, compassion and respect for others, and not of political slogans and fanaticism. For example, he was always critical of the Saudis because of their dogmatic version of Islam and their anti-Sufi attitude, which in his view produced intolerance and bigotry. As a result, he was not very popular among their followers and sympathizers: 'Someone should take Mr Eaton by the ear and lead him out of the Mosque,' said a young radical to some of his friends, 'but there were no volunteers.'[15] Eaton, moreover, used his broadcasting career and his academic credentials to contribute positively to British Islam. When he left the Centre for reasons of ill health, he continued to be involved in Muslim affairs, writing and lecturing on Islam and giving constructive advice to both senior members of the British Muslim community and government officials. Among the issues that he was concerned about and discussed were the Muslim world, British Muslim integration, the situation of Muslim women and Islamic radicalism. Eaton was saddened by the general state of decline of the Muslim world and the widespread corruption, tyranny, injustice, poverty and human rights abuses that occurred there. He was frustrated by the fact that the Muslim world, which was once the beacon of world civilization, had degenerated to such a state of ineffectuality and division: 'we are so hopeless and helpless we leave (our problems to be solved) to other people who have their own motives and their own objectives:'[16] Muslims, in his opinion, had to clean up their own backyard and not show indifference to what was taking place in their lands. The Quran condemned oppression and injustice, and apathy would lead them nowhere. As for the British Muslim community, Eaton's advice to them was to work hard, appreciate what was good in British culture and find indigenous, not imported models for living as both British citizens and

Muslims: 'it is time for the Muslims in Britain to settle down, to find their own way, to form a real community and to discover a specifically British way of living Islam.'[17] To avoid Islamophobia and achieve harmony and coexistence, British Muslims had to set an example in terms of loyalty, conduct and good citizenship in the same way as early Muslims had acted in the countries to which they migrated, thus drawing people to them and their faith: 'The most important thing is to set an attractive example. Conversions to Islam in Malaysia, South India and elsewhere came about because Muslims traders were such good men that people were drawn to belong. And now, as then, this is the most important thing because people judge, quite unfairly, by the few examples that they meet with.'[18] Anyone who spoke or dealt with Eaton will agree that he was kind and gentle to women, and highly respected and valued them; he portrayed Muslim women in particular as the backbone of Islam: strong, confident and performing valuable roles in society – in contrast to 'a lot of Muslim men (who) are basically weak'.[19] This positive attitude towards Muslim women won him a special tribute from An-Nisa Society in London; immediately after his death, the Society issued a statement lamenting his loss and stressing that it 'was saddened to learn of the passing away of the respected scholar . . . Shaikh Hasan has been a friend to An-Nisa Society since our inception 25 years ago . . . his calm and pragmatic nature gave us great encouragement and support. His writings have been a great influence on us all especially during the turbulent time of recent years.'[20] Eaton was an outspoken critic of Islamist extremism, condemning all forms of violence, including suicide bombing, and branding them as aberrations; Islam, he said, was the religion of the Middle Path, it was the religion of peace, and 'peace is always at the centre and it is never at the extremes.' For him, the path of violence was self-indulgence primarily because anger, like other strong emotions, needed to be let go, and unless it was thoroughly controlled, it would lead to self destruction, which would take with it other innocent people. Hence, those who were overcome with hatred were prepared to kill innocent people in order to express their fury. Moreover, he regarded anger as a form of drunkenness in the same way as drunkenness from drinking alcohol; both were condemned for they led to the loss of sobriety, rationality and logic. These acts, Eaton stressed, had no basis in either the Sacred Texts or Islamic history and therefore were to be condemned in the strongest possible way, for they had no place in Islam. Instead, he urged those who were angry among Muslims to adopt moderation (which was one of the main features of the Middle Way, or Islam) in all things, especially in the desire for the common good of humanity. Violence and extremisms were evil and should not be tolerated, for while the Quran commanded Muslims to be compassionate, understanding and open to others, it also emphasized being firm in the face of evil, especially if this evil came from within. Muslims were therefore required to take a stance against all those who committed violence and aggression in the name of their religion.[21] While jealously guarding his faith against any misrepresentation and untiringly supporting the community in which he was closely involved, Eaton did not shy away at times from speaking his mind or going against the views of the majority of Muslims on certain issues. In doing so, he represented a true embodiment of British Islam, English to the bone in terms of culture, values and lifestyle, but also an ardent defender of Islam. He struck a balance between his British/English identity and his Islamic faith, thus setting a good example of the view that there was no contradiction between being British and Muslim. It was this delicate harmony that made him very popular among Muslims, who used to call him the wise counsellor of the community.

Eaton was a gifted writer and a respected scholar who wrote many books and articles that have transformed the lives of many people both in Britain and around the world. One of his major works before his conversion to Islam was *The Richest Vein, Eastern Tradition and Modern Thought*, published in 1949 and twice reprinted. It was the first English account of traditional Eastern doctrines, or what is called the wisdom of the East. It also includes an exposition of the works of the two main founders of the Traditionalist School of thought. The book was originally written because Eaton was searching for the Truth, and this led him to the study of the Eastern religions, which ultimately led him to Islam. It clearly illustrates Eaton's mystical tendency and his Universality: 'The story begins many years ago in the mid-1940s when a passionate study of Eastern mysticism led me from the agnosticism of childhood and adolescence to beliefs which cried out for clarification. I can only think coherently on paper, so I wrote a number of essays on "Hindu Vedanta", "Chinese Taoism" and "en Buddhism" . . . I began to understand for the first time the heavy responsibility which falls upon those who choose to write of anything but trivial matters.'[22] The book offers an insightful critique of modern/Western life by analysing both its symptoms and its causes. Beneath the surface of this exposition, he laments the loss of the traditional foundation of the Western way of life: 'A study of Eastern ways – of life and of thought – will not offer us any kind of blueprint applicable to our own society . . . what we may reasonably hope to come to, by means of such a study, is a growing understanding of the foundation upon which the life of all traditional human societies is based, the foundation upon which our life in the West was once established, before, in pursuit of the mirage of a material heaven on earth, we broke loose and became a wonder and an abomination to the rest of the world.'[23] Elucidating certain Eastern principles of thought in order to enable Western minds to have a better understanding of Oriental thought and principles, the book would most obviously interest those attracted to traditional metaphysics, as well as those who have gained a certain appreciation for the Sacred. After his conversion, the focus of his writings became predominately Islamic, and one of his major books in this respect was his *King of the Castle. Choice and Responsibility in the Modern World.* First published in 1977–8 and then reprinted in 1990, 2006 and 2007, the book presents a unique and courageous critique of the main assumptions of modern civilization and its modes of expression, primarily from the Islamic perspective; this view, he says, 'is founded upon a belief in the essential unity of religions as deriving from a single source of Revelation, and in a perennial wisdom expressed not only through the religions but also in the myths and symbols of ancient peoples, a wisdom which may be said to inhere in the deepest level of our being so that we need only to be reminded of it in order to rediscover the truth within ourselves. This belief is in fact an extension of the Islamic perspective, for Islam is by definition the final Revelation in this human cycle and the final crystallization of that wisdom.'[24] Eaton questions the unquestioned principles of modern thought and way of life that have been taken for granted since the Renaissance and casts doubt on their ability to offer what humanity essentially needs, that is happiness and the freedom to choose one's own ultimate destiny. The main theme of the book is the human condition, or human normality – what it means to be a man or a woman from the perspective of the traditional understanding of human nature. For him, the nature of contemporary civilization is abnormal, primarily because it is cut off from the Transcendent, which has until recently dominated the lives and minds of millions of people all over the globe, and because of the resulting apathy towards the Sacred, which has legitimized or delegitimized all other forms of knowledge. This culture needs to be rejected and discarded, especially 'when it makes pronouncements upon politics or morality or upon the human situation as such.'[25] Eaton's criticism of modern thought and life is based on his belief that modern culture, despite its wealth and technological achievements, has done more harm than good to humankind: it has dehumanized men and women, making them clever animals able to exploit the earth's wealth for either their own enjoyment or the service of their society until a time when life will be extinguished and death will take them into darkness. It has stripped them of their sanctity and stability, making them fragmented, lacking any integration or wholeness and has changed the nature of human life from being God's representative on earth to a mere transient individuality: 'The age in which we live,' he says, 'stands condemned in terms of human normality precisely because it encourages men to dream their lives away in forgetfulness of their heritage and of those few things which they really need to know. Here lies the root of its sickness and there, in that heritage, is the rock to which those who refuse to slide away in the current must for ever hold fast.'[26] In view of the above, Eaton calls for the restoration of the spiritual principles of religion as the only way forward for human salvation from the current modern decadence that is based on assumptions never proved to be fact beyond any doubt. It is within the context of these different and opposing worldviews that Eaton explains why relations between the secular West and the Islamic world are still strained. This is simply because both sides of the divide, Muslims (especially pious Muslims who are still unaffected by modernity) and people in the West (especially those who are agnostic and have no real beliefs beyond the senses), find it difficult to understand each other and reconcile their views. Our author comments at length on this dichotomy as follows: 'The particular difficulty pious Muslims untouched by modernization have always had in understanding the unbeliever or recognizing him as a man of the same nature as themselves derives from the fact that, for such true believers, the truth is of their religion – the divine Unity and all that it implies – is so overwhelmingly self-evident that to deny it is like denying the desert sun when one stands in its full glare. The notion that the unbeliever's views are in some way to be respected would strike them as both foolish and wicked. On the other hand, the difficulty most people in the modern world experience in trying to understand Islam derives from the fact that the overwhelming and, above all, exclusive reality of the everyday world seems to them equally self-evident and equally unquestionable. In either case it is almost impossible to doubt what seems so obvious. Such is the power that a climate of opinion and the environment it forges have over us.'[27] Despite this enormous gulf between the two sides, Eaton recommends that Muslims try and learn more about Western culture and thought in order to be effective in society, especially in a society in which they form a minority. His *Islam and the Destiny of Man* consolidated his academic reputation and made him one of the most respected Islamic thinkers in Britain and beyond. The book became not only a bestseller – 85,000 copies were sold, leading to invitations from all over the world[28] – but also one of the most enduring books in terms of its impact on the hearts and minds of those who read it. The book transformed, and continues to transform, the lives of Muslims and non-Muslims who seek spiritual guidance: '*Islam and the Destiny of Man* brought me back to Islam,' said one of my former postgraduate students. The book is captivating not only because of its unique style of writing but also in its authentic approach and profound spiritual vision. It provides a comprehensive and well-informed account of the Islamic faith and its cultural achievements. One of the interesting issues which he alludes to in the book is the current tendency to separate the mind from the soul during the learning process, thus allowing fragmentation, inner torment and lack of serenity to develop. For him, the knowledge we learn and the wisdom we gain from various sources need to be transmitted into our substance in order to achieve the transformation; otherwise, it is useless and sterile. Wisdom cannot be kept only in the head; it has to penetrate the human substance to be effective: 'A man might spend a life reading spiritual books and studying the writings of the great mystics (and philosophers). He might feel that he had penetrated the secrets of the heavens and the earth, but unless his knowledge was incorporated into his very nature and transformed him, it was sterile . . . a simple man of faith, praying to God with little understanding but with a full heart, might be worth more than the most learned student of the spiritual sciences.'[29] In Chapter 2 of the book, Eaton deals with the tense relations between Islam and Europe/the West, and in the process he mounts penetrating critiques of those Muslim modernists and fundamentalists who have turned their backs on their intellectual and spiritual heritage, which contain effective means of facing modern and contemporary challenges. As a result, both have failed to present their faith in an adequate and authentic way: the writings of the modernists demonstrate enslavement to Western norms and thoughts while the arguments of the fundamentalists are sterile and are no longer suited to modern conditions. He begs Muslims to use the divine gift of intelligence, to write with authority and conviction and to present Islam in a language that is comprehensible to the occidental mind. As for radical Islam, Eaton attacks all forms of radicalism and regards them as an aberration in Islam and its history, commenting: 'they are purely reactive; an angry, defensive response to the hegemony of Western civilization (and) by one of those ironies with which history abounds, they have been profoundly infiltrated by Western revolutionary ideologies and, above all, by the Utopian myths which have come close to destroying European civilization. When a political fanaticism characteristic of Europe in the twentieth century is combined with Islamic fervour, the resulting amalgam is explosive.'[30] This is in contrast to the majority of traditional Muslims, who are realists and aware of human fragility and who believe that virtue cannot be imposed by force and change cannot be achieved by violence. His

Remembering God, Reflections on Islam is a further masterpiece equal in import and value to his previous classic work *Islam and the Destiny of Man*. The book, a profound spiritual analysis of the most important issues facing Muslims in the twenty-first century from a traditional Islamic perspective, deals specifically with several aspects of the relations between Islam and the West, such as the question of modernism versus traditionalism, how to live a religious/ Islamic life in the modern/post-modern secular West and how to present Islam to the Western mind, which has so far found it difficult to comprehend. The work also deals with Islamic teachings on the environment, peace and war, gender issues, the meaning of religion and remembering God, His nature and Names. Throughout the work, Eaton underlines the need for eternal/spiritual values, without which life would be a total loss. For him, religion is not just one aspect of human life; rather, it encompasses the whole life, and as such continuity with the past is essential for the future; indeed, it is the only way that leads to spiritual success: 'We forget so much of the past, but the past is still there and cannot be wiped out, unless God chooses to erase it from our record.'[31] In the Chapter 3 of the book, entitled *The Earth's Complaint*, Eaton presents a powerful presentation of the Islamic view of nature within the context of the current environmental crisis. He stresses that we are part of the natural environment, not outside it, and if we mistreat the Earth (through exploitation and conquest), we will unquestionably cause harm to ourselves and humankind as a whole; greed and wastefulness (characteristics of modern life) are major sins from an Islamic perspective that need to be avoided. The aim is to consume what we need for our sustenance, and no more; for the Earth is entrusted to us by God, and we must look after it since 'we are answerable to the "Owner of all things" for our stewardship.'[32] For Muslims, he continues, the entire Earth is regarded as a mosque; places of worship are not only conventional mosques but also the fields, the forests and the desert – all are places for prayer and therefore demand respect and care. This view is derived from the Islamic concept of *Adab*, which means correct behaviour with all the dignity that Muslims need to demonstrate at all times and in all places. As God's representatives on Earth, we need to show consideration and act virtuously not only towards our fellow human beings but also towards everything that has been created by God; 'for everything bears the imprint of His hands. The man or woman who stands, bows and prostrates in the midst of nature is a member of a universal congregation, joining in a universal prayer.'[33] Eaton attributes the current environmental crisis to the loss of harmony between God and human beings who have turned their backs on Him and abandoned their sacred role as protectors and custodians of the natural world. This he explains in the following eloquent way: 'Those who turn their backs on their Creator and forget Him can no longer feel at home in creation. They assume the role of bacteria which ultimately destroy the body they have invaded. "God's Vice-regent on earth" is then no longer the custodian of nature, and having lost his function, he is a stranger who cannot recognise the landmarks or conform to the customs of this place; alienated . . . he can see it only as raw material to be exploited. He may find riches and comfort in exploitation, but not happiness.'[34] Eaton encourages British Muslims to be active and to do their share in society to rectify the situation by adhering to the Islamic principles of moderation and avoidance of excess: animals must not be killed except for food, and even then killing must be kept to an absolute minimum; and there should be no unnecessary cutting of trees or uprooting of plants. These principles must always be borne in mind by constantly remembering God, the essential tool that shields Muslims from temptation and deviation, If this path were followed, Muslims would be in harmony with animals, plants and the Earth, which would then have no cause for complaint.[35] In the final chapter of the book, Eaton discusses the critical issue of Muslim integration and the future shape of British Islam. On this question, he is adamant that Islam will assume a British/Western shape or colour: 'The religion,' he says, 'is sufficiently universal, and sufficiently malleable to flow into different moulds in accordance with the different mentalities found amongst human communities.'[36] It has done so successfully in the past, and will continue to do so in the future without any alteration to or concern about the integrity of the essential principles of the faith. For him, a balanced approach between the letter and spirit of the religion is crucial to keeping the integrity of the faith; but ultimately compromise with the modern West is unavoidable. As to when and how this might be achieved he does not give any answer but leaves it to those 'whose priorities are sound and who know how to distinguish between the essential and the peripheral.'[37] Another important work, which he wrote in 2008, just 2 years before his death in February 2010, was *The book of Hadith*,[38] a selection of Hadith from the famous Mishkat Al-Masabih; its primary aim is to illustrate the wisdom and profound sagacity of the Prophet Muhammad, as well as his practical, day-to-day human acts. They reveal sound judgment and commentary on doctrine and principles, but also kindness and compassion; moreover, they form a spiritual guide for those seeking inner transformation. Jeremy Henzell-Thomas, who wrote the introduction to the book, speaks of the selections in the following eloquent way: 'They show the deep humanity, kindness, and beneficence of the Prophet at a time when there is a pressing need to correct not only the many distortions about him, but also the widespread misconceptions about Islam . . . They offer guidance for the deepening of knowledge, the improvement of conduct and character, and the strengthening of faith . . . above all, they remain a spiritual source of inspirational material for the transformation of Hearts, for without the Heart no injunction can ever be fully internalized, lived and embodied.'[39] Eaton's intellectual/academic contributions to Islam were not confined to the above books; he wrote dozens of articles, contributed chapters to edited books and published very short monographs on various themes of the Islamic faith[40] that demonstrate a profound knowledge of the Islamic tradition and have made a valuable contribution to the English-speaking world. Eaton and his friend and spiritual master, Martin Lings, were unique; they represented a generation characterized by remarkable intellectual rigour, high culture and above all spiritual humility. Their contribution to British Islam at both the intellectual and the spiritual level is just as incalculable as their loss not only for the British Muslim community but for society as a whole.

Chapter 6

Contemporary Case Studies: Case Study I: Tim Winter or Shaykh Abdal Hakim Murad

For our contemporary case studies, we have chosen two converts who are regarded as the most influential Muslims in terms of their impact on the future course of British Islam. They grew up in the cultural setting of the 1960s and 1970s, which was characterized by scepticism and alienation, as well as a sexual and drugs revolution. It was an era in which young people in both Europe and North America 'became disillusioned with the core values of Western societies, especially consumerism and hedonism, and experienced all sorts of alternative lifestyles and worldviews . . . and witnessed the emergence of a powerful counter culture, manifested in the hippie movement'.[1] This environment alienated those people who questioned the wisdom of living a life with no limits or boundaries and led them to seek a better alternative. Among those who belong to this category are Tim Winter, or Shaykh Abdal Hakim Murad, and Mark Hanson, or Shaykh Hamza Yusuf; although the latter is American and based primarily in America, his influence on British Muslims, especially Muslim youth, is considerable.

Tim Winter

Regarded as one of the most highly respected contemporary British converts, Tim Winter commands broad public support among British Muslims, especially among the second and third generations of British-born Muslims. By the same token, he is greatly valued in wider British society for his ability to effectively articulate Islam and Islamic issues to the non-Muslim British public, and as such he very often features in the British media, especially on BBC Radio Four, where he presents the Islamic perspective on various contemporary topics in the daily morning programme 'Thought for the Day.' He also writes regularly for British newspapers such as the *Times*, the

Independent and *Q-News International*. As a lecturer on the Divinity Faculty of Cambridge University, Winter moreover enjoys an excellent scholarly reputation among not only his colleagues at the University but also the wider British academic community and beyond, chiefly for his academic integrity and his solid knowledge of both Western and Islamic traditions – something rarely found among contemporary theologians. This has made him the most outspoken, most active, most effective and most acceptable face of Islam on both sides of the divide, the British Muslim community and wider non-Muslim British society, thus bridging the gap and reconciling the irreconcilable. Beyond Britain, Winter has various links and connections all over the world, particularly among Muslims, for he receives regular invitations from places as far away as America, Australia and China.[2] His popularity in the Muslim world was recently confirmed when his name featured in the list of the 500 most influential Muslims in the world, published by the Royal Islamic Strategic Studies Centre (RISSC) in Amman, Jordan in 2010. The Centre stated that the inclusion of his name in the list was due to the fact that 'his work impacts all fields of work and particularly, the religious endeavours of the Muslim world.'[3] Apart from his current position as Shaykh Zayed lecturer in Islamic Studies at Cambridge, he is the secretary of the Muslim Academic Trust, director of the Anglo-Muslim fellowship for Eastern Europe, director of the Sunna project, which is dedicated to publishing the Sunni Hadith collection, and the dean of the recently opened Cambridge Muslim College, to which we will return later. In 2007, Winter was adjunct professor of Islamic Studies at Hartford Seminary, Connecticut; in 2002, he became fellow at Wolfson College, Cambridge University. His secondary education started in 1973, when he was admitted to Westminster School; he then went on to Cambridge University to study Arabic, gaining a BA degree with a double first in 1983. From 1983 to 1985 he enrolled at Al-Azhar University in Cairo to pursue his Islamic studies and also to perfect his Arabic; from 1985 to 1989, he worked as the director of Almihdar Translation Office in Jeddah, Saudi Arabia, translating Arabic/English and English/Arabic commercial and legal transactions. During this period, he also gained an MA degree from Cambridge University. Since 1992, he has been a PhD candidate at Pembroke College, Oxford, working on Ottoman life and institutions. Winter is a gifted linguist: apart from Arabic, in which he feels at home, he speaks both Turkish and Persian in addition to French and Spanish. His master of Islamic languages has given him rare access to traditional Islamic manuscripts that he continues to use to consolidate and perfect his knowledge of Islam.[4]

The Road to Islam

Winter's interest in Islam seems to have developed in his early teens and continued to grow slowly but surely until he reached the age of majority both intellectually and spiritually, when he finally decided to make his home in the faith. Born in London in 1960 to a prominent Anglican family, of which he says: 'I grew up with fresh family memories of strict Sabbaths when children might only play games involving the Bible. Until my grandfather's time, too, the men of the family had taken the pledge, swearing off alcohol for life. My grandfather was the last, until in middle age, he found that occasional social drinking might be good for business. In his time that was still a momentous decision.'[5] Despite the comfortable upbringing and family atmosphere, Winter was not entirely happy or satisfied. Reading through his semi-autobiography it seems to me that there were at least two factors that troubled him at that tender age: his alienation from the modern way of life and his scepticism about the core principles of his religious beliefs. From early adolescence, Winter recalls that he started questioning the way we live and conduct our lives; the incident that triggered this pro-cess of re-assessment took place in France when he was on an exchange visit at the age of 15. He reminisces: 'In my teens I was sent off by my parents to a cottage in Corsica on an exchange with a very vigorous French Jewish family with four daughters. They turned out to be enthusiastic nudists. I remember being on the beach and seeing conjured up before my adolescent eyes every 15-year-old boy's most fervent fantasy. There was a moment when I saw peach juice running off the chin of one of these bathing beauties and I had a moment of realization: the world is not just the consequence of material forces. Beauty is not something that can be explained away just as an aspect of brain function. That was the first time I became remotely inter-ested in anything beyond the material world. It was an unpromising begin-ning you might say.'[6] Being a teenager in the 1970s, when there was no limit or boundary to what a young man or woman could do, must have had a crucial impact on his view of life and its meaning. This clearly set him on the road to look for a new direction and another worldview with a deeper meaning of life and spirituality. And this direction he found when he decided to embrace Islam, a religion that, like no other, asks of its followers strict conformity to its tenets. Even after years of making his home in Islam, Winter seems content with the way of life he has set for himself: 'I feel that I more authentically inhabit my old identity now that I operate within Islamic boundaries than I did when I was part of a teenage generation growing up in the 70s who were told there shouldn't be any boundaries.'[7]

Winter continues to be critical of the modern human condition and laments the way in which Western/modern life in all its aspects has degenerated. For him, modern life has become infertile, aimless and spiritually impoverished because human beings have decided to turn their backs on the source of their spiritual well-being in favour of an individualistic way of life whose outcomes are trivial and self-destructive. In this regard, he commends Islam and Muslims for not being willing to follow in the footsteps of the Western grandeur project and considers this a divine favour, remarking: 'Islam's "grand refusal" of the puerilization project is the great fact of our age; and the stubborn persistence of Muslims in respecting historic human normalcy in areas such as gender, sexuality, prayer, art, and the meaning of nature, is an unmistakable sign of God's ongoing favour.'[8] Winter speaks and writes about Christian doctrines, especially Trinitarian theology, more than any other British convert I have ever met or read;[9] he does not shy away from opposing it publicly or in writing and regards it as the main issue in Christian-Muslim understanding. We know that 'official credal Christianity' was behind his move first to Unitarian Christianity and then to Islam. As a teenager, he recalls that he was troubled by the doctrines of the Trinity, incarnation and atonement: with regard to the former, he argues against the complication of the nature of divine reality (referring to the three persons in one deity) and asks why ultimate reality cannot be ultimately simple? Surely, he says, 'God, the final ground of all being, does not need to be so complicated.'[10] As for the latter, he finds it troubling and intimidating: 'as a schoolboy aged perhaps nine, I had sat in services at an Anglican church in Hampstead, gazing at an enormous and bleeding Christ. How small and how guilty I felt! The message was, as the hymnal confirmed, that this suffering was the consequence of my own sinfulness. How ungrateful I would be, a voice would whisper, not to accept this heroic deed! Later (in my teenage years) I was able to call this kind of religion "blackmail". The gruesome image was oppressing me into faith.'[11] After a period of thorough research and investigation, Winter decided to migrate to Islam. Of the reasons for this, he says that Islam is a religion of the divine unity par excellence, God in Islam is one and indivisible, this Oneness is affirmed via 'two supra-rational' sources, the Quranic revelation and the mystical unitive experience; God does not need sacrifice to forgive people since he is merciful enough to forgive directly, you break through to Him directly and you communicate with Him instantly: 'in gently liberating me from the Greek web of the Trinity, He certainly showed me His existence.'[12] Moreover, the founder of the faith is human and humble but magnificent in terms of his ability to forgive when he was in a position to punish and will intercede for all sinners without any recompense. Winter, furthermore, refers to the good impression Muslims, especially Ottoman Muslims, left on him with regard to the issue of tolerance and religious diversity which they established in Europe in pre-modern times in comparison with a medieval Europe that did not tolerate any religious diversity; he explains: 'At the age of sixteen I heard my history teacher, a devout, celibate Catholic, heaping praises on the Ottomans as authors of the most tolerant and religiously-diverse society in Europe before modern times. Coupled with my religious agitations, this helped me to see that the growing acknowledgment of Judaism and (slowly) Islam by European theologians has had much to do with the sense that Latin Christian thought historically produced societies and intellectual systems characterized by a massive exclusivism. The radical division of humanity into saved and unsaved, being coterminous with the frontiers of the Church, seemed to engender a world which, unlike traditional China, India and Islam, could not tolerate diversity.'[13]

His Contribution

As in the previous case studies, it would be unjust to try and pretend that we could do justice to Winter's entire work in the limited space of this study. What we intend to do is to highlight some of his major work, citing and commenting on particular issues and drawing attention to his efforts in shaping the future of British Islam. Winter's contribution to Islam has so far been substantial, considering by his youngish age (just fifty) and the fact that his permanent academic career did not start until 1997. His overall contribution is discernible on at least two levels: at the academic level as scholar in his own right and at the popular, in particular community, level. Unlike most converts, Winter is very active and visible at both the wider societal level and the community level; committed to his adopted faith, he represents traditional Sunni Islam with its classical understanding. Within the wider society, he frequently appears in the media, explaining the subtle points of the Islamic faith or Islam's response to current affairs. One could argue that he is implicitly regarded by the wider British establishment as one of the main voices of British Islam that they can count on when they need help in understanding Islamic issues. At the community level, Winter enjoys broad social support, especially among second- and third-generation Muslims, and also commands the respect of the elderly and of community leaders. He is very often invited to community conferences and by Islamic societies at most British universities to give talks on various Islamic topics.

He believes in active engagement with the community and wider society in order to bridge the gap between the two sides and reach common under-standing. His most important community work lies in his role as the imam of Cambridge mosque, where he not only delivers the weekly Friday sermons but also gives spiritual lessens (*durus*) and organizes religious gatherings (*halaqas*) in an attempt to benefit his community spiritually and morally. His sermons focus on nurturing morally upright and proper conduct, a far cry from the fiery political rhetoric that leads to agitation and alienation. In one of his recent weekly lessons, entitled 'Love for Others', for example, he talked about the importance of having a healthy heart as a way of having a healthy community and, by extension, a healthy society. For him, Muslims must have a good heart in order to have a good community; and unless they have a pure heart, their work will be of no value to the community or to society. To acquire a pure heart they must make sure that the centre of their concern is the remembrance of God, as well as the cultivation of the principles of ethics, love, compassion and genuine empathy with others. The essence of human nature is the ability to read the feelings of other people, and when we see them suffering or insecure, we must not feel superior or arrogant and abandon them; on the contrary, we must empa-thize with them and show understanding for especially the weak and poor in society. In doing so, we can heal not only our family and our community but also the society in which we live. In this context, he stresses that Muslims should be concerned not only with the formal aspects of their religion but also with its intentions and that they should deal with other people not only on the basis of what is written in the texts or what needs and insecurities they have but also on the basis of a strong and loving heart, so that they can genuinely, through the services of other people, improve themselves and their society.[14] His other important role at the community level – and arguably his decisive contribution to both the community and British society as a whole – is his success in establishing the Cambridge Muslim College in 2009. Winter believes that the Muslim community in Britain, as elsewhere in Europe and America, cannot survive and flourish in the twenty-first century unless it has an informed leadership and that this leadership has to come from within rather than from outside. It is impossible, he asserts, to import people from other parts of the Muslim world to lead the community here in Britain since they hardly know the culture or the language of the converts and younger generations. If we do so, this will simply be a recipe for disaster. With this in mind, he set up the Cambridge Muslim College, which he describes as one of the 'institutions for the training of indigenous Ulama (religious scholars) – and I do not mean people who are carbon copies of the output of traditional Madaris in the Islamic world, I mean a good deal more risky and a good deal more adventurous. I mean people who were taught overwhelmingly in English but with good Arabic: people who are aware of the traditional curriculum and have memorized a few of the traditional texts, but also people who are profoundly aware of the nature of the modern world and the nature of the problems faced by young people; who are themselves young people and able to deal with the problems of young generation.'[15] Winter is optimistic about the success of this initiative on account of the resources available to Muslims in Britain, as well as the political and cultural freedom which characterizes British society. The College leaflet states that it 'is a non-denominational institution for education, training and research in subjects relevant to the British Muslim Community' and that it has links with neither governments nor Islamic movements and is committed to 'providing a prayerful context for strengthening *dawa* skills, and scholarly resources to support all who care about the continuing health and dynamism of Britain's Muslim community.'[16] The College, therefore, aims at preparing future British Muslim leaders who are equipped with both modern and traditional Islamic knowledge in order to cope with modern conditions and serve both their communities and wider British society. Hamza Yusuf, who directs a similar institution in America himself, describes the College as a place where students are nurtured both intellectually as well as spiritually, aspirations which modern educational institutions have fell short of, primarily because the main concern of these institutions is to develop solely the intellectual aspect of the human being, thus producing people who lack balance and wholeness.[17] Winter hopes that the institution will not only help the British Muslim community to flourish but also be able to help the Islamic world recover from its confusion and lamentable state. Academically, Winter is unquestionably an active and able scholar, his work covering a broad range of academic activities including translating, writing and editing. Winter is a gifted translator, and it is here that one notices again his immense contribution to British Islam; examples of his works in this field are *The Mantle Adorned*,[18] a collection of poems by the Egyptian poet al-Busiri (1211–94) in praise of the Prophet Muhammad, who, we are told, 'cured the poet of paralysis by appearing to him in dreams and wrapping him in a mantle'; hence the title (in Arabic: *Qasidat al-Burda*). They are regarded by Sufis as being sacred poems and have been recited by many generations on various religious occasions.[19] One of the early and major accomplishments that established his name as an expert on Islamic mysticism is the translation of two books (or chapters) from the *Revival of Religious Sciences* by Abu Hamid al-Ghazali; these are

'Remembrance of Death and the Afterlife,'[20] mainly on the spiritual methods to purify the soul and attaining a good character, and 'Disciplining the Soul and Breaking the Two Desires,'[21] which focuses on the appropriate way of dealing with sexual desire in Islam. Most of his public lectures and sermons on Islamic ethics and spirituality are inspired by these books. Other important translated works include *Seventy-Seven Branches of Faith* by al-Bayhaqi,[22] and *Selections from Fath Al-Bari* by Ibn Hajar al-Asqalani.[23] Winter's writings cover nearly all aspects of Islamic faith such as law, classical theology,[24] Sufism,[25] gender issues,[26] interfaith relations[27] and contemporary issues from the Islamic perspective,[28] especially violence and extremism. He also writes specifically on issues related to Islam and Muslims in Britain. Looking at the overall mode of expression in Winter's writings, one cannot help but discern one important issue: despite the fact that his work is thorough and academically sound, his style of writing is in most cases difficult to digest, thus obscuring some of the good ideas and arguments that he is well qualified to present. In contrast to the works of Martin Lings, for example, and more specifically those of Gai Eaton, in which the style of writing is captivating and rewarding, we find Winter's writing technique unconventional and perhaps cumbersome, especially for those for whom he writes. This issue has been raised by many students (at different levels), as well as by ordinary readers, who include non-Muslims, born Muslims and converts; of these three groups the latter two are his main readers. Similarly, the way he describes those who disagree with them is rather indelicate.[29] In all his works, whether related to more general Islamic themes or associated with Islam and Muslims in Britain, Winter adopts the traditional mainstream Sunni perspective of Islam. For him, Sunnism combines traditional wisdom and the texts so as to produce prudence, pragmatism and a successful strategy for responding to and dealing with difficult situations in order to protect the Umma. Hence, for him, it is a credible alternative for confronting the current challenges facing the Muslim world. Nowhere is this approach more crystal clear in his writings than when he deals with the issues of Islamic radicalism, terrorism and suicide bombings. For example, in one of his articles, entitled 'Bombing without Moonlight, the Origins of Suicidal Terrorism', he criticizes Islamic radicalism and argues against its Islamic authenticity: according to him, the phenomenon has nothing to do with mainstream Sunni Islam; on the contrary, it has its origins in Western modernity. 'Islamic *ghuluww*,' he says, 'at least in its currently terroristic forms, betrays a European etiology. It borrows its spiritual, as well as its material, armament from Western modernity. This, we may guess, marks it out for anachronism in a context where intransigence is xenophobic.'[30] It is a by-product of globalization, and if Islamic radicalism 'has a future, it will be because modernity has a future, not because it has root in Islamic tradition. That tradition, indeed, it rules out of order, as it dismisses the judicial, theological and mystical intricacies of mediaeval Islam as so much dead wood. The solution . . . must be a counter-reformation, driven by our best and most cosmopolitan heritage of spirit and law.'[31] To prove his point, he insists that over the last 50 years (and even before) especially Sunni Islam has been cautious and self-examining but not militant in responding to the imposition of modernity on its societies, and with few local exceptions 'a doctrine of generic jihad against the West has been conspicuous by its absence.'[32] The Islamic zealots, products of Western education on the fringes of Islamic tradition, are unhappy, like ibn Taymiya before them, with the accommodationist course adopted by mainstream Sunni Islam in the face of Western imperialism and modernity. This pragmatic stance was and continues to be 'conciliatory, cautious, and disciplined, seeking to identity the positive as well as the negative features of the new global culture (while the militants) insist on totalitarian and exclusionary readings of the law and the state.'[33] In view of all this, he concludes that militant Islam, including al-Qaida, 'is inauthentic: it rejects the classical canons of Islamic law and theology, and issues *fatwas* that are neither formally nor in their habit of mind deducible from medieval exegesis'.[34] Therefore, they will not be beaten but through Sunni normalcy, precisely because they were anti-Islam before being anti-West. On the issue of 'soft targets' and 'suicide bombings,' Winter states that these are certainly not Islamic phenomena but part of secular/Western heritage, giving as examples the way Europeans and Americans dealt with German and Japanese cities during the Second World War to corroborate his argument. He insists that the roots of suicide bombings go back to Buddhist / Hindu rather than Islamic tradition; the Islamic genealogy of the practice is very recent, going back to Palestinian and Shia Lebanese guerrillas, who learnt the practice from the 'black Tigers'. Having said this, however, 'there is also a strong Western precedent, in pagan antiquity, in early Judaism and in Christianity'[35] that allowed room for a culture of suicide warfare in Western tradition that has no parallel in Islamic tradition. Our author is emphatic on this point: 'let no-one claim, then, that suicide bombing is alien to the West. It is a recurrent possibility of Europe's heritage. What needs emphasizing, against the snapshot thinking of the journalists, is the absence of a parallel strand in Islamic thinking. For Islam, suicide is always forbidden; some regard it as worse than murder. Many Biblical stories are re-told by Islam, but the idea of suicidal militancy is entirely absent from the scriptures. Saul's suicide is not present in the Koran, nor do we find it in Tabari's great Annals. The Koranic Jonah does not ask to be pitched overboard, and Job does not pray for death. Similarly, the suicidal *istishhad* of Samson is absent from the Koran and Hadith, no doubt in line with their insistence on the absolute wickedness of suicide.'[36] Islamism with its alien practices is therefore not Islam; it is the child of Western modernism, precisely because it embraces everything that is modern and rejects everything that is traditional and spiritual. Describing it in a more passionate way, he goes on to say: 'Islamism is modern in very many ways. It is modern in its eagerness for science and its hatred of "superstition". It is modern in its rejection of all higher spirituality. It is modern in its rejection of the principle of tradition, and, despite itself, cannot but impose the insecurities of Western-trained minds on scripture. Intertextuality and the community of sages are barred. The theopolitics of classical Islam, where both scholarship and the state are invigorated by mutual tension, is replaced by the finally Western model of the ideological totalitarian state, with a self-appointed clerisy requiring absolute control over policy and the Shari'a.'[37] In this respect, Islamism offers a totalitarian model in which people's freedom and movements are controlled and restricted rather than an environment that allows for options and various regional expressions. Hence, it is a perversion far removed from Islam, especially mainstream Sunni Islam, which has the ability to contain and ultimately defeat this vice. Underpinning his whole argument is in my opinion a clear message to Britain and, by extension, to Europe and America that Islam, especially traditional Sunni Islam, which is cautious, pragmatic and accommodationist, has nothing to do with Islamism, which in his opinion is a mirror of the worst of the Enlightenment. It is the former that he wishes British Islam to be based on, and this is what he endeavours to further not only through his writings, public lectures, official advice and weekly sermons but also through his Cambridge Muslim College. His works on Sufism reveal affection for traditional Sufism championed by his role model and inspirer al-Ghazali, and he regards traditional Sufism as the only way out of the disequilibrium prevailing among contemporary Muslims. For him, a spiritual revival is the precondition for the restoration of balance and equilibrium; the dislocation brought about by modernism can only be overcome through inner transformation. To achieve this goal, there should be a process of intellectual maturation that would yield a vision of contentment, happiness and deep affection for others. Muslims must deepen their hearts and fill them with the Islamic virtue of respect, tolerance, tenderness and harmony. To achieve this, Muslims must ensure that moral reform – essential for collective societal success – is not solely judged by conformity to the law (something which is very easy to do) but essentially by a genuine transformation of the soul, for there is very little value in visible conformity to the law if this conformity does not lead to a righteous disposition of the heart. To be judgmental and preoccupied with the outward appearance of uprightness is to miss the essential aim of revelation:[38] 'For it is theological nonsense to suggest that God's final concern is with our ability to conform to a complex set of rules. His concern is rather that we should be restored, through our labors and His grace, to that state of purity and equilibrium with which we were born. The rules are a vital means to that end, and are facilitated by it. But they do not take its place.'[39] Failing to grasp this principle intellectually would lead, as is the case with current modern religiosity, to a mode of piety that is empty and deprived of spiritual nourishment, its main characters marked by narrow-mindedness, intolerance and exclusiveness: 'Even more noticeably, it produces people whose faith is, despite its apparent intensity, liable to vanish as suddenly as it came.'[40] Winter concedes that in our present age, it would be difficult to reach the intended state of perfection, but Muslims must do their best in the circumstances. However, he warns them not to be arrogant, self-righteous and critical of others; rather, they should try and understand the weakness of human beings: 'There is too much judgement of others and not enough judgement of ourselves, there is too much self-righteousness and not enough self knowledge, and one way in which we can heal that is to remember that people's weakness in this age is very understandable, it is an age in which it is difficult to do the basics let alone the perfection that is demanded of us.'[41] The quest for inner transformation is nowhere more needed than for those Muslims living in Britain and, by extension, in the West; in fact, he regards it as an obligation on them. Winter explains that the migration process to minority settings has led to a de-spiritualization of Muslim communities, mainly because it is easy to import and implant the husk, the shell and the formal principles of the religion, but it is difficult to do so with the spirit, which by its very nature is more settled and linked to spiritual places far away from the new setting. This has led to religious disfiguration, where the emphasis has been on the formal level of the religion at the expense of its spiritual aspect. Hence, many Muslim groups and organizations in the West tend to be outward, dry, exoteric, hard and intolerant: 'arguments,' he says, 'among Muslim organisations in the West for the most part tend to be on the formal level of religion, the level of Islam, sometimes Iman, but never Ihsan, so the religion is unbalanced in favour of the formal aspect of it (and here is where the problems lies) with the Muslim Communities in the West – we imported the husk and left the kernel.'[42]

The de-spiritualization process has been accentuated by the fact that Western settings are not conducive to spiritual nourishment; on the contrary, everything is calculated to question and challenge religion. To avoid spiritual erosion, spiritual life becomes more indispensable for Muslims living in the West than those living in the Islamic world. As a strategy for survival in the West, he suggests that Muslims should be aware that outward forms alone will not sustain their spiritual survival and will appeal to neither converts nor second and third generations, primarily because the outward form of religion is not rich enough to sustain people. It is spirituality, or Sufism, the spiritual aspect of the faith, that will give Western Muslims the stimulus and the spiritual protection to live a devotional life and be dynamic, constructive and inclusive.[43] Other aspects of his writings on British Islam also include the questions of Muslim loyalty and integration. Winter insists that the integration of the Muslim community into the wider British society is essential for its survival in the long term. He urges Muslims to interact and engage regularly with wider non-Muslim society on the basis of the nobility and integrity of conduct in order to win over their trust and respect, maintaining as he does that people will not understand the true nature of Islam 'by being shouted at by some demagogue at Speakers Corner, or by reading some angry little pamphlet pushed into their hand by a wandering distributor of tracts'.[44] They will learn and understand the faith only when Muslims interact with them honourably and respectfully. Isolation will lead them nowhere and 'those who believe that Muslim Communities can only flourish if they ghettoise themselves and refuse to interact with majority communities would do well to look at Chinese history. Many of the leading mandarins of Ming China were in fact Muslims. Wang Dai-Yu, for instance, who died in 1660, was a Muslim scholar who received the title of 'Master of the four Religions' because of his complete knowledge of China's four religions . . . Many of the leading admirals in the navy of the Ming Empire were practising Muslims.'[45] He reminds them that the Chinese case was the norm rather than the exception; Islam allows room for particularities and adaptation in minority settings, and throughout their history Muslims have managed to integrate into the guest society and display good citizenship. British Muslims, he continues, must focus on building their own British Muslim identity that is based on the essential Islamic principles and wed to the best of British values 'and quietly but firmly ignore the protests both of the totalitarian fringe, and of the importers of other regional cultures, such as that of Pakistan, which they regard as the only legitimate Islamic ideal'.[46] Winter is thus adamantly in favour of the creation of a British Islam that is rooted in British values of openness, respect and tolerance. He thinks that, more than any other European country, Britain has the advantage of nurturing such an expression of faith: first, unlike Continental countries, Britain has a long-standing tradition of religious non-conformity (Britain was the first European country to sever its relations with the Papacy which was enforcing absolute religious conformity throughout Europe). Second, right-wing xenophobic groups are less visible in contemporary Britain than in other European countries. For example, the National Front party is not popular and its views find expression only on the fringe of British politics while its counterparts in other European countries are prominent in domestic politics, often polling a fair percentage of votes in elections. Finally, there is some form of intersection between moderate, moral Islam and 'common sense English nature'[47] that could create a positive climate for the development of British Islam. In this connection, he affirms: 'Islam is a universal religion . . . it works everywhere . . . once we have become familiar with it, and settled into it comfortably, it is the most suitable faith for the British. Its values are our values. Its moderate, undemonstrative style of piety, still waters running deep; its insistence on modesty and a certain reserve, and its insistence on common sense and pragmatism, combine to furnish the most natural and easy religious option for our people.'[48] To achieve this goal, Winter constantly encourages the Muslim community to show loyalty and make Britain their emotional home; for there is no place for those who are not interested in peaceful co-existence with their fellow citizens and whose hearts and minds are on other continents. He urges Muslims to play an active role in building a just and prosperous Britain, reminding them that Islam emphasizes loyalty wherever Muslims live, including a minority setting, and calls on them to make it their duty to cooperate and work within the framework of the laws laid down by the majority, non-Muslim lawmakers. The main aims of the Shariah with regard to the rights of life, religion, honour and a free mind are all protected by British law; indeed, they are more widely respected in Britain than in some legal systems in the Muslim world![49] He also stresses that Muslim loyalty must be effective both in times of peace and in times of war, citing the Hanafi school of law (the majority of Muslims in Britain are Hanafis), which affirms the sanctity of the pact which Muslims as a minority sign with non-Muslim rulers; it asks them to respect the law of the land and not to commit any crime that might endanger the peace and security of the state, even if this state is at war with a Muslim country.[50] In order to flourish, gain influence in society and prevail over xenophobic voices that accuse Muslims of planning to overtake their adopted country, Winter advises the Community to: first, show a sense of belonging and a deep commitment to British society; second, demonstrate a willingness to accept some form of cultural compromise; third, invest great energy in learning British / Western cultures to find elements of convergence between the two worldviews (the two latter points being crucial in achieving social integration); fourth, 'de-ideologise Islam' by opposing anti-British/anti-Western readings of the texts and encouraging less ideological, as well as more spiritual and ethical readings of the tradition (there are many interpretations of Islam that are inclusive and tolerant – focusing on one interpretation to fit ideological agenda is a reflection of Modern Muslims' ignorance of the intellectual and spiritual richness of their tradition); fifth, adhere properly to the Islamic rules on the 'correct conduct of guests', which is absolutely essential (if the community is not happy with certain aspects of domestic or foreign policy, an appropriate response could be beneficial whereas protesting and demonstrating against the host culture would be extremely unwise). 'Rigorism, discourtesy and narrow-mindedness, the tedious refuges of the spiritually inadequate and the culturally outgunned, end up reinforcing the negative attitudes that they claim to repudiate. Conversely, a reactivation of the Prophetic virtue of *rifq*, of gentleness . . . will make us welcome rather than suspected, loved and admired rather than despised as a community of resentful failures.'[51] Winter wants Muslims in the West to emulate early Muslim immigrants to Abyssinia who impressed their hosts by their conduct, courtesy, eloquence and humility, ultimately winning them over and inducing them to offer all the respect and protection they needed. For him, this could be achieved if Muslims regained their traditional Islamic spirituality, which would transform their innermost selves and allow them to cultivate lasting civilizational monuments (as did their ancestors before them) that would demonstrate the 'quality of their souls' and their capacity to contribute positively to British/Western societies.[52] Winter is heavily involved in inter-religious relations, especially in the dialogue between the three monotheistic religions, where there is so much common ground.[53] The aim is to focus on the points of convergence, build up mutual respect and understanding and bypass previous conflicts and disputes in order to achieve healing. Although the context in which the following statement was made may be different, it nevertheless reflects his genuine attempt to reach common understanding within the framework of interfaith dialogue. He says: 'We need to spend less time revisiting old disputes, and concentrate on healing the present. We have all made slips in the past; to make them permanent barriers to acceptance and reconciliation surely frustrates the purposes of God.'[54] There is no doubt about Winter's huge contribution to Islam in general and British Islam in particular, and this contribution will become even more evident in future when one considers his broad and intense involvement in Muslim affairs. He is passionate about his adopted faith and fervently wishes that it will assume its rightful and deserved place as a universal religion both globally and in British / Western contexts. His model and source of guidance is mainstream medieval Sunni Islam with its intellectual, legal and spiritual vigour as well as its artistic and aesthetic spirit. Despite the fact that his Arabic, both written and oral, is perfect (even his accent is rather classical) and that he has studied, lived and worked in the Arab world, Winter never developed an affection for the Arabs in the same way as Martin Lings, for example. In fact, one might intuit some form of aversion towards them; both his writings and public lectures are conspicuous in their lack of any reference to Umayyad, Moorish and Abbasid achievements; clearly his appreciation lies in the Seljuk/ Ottoman/ Turkish part of the Muslim world. At the personal level, Winter is polite, respectful and formal but at the same time reserved and shy. His reserved nature has been understood – or misunderstood – as an indication of middle-class arrogance and haughtiness, an impression that has been formed among Muslims and non-Muslims alike. However, the majority of people who have expressed this feeling are converts, perhaps because they are more conscious of class division than born Muslims, who overwhelm-ingly descend from immigrant families with peasant origins. Having said this, Winter is a man of integrity and goodness, and his work is highly valued on both sides of the divide. Islam, especially British Islam, is certainly lucky to have him within its abode.

Chapter 7

Contemporary Case Studies:
Case Study II: Mark Hanson or
Shaykh Hamza Yusuf

Although Hamza Yusuf is an American national and based primarily in the United States, his influence on British Muslims, especially second- and third-generation Muslims, is enormous – hence his inclusion in this research study of predominantly British converts. Yusuf is regarded as one of the most popular and influential Muslim converts in the United States as well as the United Kingdom; he commands broad public support both among Western converts (he is well known among converts not only in America and Britain but also throughout Europe) and among Muslim immigrants, especially those in the second and third generations. He is also well known in the Middle East, especially the Arab world (through his educational television show entitled 'Rihla', specially designed for the Arab world – and which has proved to be a great success), where he enjoys considerable support and respect among traditional religious scholars such as Shaykh Abdallah ibn Bayyah and Shaykh al-Habeeb al-Jefri. He has worldwide connections with Muslims and he is very often invited to lecture not only to Muslims but also to wider Western public audiences interested to know his views on Islamic issues. Yusuf thinks that the internet and information technology has, for the first time in history, opened up avenues for Muslims to introduce their religion to the world instead of allowing others to tell the world what Islam is about and what Muslims believe and practise. He encourages Muslims to use this opportunity to explain the true nature of Islam to the outside world, stating: 'We are not telling people who we are; we are letting other people define who we are. They are saying, "These are devil worshippers; these are people that are violent." This is the type of environment that has been created by the seeds of hatred that have been sown in the hearts of too many people in the West. People in the West are generally good; but if you brainwash people, if you give them messages day in and day out, they will begin to believe those messages, and then they could do the most heinous things.'[1] In order to improve the image of Islam, he uses the internet extensively to inform people, especially in America and Britain, about the authentic principles of the faith. Moreover, his audio and video cassettes are to be found around the globe. His popularity is based on many factors: first, his charismatic and magnetic nature, which permeates much of his discourse; second, his ability to communicate effectively with his audience, not only in the English language but also – and most importantly – in the classical Arabic that he is so well versed in, fascinating ordinary Arab people who speak only colloquial Arabic. He also captivates his Western listeners, the Guardian describing his speech as follows: '[Yusuf] has a rare cultural fluency, shifting easily between the Bible and the Koran, taking in, within a few breaths, Shakespeare, Thoreau, John Locke, Rousseau, Jesse James, Dirty Harry and even, at one point, the memoirs of General George Patton.'[2] Third, his solid knowledge of the Quran, Hadith and other classical Islamic sciences combines with a broad and deep know-ledge of Western thought and culture, giving him an advantage over those who teach or preach Islam but lack either the Islamic or Western compo-nent. Last, but not least, there is his 'ability, while imparting these jewels of tradition, to communicate at the same time a spirit compounded of bound-less enthusiasm, total commitment, unshakeable certitude, and overflowing love: qualities that have brought out the eternal freshness and inexhaust-ible vitality of the sources of (the Islamic) tradition to the many Muslims today, whose receptivity to these sources of truth is, alas, sorely in need of regeneration . . . the effect of his . . . talks is to enhance this receptivity to the essential elements of traditional Islam.'[3] In doing so, he unquestionably helps Muslims to find spiritual regeneration, something greatly lacking in the material world in which we live today.

The Road to Islam

Yusuf was born to a Greek Orthodox mother and Catholic father in Washington state in 1960 but grew up in northern California; he traces his family origins to a mixture of Scottish, Greek and North European roots. Both parents were well educated and broad minded with a keen interest in social, political and educational affairs. He recalls that his father liked poetry, especially English poetry, while his mother was active in the civil rights movement: 'She was very opposed to the Vietnam war,' he says, 'so we grow up with a lot of social awareness (and) understood that this country has a lot of inequities . . . that's the type of background we were raised in.'[4]

He speaks highly of his mother as a spiritual person, quite open to other religions, and recalls that she used to take him to the synagogue, mosque, Hindu temple and Buddha *vihara* in order to expose him to other religions.[5] Yusuf went to schools and had a good education but just before starting junior college in 1977, at the age of 17, he had a serious car accident that brought him close to death: 'I think for me it was a confrontation with death at an early age . . . I became interested in what happens after death. And I began to study what various traditions have to say.'[6] After a period of reflection and reading, he embraced Islam. Yusuf explains the story of his conversion in the following way: 'I did not want to become Muslim . . . because I was very young, 18, I had not sown my wild oats yet, as they say in America . . . But I just realized it was right . . . Winston Churchill said, "I have bumped into the truth a few times in my life, and I quickly get up and brush myself off, and get along with it." Well, I bumped into the truth a few times, and I had a choice to brush myself off and get on with it, or to become Muslim, and . . . I chose to become Muslim.'[7] Yusuf's encounter with Islam started with the Quran rather than with a Muslim person, and he relates that the person who led him to the holy book was the late Martin Lings. While he was browsing through the shelves of a spiritual bookshop, his eyes spotted a book entitled *The Book of Certainty* by an author of a foreign name called Abu Bakr Siraj ad-Din (he later discovered that the book's author was the same person as the late Martin Lings). Since he was looking for certainty, he bought the book and started reading it; the book quoted extensively from the Quran and offered a commentary on it. Shortly afterwards, and as a result of a life-changing event, he bought a copy of the Quran 'and began to read a very personal revelation that would compel me to convert to the religion of Islam'.[8] Yusuf officially became Muslim 1 month before his 18th birthday while he was studying at college, but 6 months later he left the college and went to England, where he joined Abdul Qadir al-Sufi's community.[9] He studied Islam with this group for few years before leaving for the Middle East (United Arab Emirates, Saudi Arabia, Algeria, Morocco and Mauritania),[10] where he studied Arabic and Islamic sciences in a traditional way from some of the great traditional scholars, chief among them being Murabit al-Hajj from Mauritania, of whom he speaks very highly.

His Contribution

After 10 years abroad, he returned to the United States and embarked on a degree in nursing at the Imperial Valley College, followed by another degree in religious studies from San Jose University.[11] For a while, he taught classes on Islamic subjects in the San Francisco Bay area, but then he set up the first Islamic institute (called Zaytuna) in 1996 in Berkeley, California, of which he is currently the director. The Institute is now seeking accreditation from the Western Association of Schools and Colleges in order to be the first 4 year Muslim College accredited in the United States; at the moment it offers two majors: one in Islamic Law and Theology and one in Arabic language. Yusuf hopes to broaden the College's curriculum in the future to include other classical subjects, along with subjects related to contemporary Islamic issues.[12] The Institute has acquired a good reputation for teaching traditional Islamic sciences and the Arabic language, as well as for coaching pedagogical methods. It is increasingly gaining both moral and financial support from the community and even beyond: for example, the current mufti of Egypt, Ali Gomaa, stated that '[t]hings like the Zaytuna College are definitely step in the right direction'[13] and commenting that it would lead to improved relations between Islam and the Western world. Apart from a full-time 4 year degree, the College also runs a programme of *Deen Intensive Courses* for a short period of one week or weekends, as well as for longer periods of about 2 months usually during the summer break and taking place in various locations (this year, for example, in Spain), usually at historical Islamic sites. In addition to his responsibility as director of the Institute, Yusuf also gives lectures in America and Britain, where he continues to be a regular visitor. Since the September 11 attacks on the United States, Yusuf has assumed a prominent role not only in the US but also worldwide, becoming a member of many organizations including C100, a division of the World Economic Forum that aims at bridging the gap and building understanding between the West and the Muslim world; his views are sought regularly not only by the media but also by leaders and heads of states (including former president, Bush Jr., who sought his advice after the September 11 attacks, and prominent members of the British government under former prime minister, Tony Blair).[14] In Britain, he is a familiar face in the British media and a sought-after interviewee by BBC radio and television, as well as by newspapers, chief among them being the *Times* and the *Independent.* I recall my meeting with him in Oxford early this year, which was arranged for me by his agent in London. I was supposed to meet him at 11am in a luxury hotel in the city centre, but by the time I had arrived to meet him, I was told that I would have to wait for a while as Yusuf was already in the middle of an interview with someone from the BBC! However, it took three hours for Yusuf to finish his interview with the BBC, leaving me waiting from 11am until 2pm! But at least I managed to get half an hour of his time! Yusuf's contribution to and influence on British Islam continues to be considerable and effective, operating in my opinion through at least three media: his public lectures/sermons (by far the most effective source of his impact on British Muslims), his written works and his institution, the Zaytuna. Yusuf considers Britain his second home, sometimes paying more frequent visits than to other American states; he has an agent in London, who organizes his regular trips to the UK. His links with British Muslims go back to as early as the 1990s, when his name and lecture tapes started to spread among Muslim youth, especially in London and Birmingham, a town which Yusuf used to visit regularly to give public lectures/sermons. I remember that in 1994–5 one of my undergraduate students, a convert living in Birmingham, drew my attention to Yusuf and spoke highly of him; to prove his point he bought me a number of tapes of his lectures/sermons as a gift. His lectures/sermons deal with various Islamic subjects, but also with Muslims in Britain and America, Islamic radicalism, interfaith relations and Islam and the West. The Islamic subjects he lectures on include the core texts of Islam such as the Quran, Hadith, Islamic law, especially Maliki law, and other guiding precepts of the faith, but he also speaks on current social, political, economic and moral/ethical issues. With regard to social issues, for example, he talks about the decay of modern society, which he describes as the society of the dead due to the death of the spirit or the soul. To bring it back to life, society needs to be regenerated: people have to recognize the purpose of their lives – why they were created and what they were created for – and then set out and strive to achieve that goal, which is to be close to the spirit. This is human nature. He laments the fact that contemporary human beings are wasting their one precious, short life; the modern material orientation is not the life human beings were created for; materialism will not make humans feel alive and happy; the only thing that makes them alive is to live a spiritual life. The decay of society has had a huge impact on the welfare of the modern family, leading to increases in domestic abuse and family break-ups; thus, he warns Muslims to be vigilant and on their guard. In this connection, Yusuf refers to domestic violence among Muslims, especially against Muslim women, stressing that marriage seeks first and foremost to protect individuals by finding tranquillity in another person so that they should not become brutish. Hence, marriage is a civilizing process aiming at allowing people to be human, and partners in marriage need to respect each other and find protection in one another. He reminds them that oppression is prohibited in Islam, for Muhammad said in Hadith Qudsi that Allah says: 'O my servants, I have forbidden oppression for myself and have made it forbidden amongst you, so do not oppress one another.'[15] Therefore, if Muslim men mistreat their wives, they are violating God's command and following patriarchal *jahiliyyah* (ignorance) rules. Yusuf rejects the claim by some that the Quran allows for women to be beaten by their husbands, maintaining that the verse has been misinterpreted;[16] for the verse does not refer to all women but only to those women who enter into a state of disobedience (not to her husband but to God). In this case, the husband has to first advise her; if she continues, the next stage is not to have intimacy with her; if she carries on in her state of disobedience; the third stage is not to beat her, as the word *dharaba*[17] is commonly interpreted, but, according to Yusuf, to get angry with her and inform her that the situation is serious. Yusuf insists that whoever asserts that the verse permits men to beat their wives is wrong; in his view even slapping is prohibited, and he reminds them of the example of the Prophet Muhammad (whose *sunnah* ought to be followed), who never in his life struck a child or a woman. Yusuf emphasizes that if men use this verse to express their anger and rage about their wives, they must be punished by the proper authority; he recommends a specific punishment for those who beat their wives primarily because the moral principles are no longer upheld.[18] On another occasion, he talks about the obsession of some Muslim men with the issue of women's head covering; he rejects forcing women to cover their heads and instead recommends that proper advice be given to make them aware that it is a religious obligation. He condemns those who use force against women who decide not to cover their heads and warns them that they are committing heinous crimes against them in violation of Islamic principles that stress the protection and respect of women. In addition, Yusuf has spoken on the rights of women in Islam and taken a strong stance on defending these rights, stressing that Islam grants women full rights, but the abuse of these rights arises when Muslim men abandon the teachings of Islam on women. To prove his point, he invokes the Prophet Muhammad, who is reported to have said: 'No one honours a woman except an honourable man, and no one demonizes a woman except a demeaning human being.'[19] In his view, and also from a cosmological perspective, women symbolize the virtue of mercy while men stand for the virtue of justice; both have to work together and respect each other in order to achieve harmony in society. Yusuf thinks that the mistreatment of women is a global issue rather than a specifically Muslim phenomenon. He calls on women to use their power and potential to transform society for the better; he believes that human society needs more feminine influence to redress the imbalance arising from male dominance, which has had an unhealthy impact on the human condition. And unless this imbalance is resolved, humanity will continue to suffer.[20] With regard to the political and economic spheres, Yusuf believes that there is no perfect human society on the planet despite any claims to the contrary. For him there is no equality in the world primarily because people are not equal in talents and gifts; there is only equality in mathematics, and the only place where equality can be achieved in society is before the law.[21] The talk about creating an egalitarian state or society is a myth, for there has never been an impartial society on this planet; this is a modern misconception, he says, in which modernity desires to create a better world and a perfect society. This is a utopia and 'all utopian ideologies have (ultimately) led to a dead end; Marxism was utopian, Socialism is utopian.'[22] Islam, by contrast, is not a utopia; it acknowledges that there is a utopian place, but it is not here, not in this world; rather, it is in the second world, the hereafter. In the meantime, Islam encourages individuals to cast off of their dysfunctional status, and if enough of them followed suit collectively, society would be improved, but not perfected.[23] In his lectures/sermons, Yusuf is highly successful in explaining and transmitting the moral and ethical principles of Islam such as uprightness, sincerity, respect, generosity, humility (not false modesty) and loyalty; by the same token, he warns against the moral dangers of hypocrisy, ostentation, deceit and bigotry, strongly emphasizing the need for an inner struggle (*mujahaha*) against the errors of one's own soul. In his opinion, *jihad* 'is the highest principles of struggle against what is wrong in the world. I (have) never understood it to mean the use of indiscriminate violence against innocent people and civilians. I understand it to be a spiritual struggle within the heart as well as a social struggle in activism . . . when it is appropriate.'[24] Thus, for him, there is a great need for Muslims to purify their souls from the current anti-spiritual vitiation of their lives and achieve moral rectitude. This becomes more important for those Muslims living in the West, for example, in Britain. Hence, he urges them to be good citizens, live within the law and try to be exemplary followers of Islam; to achieve this, Muslims must follow the example of the Prophet Muhammad, who treated his opponents with magnanimity. For example, they must try and enter into a dialogue with people in a sincere way and avoid being rude to them; for 'a Muslim never curses people, never speaks ill of people and finds faults in them . . . treat people in the best way (and) interact with beautiful character. If they do injustice to you, you have the right to do defend yourself, but if you are patient, that is better.'[25] Yusuf makes it clear that the best way of dealing with oppression and injustice is to contain them by answering wrongs with rights, by fighting wrongs with rights rather than fighting wrongs with wrongs. In doing so, Muslims would rise above their egoism and set a good moral example that might impress people around them who would in turn act in a sincere way.[26] It is important to stress that Yusuf's approach or message, whether in his lectures/sermons, writings or teaching, is orthodox and 'rooted so deeply in the "original" of the Islamic tradition. The best of what he speaks (and writes) about in his many talks and lectures is traditional Islam – the teachings of the Quran and of the Prophet, orthodox fiqh, the spiritual principles of normative Sufism. It is this Islam – faithfully transmitted from generation to generation, an Islam that is broad and deep, legally circumspect and spiritually rich, ethically demanding and aesthetically sensitive – that he learned from his traditional shuyukh, and it is this that he in turn (expresses) and teaches to the best of his ability.'[27] It is on the basis of these principles that Yusuf continues to speak out against violence, radicalism and terrorism, stressing that the killing of civilians is alien to the Islamic tradition, and there is no justification for it in the holy texts. Both the Quran and the Hadith prohibit these heinous acts. The Quran says that 'if you kill one human being without right, it is as if you killed all of humanity';[28] similarly, the Prophet Muhammad is reported to have said: 'Be aware of extremism in religion because it is extremism in religion that destroyed the people before you.'[29] Hence, there is no legitimacy for violence whatsoever. Like Winter, he insists that this is a modern phenomena that has its roots in Western tradition, and those Muslims who use it have certainly been influenced by it; therefore, the only way to contain and combat it is to address certain contemporary problems and encourage the traditional teachings of Islam.[30] As a Western convert to Islam, Yusuf is in a good position to try and help influence the discourse of the relationship between the two worlds; he knows Western culture, but also studied traditional Islam in the Middle East. Hence, he is well versed in both traditions and naturally sensitive towards both of them. Since the September 11 attacks, he has been working hard towards bridging the divide: he has very often appeared in the media, as well as at international forums and high-profile conferences. Yusuf believes that ignorance on both sides has led to misunderstanding and fostered hatred: the West is usually judgemental and has preconceived notions about Islam while Muslims are partial and have distorted ideas about Western culture. Therefore, each side has to learn more about the other's history and contributions to world civilization; for 'to be aware of others' accomplishments and the indebtedness we have to so many people is to appreciate and begin to respect all members of the human family'.[31] The world, he says, has become so small and interdependent that we cannot afford to live aloof and ignorant of one another; this is especially true of Islam, a religion that has 1.5 billion followers worldwide, with more than 30 million of them living in Europe and America. He encourages the West to learn more about Muslim contributions to the overall progress and improvement of Western life and to benefit from the way Islam integrated science and religion and handled race and ethnicity, in both of which Muslims have historically been very successful.[32] Yusuf is keen to stress that current tensions result from ignorance, and demeaning the other is one of the most important issues facing humanity today. Therefore, knowing and respecting one another is a prerequisite for peaceful co-existence. 'The human family,' he reminds us, 'is a great one, and the Muslim branch is certainly worth knowing.'[33] Yusuf, moreover, urges the West to understand Muslim frustration and attempt to redress past issues;[34] likewise, he asks Muslims to stop pointing their finger at the West for their difficulties and start a serious self-examination as to what went wrong with them.[35] The dialogue and inter-faith relations between world religions is a further area in which Yusuf is closely involved. His approach to this question is based on the fact that humanity is like a tree with different branches: human beings are all children of Adam and Eve, or what Muslims call *Banu Adam*; hence, they should work together against all wrongs and struggle for what is right. Furthermore, people need to respect one another and celebrate their diversity;[36] he stresses that the Quran has a pluralistic worldview that recognizes religious diversity[37] and allows people to manifest their religiosity according to the dictates of their belief systems: 'It is clear', he says, 'that diversity is an expression of the divine itself.'[38] The same dictates can be found in the Hadith of the Prophet, in which he is reported to have said: 'Whoever hurts a non-Muslim citizen hurts me, and whoever hurts me has vexed God.'[39] For Yusuf, humanity is the common ground that binds people together irrespective of their creed, race or colour; thus, 'a human is inviolable by virtue of his or her humanity, even before the inviolability of shared faith'.[40] Yusuf believes that in view of the problems facing humanity today it behoves people of different faiths to cooperate and put aside their differences; for they might talk of the sacred in different ways and in different languages, but the essence of the sacred is one and the same.[41] In the light of the above, Yusuf urges both Muslims and non-Muslims to show homage and reverence not only to the Abrahamic faiths (which is already an obligation for Muslims) but also to other traditions such as Hinduism, Buddhism and Shintoism; for these are wisdom traditions that contain benefits for humanity, affirming the Quranic assertion that whatever benefits people remains on Earth. The fact that they have survived the test of time is indicative of the benevolence contained in them; otherwise, they would have disintegrated a long time ago.[42] Before ending this section, I would like to comment on Anne Sofie Roald's remark, mentioned in her book, that Yusuf's 'speeches do not appeal particularly . . . to academics'.[43] I find this observation very insulting to many intelligent and educated people who listen to his speeches and find his message revealing. To give only a few examples as an illustration, Dr Reza Shah-Kazemi, one of the most respected scholars of comparative religion in not only Britain but also the United states, stated that he had listened to more than thirty of his tapes in 1 year and found his 'speeches' rewarding.[44] In answer to a question on the scholarly impact of Yusuf, Dr Ian Draper of the department of Theology and Religion at the University of Birmingham stated that if he were to be given the choice between listening to Tim Winter or Hamza Yusuf, he would certainly choose the latter: 'I found his knowledge of both Western and Islamic traditions amazing,' he commented.[45] She also writes that Yusuf 'is a rhetorician rather than an intellectual (because) he does not write much'.[46] First, I find it difficult to make an organic connection between being an intellectual and being a writer; not every intellectual is necessarily a good writer and vice versa. Moreover, some scholars may not have written much, but their academic integrity is intact: Tim Winter, for example, has not written a great deal in terms of being an author or editor of books, but no one would question his intellectual and/or academic capabilities! Second, contrary to what Dr Roald claims about his lack of writing, Yusuf does indeed produce scholarly works: he writes some good articles on the subtleties of the Islamic faith that show a solid knowledge of traditional Islam – something scarcely found among 'intellectuals/academics' in departments of sociology, anthropology or political sciences. But, most importantly, Yusuf translates classical Islamic works and poetry; and here, as in the case of Tim Winter, is where his academic contribution lies, unless Dr. Roald does not consider the translation of classical texts and contemporary books to be scholarly production. Among his major works,[47] which have had a major impact on British Muslims, especially Muslim youth, is the 'Purification of the Heart'.[48] I remember one of my theology students being so impressed by the book that he bought me a copy as a present. The book looks at how Islam deals with the spiritual cures of the heart from diseases such as malice, rancour, envy, hatred, lust and other afflictions and illustrates how people of various religious backgrounds can benefit from these teachings and techniques. This was followed by another major book, the translation of the *Creed of Imam Al-Tahawi*,[49] one of the most respected classical texts that deal with the articulations of Islamic faith and Muslim belief. Of this work John Esposito observes: '[It] is an important contribution to scholarship and to Muslim self-understanding. This fluid and accurate translation provides access and insight into a major scholastic work that sets out core Islamic beliefs/doctrines. It will be welcomed by Muslim and non-Muslim researchers alike.'[50] The third and final medium through which Yusuf has an impact on British Islam is through Zaytuna College, of which he is the co-founder and director. Since its inception in 1996, an increasing number of British students have been attending the college not only to take part in workshops and conferences but also to learn Arabic and traditional sciences. A programme that has been very popular among young British Muslims is the annual *Deen Intensive Program*, which takes place in the summer break and which aims 'to connect participants to the rich intellectual heritage that we have inherited from our scholars . . . and is dedicated to the preservation and dissemination of the core sacred sciences of Islam from traditional sources.'[51] During this intensive programme, students are taught a number of Islamic subjects from the traditional perspective. The popularity of the programme derives not only from the methods and subjects of teaching but also from the fact that Yusuf and Tim Winter are two of the main lecturers in the programme. The fact that Winter also teaches there is an indication of the degree of Yusuf's impact on British Islam, for these two scholars seem to work together and from the same platform. They are also close friends and support one another in their aims to strengthen traditional Islam among the Muslim communities in their respective countries. One of the main results of this collaboration has been the setting up in 2009 of the Cambridge Muslim College along the lines of the Zaytuna College in California; and Yusuf continues to be the main promoter of this newly established traditional Islamic institute in Britain. Moreover, he has come to be regarded as something of a pioneer in establishing this kind of institution[52] not only in America but also in Britain and Europe. At the personal level, Yusuf is open, modest and easy to talk to, and this is the reason why he is so popular among British youth. Unlike Winter, he has developed a special affection towards Arabs, and he is at home in the Arab world, to which he is a regular visitor. His writings, lectures and sermons reflect his admiration for Arabs and contain references to their contributions to and heritage within the broader Islamic world. He always points out that although Islam is a universal religion, it nevertheless has a certain Arabian flavour. In the light of the above, one can conclude that Yusuf's contribution to British Islam is as immense as it is distinctive, and gives rise to hope for the future. His message has had a great impact on many young British people since it gives them confidence and inspires them to practise moderation. Ed Husain, for example, a former member of a radical Islamic group in

Britain, stated in his book *The Islamist* that he left the group because he was inspired by the moderate, non-political teaching of Hamza Yusuf.[53] My main concern is that he has taken on too many responsibilities and that this might ultimately work to the detriment of what he is good at: namely teaching, writing and presenting powerful public lectures.

Conclusion

In recent years, Islam has become a prominent religion in Western Europe; this is due not only to migration but also to the growing number of indigenous Europeans converting to Islam. There are now small but significant numbers of native European Muslims in nearly all western European countries. A number of these converts are professionals, philosophers, diplomats and even celebrities. Conversion to Islam among western Europeans is not as new or unheard-of a phenomenon as some would claim; in the past, several notable Europeans met Muslims or encountered Islam through reading the texts or other material on the Islamic tradition and decided thenceforth to embrace the faith. Thus, to say that conversion to Islam in western Europe is a new phenomenon is incorrect from a historical point of view. However, this phenomenon has recently gained significance as the numbers of converts increased and the process of conversion became more frequent, leading to the emergence of small but active indigenous groups in each European country, which desire to promote Islam as a normal religion within their own particular settings.

Like the rest of western Europe, Britain has witnessed an increase in the number of indigenous converts; these have come from diverse backgrounds and represent all classes of British society. A notable feature in the British context is that among those who have adopted the faith are prominent figures from privileged backgrounds and who have enjoyed a good education. Some of those whom the book has focused on, especially in the case studies, have worked (and are still working) assiduously not only to normalize Islam but to form a British Islam that could become part and parcel of the overall British religious landscape.

My choice in no way belittles or excludes the valuable work and contributions that continue to be undertaken by other active converts in this field. Rather, it is based on many practical factors such as the theme of the book, which is predominantly intellectual or spiritual; accessibility (it proved difficult even to contact some of them); permission (some scholars refused to take part or preferred their names to be kept anonymous, mainly due to career mobility or fear of unpredictable reactions – I know at least two professors who prefer to keep their conversion private); and their effective-ness and broader public support, especially among members of the Muslim community. The case of Hamza Yusuf is special on account of the fact that his contribution to British Islam is unquestionably manifest. Nonetheless, I believe that the work done by each one of them is ultimately valuable, aiming as it does at advancing the cause and formation of British Islam. Their activism and dedication to the future of Islam cannot be overlooked; they believe that Islam has much to offer to British society and have always worked towards that objective. They have never ceased to be genuinely committed to the well-being of British society; they are not (and never were) 'the fifth column,' as some fanatical or uninformed groups have suggested, nor are they traitors who have abandoned their culture and tradition. On the contrary, they continue to be British to the letter, proud of the authen-tic British values and ideals which they have been striving to incorporate into the universal Islamic principles of fairness and justice.

Neither have they abandoned or defamed Christianity. Rather, their religious faith is re-affirmed by their adoption of the new faith, for Islam accepts and recognizes Christianity as an integral part of its Abrahamic tradition. They are at home with Islam, for '[d]espite all the stereotypes of Islam being the paradigmatic opposite to life in the West, the feeling of conversion is not that one has migrated but that one has come home. I feel that I more authentically inhabit my old identity, now that I operate within Islamic boundaries, than I did when I was part of a teenage generation . . . who were told there should not be any boundaries.'[1] They are not amenable to the pronouncements of any ethical or cultural replica that is imported from outside Britain; on the contrary, they integrate their British identity harmoniously into the Islamic religion and illustrate that traditional Islam, which is pragmatic, broad, open, spiritual and cosmopolitan, is 'far from destroying or diminishing identification with one's indigenous culture, on the contrary leads one to appreciate more deeply and to enhance all that is noble, beautiful and good therein. To the specious argument that Islam is inherently incompatible with traditional British values, [these people provide] an eloquent living refutation.'[2]

The following reasons, in my opinion, lead one to believe that some form of British/English Islamic culture might be achieved: first, Islam – historically speaking and despite its Arabian origin – never imposed Arabism on non-Arab Muslim peoples to whose lands it spread; it encouraged conquered populaces to convert to the faith and accept its principles and practices, but it did not force them to accept Arabism. Islam accepts and respects race, diversity and ethnicity, and when it prevailed in the conquered territories, local customs, ideals and values were nurtured rather than suppressed and led to the emergence of different expressions of Islam such as Persian, Turkish, Indian or Malaysian Islam. It is the same water but it takes on the colour of the vessel. Second, there are certain British values that are as profound as they are universal, and these resonate well with Islam. English people in particular, despite committing atrocities in the historical past, have a tremendous sense of fairness and fair play – a positive quality and a British quality which is not true of, for instance, certain Mediterranean cultures in Europe. Further, liberalism and progressive attitudes are something positive in British social history (the anti-slavery movement, women's rights and the notion of human need – Florence Nightingale, who had a universal view of human need, was more committed to the anti-colonial movement in India than in many other of the activities she was involved in). Third, Muslims need to recognize that although they were once the great promoters of religious and racial tolerance, Britain – and by extension Europe and America – have surpassed them in this respect.

Muslims, therefore, need to recognize these positive elements of British/ Western culture and should not look upon it generally as being decadent and sexually promiscuous. There are undoubtedly things which also trouble many British/Western people; but they do not constitute what Britain/the West is. There are positive elements in British culture and history that Muslims in Britain can benefit from; once this is recognized, a process of constructive union between the traditional universal principles of Islam and what is best in the British values mentioned above can take place, which would allow this form of British Islam to materialize. This process has already begun, for these scholars have prepared the ground: they have managed to re-establish the centrality of traditional Islam that is rooted in authentic sources of the faith, as opposed to the reactionary, anti-colonial and political variety of Islam. They are inspiring and encouraging young people to follow in their footsteps and learn traditional, spiritual Islam, as opposed to radical, revolutionary Islam.[3] They have succeeded in restoring the good name of Sufism as the rigorous Islamic tradition of spirituality and have helped to promote the idea of Western intellectual Islam in the sense that Muslims in the West can produce their own scholars and their own intellectuals.

The Muslim community in Britain must capitalize on these achievements and support this group; it must make sure that the leadership of the British community is not a foreign leadership. There should be a British leadership, even if this leadership may come from the convert group (if sufficiently competent), and to do so, Muslims must rise above their tribalism, ego and family networking. They must, moreover, create think-tanks and forums to address their own social problems, of which there are a great many. In doing so, Muslims in Britain will ensure the survival of a healthy, constructive and dynamic Islam rather than an isolated and marginalized Islam.

Notes

Introduction

[1] L. Rambo and C. Farhadian, *Converting: Stages of Religious Change*. In C. Lamb and M. Bryant (eds), *Religious Conversion, Contemporary Practices and Controversies*, Cassell, London, and New York, 1999, p. 23. More on this subject, see, Lewis Rambo, *Understanding Religious Conversion*, Yale University press, New Haven, 1993.

[2] See for example the most recent article on the subject by Jerome Taylor and Sarah Morrison 'The Islamification of Britain: record number embrace Muslim faith', *The Independent on-line*, Tuesday, 4 January 2011.

[3] A recent study on this issue by K. Brice 'A Minority within A Minority: A report on Conversion to Islam in the United Kingdom', Faith matters, published this year (2011), estimates the number of British converts to Islam up to 100,000. But yet again some have cast doubt on the accuracy of the figure, see the independent, Op. Cit.

[4] Yasin Dutton, *Conversion to Islam: Quranic Paradigm*. In C. Lamb and M. Bryant (eds), *Religious Conversion*, op. cit., pp. 151–3.

[5] Ibid., p. 153.

[6] The Quran, 7:172, cited in Tim Winter, *Conversion as Nostalgia: Some Experiences of Islam*. In M. Percy (ed), Pervious *Convictions, Conversion in the Present Day*, SPCK (Society for Promoting Christian Knowledge), London, 2000, pp. 95–6.

[7] Yasin Dutton, *Conversion to Islam*, op. cit., pp. 153–6.

[8] Personal communication, Lancaster, October 1997.

[9] http://thetruereligion.org/mum.htm, accessed at 11.3.2003.

[10] Personal communication, Amsterdam, March 2003.

[11] http://www.thetruereligion.org/yfm.htm, accessed at 10.3.2003.

[12] http://thetruereligion.org/mum.htm, accessed at 9.9.2003.

[13] http://www.thetruereligion.org/yfm.htm, accessed at 11.9.2003.

[14] Tim Winter, *Conversion as Nostalgia*, op. cit., p. 108.

[15] British Muslims Monthly Survey, 2002, Vol. 10:1, Centre for the Study of Islam and Christian-Muslim Relations, Department of Theology, University of Birmingham, pp. 8–9.

[16] Tim Winter, *Conversion as Nostalgia*, op. cit., p. 108.

[17] Ibid., pp. 107–8.

[18] British Muslims Monthly Survey, 2002; see also Amina Wadud, *American Muslim Identity: Race and Ethnicity in Progressive Islam*. In Omid Safi (ed), *Progressive Muslims, on Justice, Gender, and Pluralism, One World*, Oxford, 2003, p. 275.

[19] http://thetruereligion.org/mimima.htm, accessed at 14.10.2003.

[20] Personal interview, Birmingham, September 2003.

[21] Tim Winter, *Conversion as Nostalgia*, op. cit, p. 100.

[22] http://thetruereligion.org/mum.htm, accessed at 14.10.2003.

23 Tim Winter, *Conversion as Nostalgia*, op. cit., p. 100.

24 http://www.unn.ac.uk/societies/islamic/women/women3.htm, at accessed 15.2.2003.

25 http://www.usc.edu/dept/MSA/newmusilm/karima.html, accessed at 10.2.2003.

26 http://thetruereligion.org/mum.htm, accessed at 3.3.2003.

27 H. Haleem, 'Experiences, Needs and potential of New Muslim women in Britain' in H. Jawad and T. Benn, *Muslim Women in the United Kingdom and Beyond, Experiences, and Images*, Brill, Leiden, 2003, p. 94.

28 The Quran, 33:32.

29 The Quran, IV: 124–5

30 On this see, Haifaa Jawad, *The Rights of Women in Islam: An Authentic Approach*, Macmillan, London, 1998, pp. 11–14 and p. 26.

31 A. Schimmel, *Mystical Dimensions of Islam*, The University of North Carolina press, Chapel Hill, 1975, pp. 426–9.

32 A. Schimmel, *My Soul is a Woman, the Feminine in Islam*, Continuum, New York, 1999, p. 21.

33 Ibid, pp. 34–5.

34 For more see, Farid Al-Din Attar, *Muslim Saints and Mystics*, Arkana, London, 1990, pp. 39–51.

35 A. Schimmel, *Mystical Dimensions of Islam*, Op. Cit, pp. 426–7 and pp. 430–5. Also, see, Seyyed Houssein Nasr, *Traditional Islam in the Modern world*, Kegan Paul international, London, and New York, 1987, pp. 47–58. On the activities of Sufi women see, Javad Nurbakhsh, Sufi Women, Khaniqahi-Nimatullahi Publications, New York, 1983.

36 For more on this issue, especially on the lack of Spirituality in the Western World see the good book by Philip Sherrard, *The Rape of Man and Nature: An Enquiry into the Origins and Consequences of Modern Science*, Golgonooza Press, Ipswich, 1987.

37 http://www.usc.edu/dept/MSA/newmuslim/karima.html, accessed at 4.3.2003

38 Saadia Khawar Khan Chishti, 'Female Spirituality in Islam' in Seyyed Hossein Nasr, *Islamic Spirituality*, Cross Road, New York, 1987. p. 204.

39 A. Schimmel, *My Soul is a Woman*, p. 89 and p. 93.

40 Cited in Aliah Schleifer, *Mary the Blessed Virgin of Islam*, Fons Vitae, Louisvill, KY, 1997, p. 63.

41 Margaret Smith, *Rabia the Mystic and her Fellow Saints in Islam*, Cambridge University Press, Cambridge, 1984, p. xxx.

42 Margaret Smith, *Rabia the Mystic and her fellow Saints in Islam*, pp. 2–3.

43 A. Schimmel, *My Soul is a Woman*, Op.Cit, p. 105.

44 Michel. Chodkiewicz, *The Seal of the Saints*, Gallimard, Paris, 1986, p. 126.

45 A. Schimmel, Op.Cit, p. 103.

46 R. Austin, 'The Feminine Dimensions in ibn Arabi's Thought', *Muhyiddin ibn Arabi Society Journal, Vol 2*, 1984, p. 12.

47 Reza Shah-Kazemi, 'Women in Islam: A Reminder to the Taleban', London, Dialogue, 1996, p. 2.

48 Sachiko Murata, *The Tao of Islam*, State University of New York Press, Albany, 1992, pp. 8–9.

49 Ibid, p. 9.

50 Ibid, p. 89.

51 Ibid, p. 9.

52 Reza Shah-Kazemi, Op.Cit, p. 2.

[53] Kate Zebiri, British Converts Choosing Alternative Lives, One World, Oxford, 2008, pp. 1–5.

[54] One can also mention the autobiography by Lucy Bushill-Matthews, *Welcome to Islam: A Convert's Tale*, Continuum, London, 2008.

Chapter 1

[1] See Jan Rath et al., *Western Europe and its Islam*, Brill, Leiden, 2001, p. 24.

[2] See Gerholm and Lithman (eds), *The New Islamic Presence in West Europe*, Mansell Publishing Limited, London and New York, 1988.

[3] See Jorgen. Nielsen, *Muslims in West Europe*, third edition, Edinburgh University Press, Edinburgh, 2004, p. 1.

[4] See S. Allievi, 'The Muslim Community in Italy', in Nonneman et. al. (eds), *Muslim Communities in the New Europe*, Ithaca Press, Reading, 1996, p. 315.

[5] See P. Lewis, *Islamic Britain*, I.B. Tauris, London, 1994, pp. 10–11; see also H Ansari, *The Infidel Within*, Hurst and Company, London, 2004, p. 26.

[6] A. Hourani, *Islam in European Thought*, Cambridge University Press, Cambridge, 1991, p. 7.

[7] See Norman Daniel, *The Arabs and Medieval Europe*, Longman, London, 1975; A. Hourani, Islam *in European Thought*, Cambridge University Press, Cambridge, 1991.

[8] R. Ballard, 'Islam and the Construction of Europe' in Shadid and Koningsveld (eds), *Muslims in the Margin. Political Responses to the Presence of Islam in Western Europe*, Kok Pharos Publishing House, the Netherlands, 1996, p. 26.

[9] On this issue, see N.I. Matar, 'Turning Turks: Conversion to Islam in English Renaissance Thought', Durham University Journal, LXXXVI (1), 1994, pp. 33–41; N.I. Matar, 'The Renegade in the English Seventeenth-Century Imagination', Studies in English Literature 1500–1900, Vol 33, 1993, pp. 489–502.

[10] N. Clayer and E. Germain (eds), *Islam in Inter-War Europe*, Hurst and Company, London, 2008, p. 6.

[11] Ibid., p. 6.

[12] Ibid., p. 67.

[13] Ansari, op. cit., pp. 27–8; see also, Peter Mansfield, *The Arabs*, Penguin Books, London, 1982.

[14] Ansari, op. cit., pp. 31–51.

[15] See Jorgen Nielsen, *Muslims in West Europe*, Edinburgh University press, Edinburgh, 1991; S. Vertovec, and G. Peach, (eds), Islam in Europe. *The Politics of Religion and Community*, bastingstoke, Macmillian, London, 1997; D. Westerlund and I. Svanberg, (eds) *Islam Outside the Arab World*, St Martin's press, New York, 1999, especially pp. 315–40; and T. Ramadan, *Western Muslims and the Future of Islam*, Oxford University press, Oxford, 2004.

[16] In historical terms, some sources state that European conversion to Islam started as early as 1500–1600, when large numbers of Europeans converted to Islam. These were mainly a 'mixed bag of adventurers, pirates, slaves seeking their freedom, mercenaries and traders, some of whom went on to enjoy distinguished careers in politics or military life.' See, Zebiri, *British Muslim Converts*, Op. Cit., p. 32.

[17] Seyyed Hossein Nasr, *Sufi Essays*, ABC International Group, Kazi publications, Chicago, (third edition), 1999, p. 162.

[18] For more information on his early years see Robin Waterfield, *René Guénon and the Future of the West*, Sophia Perennis, Hillsdale, New York, 2002, pp. 12–27.

[19] For more on his relationship with Agueli see Waterfield, ibid., pp. 28–31.

[20] Ibrahim Kalin, René Guénon, www.cis-ca.org/voices/g/Guénon-mn.htm.intor, accessed at 12. 8. 2009.

[21] See René Guénon, *East and West* (translated by Martin Lings), Sophia Perennis, Hillsdale, New York, 2004, (first published in French in 1924).

[22] René Guénon, *The Crisis of the Modern World* (translated by Marco Pallis, Arthur Osborne and Richard C. Nicholson), Sophia Perennis, Hillsdale, New York, 2004, (first published in French in 1946).

[23] René Guénon, *The Reign of Quantity and the Signs of the Times* (translated by Lord Northbourne), Sophia Perennis, Hillsdale, New York, 2001 (first published in French in 1945).

[24] See www.cis-ca.org/voice/g/guenon-mn.htm, accessed at 21.07.2008.

[25] See www.seriousseekers.com/Teachers%20Contributors/teachers_priority, accessed at 21.7.2008.

[26] Ibid.

[27] Muhammad Asad, *The Road to Mecca*, Gibraltar, Dar Al-Andalus, 1980, (First published in 1954), pp. 51–55

[28] Ibid., pp. 55–6.

[29] Ibid., pp. 56–74.

[30] Ibid., pp. 101.

[31] Ibid., pp. 309–10.

[32] Muhammad Asad, *Islam at the Crossroads*, Arafat Press, Lahore, 1937.

[33] Muhammad Asad, *This Law of Ours and Other Essays*, Islamic Book Trust, Kuala Lumpur, 2001.

[34] Muhammad Asad, *The Message of the Quran*, The Book Foundation, London, 2003.

[35] T. Burckhardt, 'Traditional Science', *Studies in Comparative Religion, Vol. 16*, No. 1–2, Winter–Spring, 1984, p. 87.

[36] T. Burckhardt, *Traditional Science*, op. cit., pp. 84–6.

[37] T. Burckhardt, *Moorish Culture in Spain*, Fons Vitae, Louisville, KY, 1999, pp. 206–8.

[38] See www.allamaiqbal.com, accessed at 12. 1. 2009.

[39] See Michon, Jean-Louis. 'Titus Burckhardt in Fez ', *Studies in Comparative Religion, Vol. 16*, Nos 1 and 2, 1984, pp. 57–62. See also Titus, Burckhardt. Fez: City of Islam, Islamic Texts Society, Cambridge, 1992.

[40] T. Burckhardt, *Art of Islam: Language and Meaning*, World Wisdom, Bloomington, Ind, 2009.

[41] T. Burckhardt, *Fez: City of Islam*, Islamic Texts Society, Cambridge, 1992.

[42] T. Burckhardt, *Moorish Culture in Spain*, Fons Vitae, Louisville, KY, 1999.

[43] Seyyed. Hossein. Nasr 'Foreword' in William Stoddart (ed), *The Essential Titus Burckhardt: Reflections on Sacred Art, Faiths and Civilisations*, World Wisdom, Bloomington, Ind, 2003, p. xvi.

[44] T. Burckhardt, 'The Void in Islamic Art', *Studies in Comparative Religion*, Op. Cit, p. 82.

[45] See www.Allamaiqbal, accessed at 12. 1. 2009 and www.cis, accessed at 1. 4. 2009.

[46] See T. Burchardt, *Universal Man, Abd al-Karim al-Jili: Extracts Translated with Commentary*, Beshara Publication, England, 1983.

[47] T. Burckhart, *An Introduction to Sufi Doctrine*, World Wisdom, Bloomington, Ind, 2008.

48 Seyyed Hossien Nasr, 'With Titus Burckhardt at the Tomb of Ibn Arabi', *Traditional Islam in the Modern World*, Kegan Paul international, London and New York, 1987, p. 294.

49 S. H. Nasr, *Traditional Islam in the Modern world*, Op. Cit, pp. 291–2.

50 See www.informationislam.com/articles.aspx?cid=1&acid=207aid=150; www.islamonline.net/livedialogue/english/Guestcv.asp?hGuestID=ufM0Xx, accessed at 20. 3. 2008.

51 Murad Hofmann, 'Journey to Islam' *Diary of a German Diplomat*, The Islamic Foundation, Markfield, 2001, p. 47.

52 Murad Hofmann, *Journey to Makkah*, Amana Publications, Beltsville, Maryland, 1998, p. 28.

53 Ibid., p. 30.

54 Ibid., pp. 30–1.

55 Ibid., pp. 31–2.

56 Ibid., pp. 33–6.

57 Ibid., p. 37.

58 The Quran: 53:38.

59 Murad Hofmann, *Journey to Makkah*, op. cit., pp. 30–40.

60 Ibid., pp. 40–1.

61 Murad Hofmann, 'Journey to Islam', *Diary of a German Diplomat*, Op. Cit.

62 Murad Hofmann, *Journey to Makkah*, Amana Publications, Beltsville, Maryland, 1998,

63 Murad Hofmann, *Islam and Quran*, Amana Publications, Beltsville, Maryland, 2007.

64 Murad Hofmann, *Religion on the Rise, Islam in the Third Millennium*, Amana Publications, Beltsville, Maryland, 2001.

65 Murad Hofmann, *Islam: The Alternative*, Amana Publications, Beltsville, Maryland, 1999.

66 See www.geocities.com, accessed at 30. 5. 2008.

67 On all the above issues see Murad Hofmann, *Islam: The Alternative*, Amana publications, Beltsville, Maryland, 1999 and *Islam in the Third Millennium*, Amana publications, Beltsville, Maryland, 2001. See also: www.islamonline.net/English/contemporary/2002/05/article3-a.shtml, accessed at 16. 4. 2009.

68 See www.worldwisdom.com/public/library/defult.aspx, accessed at 5. 3. 2009.

69 Jean-Baptiste Aymard and Patrick Laude, Frithjof Schuon. *Life and Teachings*, State University of New York Press, Albany, 2004, p. 8.

70 See www.religioperennis.org, accessed at 5. 3. 09.

71 Jean-Baptiste Aymard and Patrick Laude, op. cit., pp. 7–15.

72 Ibid., p. 15.

73 Ibid., pp. 18–24.

74 For more on his personal life see ibid, pp. 5–54. See also S.H. Nasr, (ed.) The Essential Frithjof Schuon, World Wisdom, Bloomington, Ind, 2005, pp. 5–52.

75 Frithjof Schuon, *The Transcendent Unity of Religions* (translated by Peter Townsend), Faber and Faber, London, 1953.

76 Frithjof Schuon, *Understanding Islam*, World Wisdom Books, Bloomington, Ind, 1998.

77 Frithjof Schuon, *Islam and the Perennial Philosophy* (translated by Peter Hobson and S.H. Nasr), World of Islam Festival Publishing Company, London, 1976.

78 See http://revertmuslims.com/forum/index.php?showtopic=1309, accessed at 13. 2. 2009.

79 S. H. Nasr, *The Essential Frithjof Schuon*, op. cit., p. 50.

Chapter 2

[1] http://www.euromuslim.net/index.php/islam-in-europe/country-profile/profile-of-the, accessed at 23.2.2010.

[2] Ibid., see also Ali Kose, *Conversion to Islam, A Study in Native British Converts*, Kegan Paul international, London and New York, 1996, p. 11.

[3] See M. Rodinson, *Europe and the Mystique of Islam*, I.B. Tauris, London, 1988, pp. 33–7.

[4] http://www.euromuslim.net/indx.php/islam-in-europe/country-profile-of-the, accessed at 23.2.2010.

[5] See Jorgen Nielsen, *Muslims in West Europe*, Edinburgh University Press, Edinburgh, second edition, 1995, p. 4.

[6] See M. M. Ally, *History of Muslims in Britain*, 1850–1980, unpublished MA dissertation, University of Birmingham, 1980, pp. 41–7.

[7] See *The Islamic Review*, January, *Vol XXIII*, No. 1, January 1935, p. 23.

[8] See www.absoluteastronomy.com/topics/Henry_Stanley,_3rd_Baron_Stanley_of_Al, accessed at 23.3.2010.

[9] See www.wokingmuslim.org/pers/quilliam/rev-re12.htm, accessed at 23.2.2010.

[10] Ibid.

[11] William Facey, 'From Mayfair to Mecca, Lady Evelyn Cobbold's pilgrimage in 1933', public lecture at IAIS, Exeter University, April 2009.

[12] Lady Evelyn Cobbold, *Pilgrimage to Mecca*, New edition, Arabian publishing, London, 2009, p. 89.

[13] Ibid., pp. 89–90.

[14] William Facey, 'Mayfair to Mecca', *Saudi Aramco World, Vol 59*, no. 5, 2008, at www.saudiaramcoworld.com/issue/200805/mayfair.to.makkah.htm, accessed at 30.3.2010.

[15] Ibid., see also his public lecture cited above.

[16] In addition to her decision to publish her pilgrimage diary, Lady Evelyn also delivered a public speech in December of 1933 on the occasion of the birthday of the Prophet Muhammad, which was held by the Muslim Society of Britain in London. In her speech, she talked sympathetically and passionately about the moral life of the Prophet Muhammad, especially his message of tolerance and the necessity of acquiring knowledge. She ended her speech by advising Muslims to follow in his footsteps, live a moral life and adhere to their faith. The Islamic Review commented on her speech as follows: '[the lecture] went a long way to help Muslims, steeped in love for the Holy Places, to live for a brief space of time in the days of the Holy Prophet. As to non-Muslims, it went a long way to impress indelibly the brilliant speech which Lady Evelyn had already made'; see The Islamic Review, Vol XXII, No. 3, March 1934, p. 72.

[17] All the passages quoted are taken from The Islamic Review, Vol XXIII, No. 1, January 1935, pp. 23–4.

[18] Lady Cobbold, *Pilgrimage to Mecca*, op. cit., p. 123.

[19] See Marcia Herman, 'Roads to Mecca: Conversion Narratives of European and Euro-American Muslims', *The Muslim Worm*, Vol. LXXXIX, No. 1, January 1999, pp. 57–8.

[20] See, for example, *The Islamic Review*, March 1934, and January 1935. See also the account of the funeral service and her burial, which was produced as a report in

the Woking mosque and sent to Lahore in 1963; it can be found at: www.woking-muslim.org/pers/ez_cobbold/index.htm, accessed at 19.2.2010.

[21] The Quran: The Light, Chapter 24, verse 35. The Imam who conducted her funeral was so moved by her attachment to the faith that he wrote the following words in his report: 'Glory be to Allah, what love for Islam! On the one hand there is the far-off Scotland and an independent-minded woman of authority – yet Islam possesses such great power as to capture her, and it is a capture by which Islam has planted on top of a high mountain in Scotland, in the midst of a gathering of the aristocracy and nobility, the declaration: Allahu nur-us-samawati wal ard.' See: www.wokingmuslim.org/pers/ezcobbold/index.htm, accessed at 19.3.2010.

[22] See *The Islamic Review*, Vol. 2, No. 2, February 1914, pp. 64–5. See also, the official website of Woking mission.

[23] See www.Masud.co.uk, accessed at 17.10.2010.

[24] Ibid.

[25] *The Islamic Review*, Vol. 2, no.2, February 1914, pp. 64–5.

[26] See the article at the official website www.masud.co.uk, accessed at 20.10.2010.

[27] *The Islamic Review*, February 1914, Op. Cit, p. 64–5.

[28] See Tim Winter, *Muslim Songs of the British Isles*, Quilliam Press, London, 2005, p. 6.

[29] This poem has been set to music and re-published in: Tim Winter, *Muslim Songs of the British Isles*, Op. Cit, p. 21.

[30] See all of the above poems and more at: www.Masud.co.uk, accessed at 12.2010.

[31] Yahya Birt thinks that Parkinson was a systematic writer and that he was more systematic in his writings than William Quilliam. I am unable to affirm this assumption, given the fact that no record has yet been found of scholarly works by Parkinson. Perhaps, this issue will have to wait until a new detailed study of Parkinson (which Birt told me he intends to undertake in the near future) has been conducted. Personal interview, Markfield, September 2010.

[32] See *Islam-Our Choice*, Begum Aisha Bawany, Karachi, abridged edition, 1967, p. 8.

[33] See Eric Rosenthal, *From Drury Lane to Mecca*, Sampson Low, London, 1931, pp. 3–11.

[34] Cited from ibid., p. 15.

[35] Ibid., p. 15.

[36] T. J. Winter also claims that he was the 'first British Guest of Allah'. See www.lastprophet.info/en/tim-winter/the-first-british-guest-of-allah.html, accessed at 15.2.2010.

[37] See Eric Rosenthal, From Drury Lane to Mecca, op. cit., p. 41.

[38] See M. Herman, 'Roads to Mecca: Conversion Narratives of European and Euro-American Muslims', op. cit., p. 65.

[39] Ibid., pp. 23–58.

[40] *The Independent on-line*, 2 January 2009.

[41] Ron Geaves, Islam in Victorian Britain, the Life and Times of Abdullah Quilliam, KUPE publishing, Markfield, 2010, p. 15.

[42] See *The Independent on-line*, 2 August 2007.

[43] Ron Geaves, *Islam in Victorian Britain*, Op. Cit, pp. 123–4.

[44] Ibid., p. 291.

[45] Ibid., pp. 144–62.

[46] Ibid., p. 164.

[47] J. Nielsen, *Muslims in West Europe*, second edition, Edinburgh University press, Edinburgh, 1995, p. 5.

[48] *The Independent on-line*, 2 January 2009. See also Geave, *Islam in Victorian Britain*, op. cit., pp. 284–313.

[49] See www.wokingmuslim.org/pers/headley/headley-press.htm, accessed at 19.2.2010. See also www.wokingmuslim.org/pers/headley.htm, accessed at 19.2.2010.

[50] See Islam-Our Choice, op. cit., p. 1.

[51] On the issue of his religious upbringing and inner feelings, see Lord Headley, The Affinity between the Original Church of Jesus Christ and Islam, trust for the encouragement and circulation of Muslim religious literature, the Mosque, Woking, 1926, pp. 26–9.

[52] See *The Islamic Review, Vol XI*, No. 6, June-July 1923, p. 206.

[53] See Lord Headley, A Western Awakening to Islam, 1914, p. 32, at www.aaiil.org, accessed at 2.3.2010.

[54] Ibid., p. 62.

[55] Lord Headley, The Affinity between the Original Church of Jesus Christ and Islam, op. cit., p. 40.

[56] Ibid., pp. 32–3.

[57] See Lord Headley, *The Great Prophets of the World*, The Mosque, Working, 1923, p. 48.

[58] For more detailed information see, Lord Headley, ibid.

[59] See Ali Kose, *Conversion to Islam*, op. cit., pp. 14–15.

[60] Lord Headley, 'President's Address, British Muslim Society', *The Islamic Review, Vol. III*, No.1, January 1915, p. 9.

[61] See M. Ally, *History of Muslims in Britain*, op. cit, pp. 72–3.

[62] Lord Headley, *The Islamic Review*, op. cit., p. 10.

[63] Ibid., p. 15.

[64] Ibid., pp. 11–12.

[65] Ibid., p. 13.

[66] M. Ally, *History of Muslims in Britain*, op. cit, pp. 75–7.

[67] For more information see, *The Islamic Review, Vol. XI*, No. 1, September, 1923, pp. 301–13. *The Islamic Review, Vol. XI*, No. 12, December 1923, pp. 443. *The Muslim Outlook, Vol. II*, No. 55, February 1926, pp. 1–2. See also the Woking Muslim mission website.

[68] Anne Fremantle, *Loyal Enemy*, Hutchinson and Co, London, 1938, pp. 7–16.

[69] Peter Clark, Marmaduke Pickthall, *British Muslim*, Quartet, London, Melbourne, New York, 1986, pp. 8–9.

[70] Anne Fremantle, Loyal Enemy, op. cit., p. 27.

[71] Ibid., p. 30.

[72] See Tim Winter, www.masud.co.uk/ISLAM/bmh/BMM-AHM-pickthall_bio.htm, accessed at 19/02/2010.

[73] Cited from ibid.

[74] Cited from Anne Fremantle, *Loyal Enemy*, op. cit., p. 81.

[75] Peter Clark, 'introduction' *Said the Fisherman*, novel by Pickthall, Quartet Books, London, 1986, pp. 2–3. You can see an earlier version by Pickthall, *Said, The Fisherman*, Methuen, London, 1919.

76 Tim Winter, www.masud.co.uk/ISLAM/bmh/BMM-AHM-pickthall_bio.htm, accessed at 19/02/2010.

77 All quotations are from Marmaduke Pickthal, *Said the Fisherman*, Introduction by Peter Clark, op. cit., p. 1.

78 Peter Clark, Marmaduke Pickthall, *British Muslim*, op. cit., p. 26.

79 Anne Fremantle, Loyal Enemy, op. cit., p. 228.

80 M. Pickthall, *Said The Fisherman*, especially the introduction to the book by P. Clark, Op. Cit.

81 Peter Clark, Marmaduke Pickthall, *British Muslim*, op. cit., p. 42.

82 Anne Fremantle, *Loyal Enemy*, op. cit, p. 296.

83 Marmaduke Pickthall, *Said The Fisherman*, with introduction by Peter Clark, p. 7.

84 Anne Fremantle, *Loyal Enemy*, p. 320.

85 Ibid., pp. 321–2.

86 Most of his writings on Islam can be found in this journal; some of his sermons and lectures were published as booklets.

87 Peter Clark, Marmaduke Pickthall, *British Muslim*, op. cit., p. 38.

88 See Marmaduke Pickthall, *The Cultural Side of Islam*, Kitab Bhavan, New Delhi, second edition (first edition was published in 1927), 1981, especially Chapter Two, pp. 23–47.

89 Ibid., p. 44.

90 Ibid., p. 54.

91 Ibid., p. 59.

92 Ibid., pp. 59–65.

93 Ibid., p. 91.

94 Ibid., p. 90

95 Marmaduke Pickthall, *The Position of Women in Islam*, Umma Publishing House, Karachi, (no date), p. 7.

96 Ibid., pp. 8–9.

97 See Chapter Seven of his book *The Cultural Side of Islam* cited above, especially pp. 152–60.

98 Marmaduke Pickthall, *The Meaning of the Glorious Quran, Text and Explantory Translation*, The Muslim World League, New York, 1977, translator's foreword, p. iii.

99 Anne Fremantle, *Loyal Enemy*, p. 420.

100 Seyyed Hossein Nasr, *Islam: History, Religion, and Civilisation*, Harper One, New York, 2003, p. xv.

Chapter 3

1 S.H. Nasr, 'The Heart of Islam', *Enduring Values for Humanity*, Harper San Francisco, New York, 2004, p. 310.

2 For an in-depth discussion of all these issues, see the following: René Guénon, *The Crisis of the Modern World*, Sophia Perennis, Hillsdale, New York, 2004 (first published 1927), *The Reign of Quantity and the Signs of the Times*, Sophia Perennis, Hillsdale, New York, 2004, (first published 1945) and East and West, Sophia Perennis, Hillsdale, New York, 2004, (first published 1924). On contemporary spiritual poverty, see Seyyed Hossein Nasr, *Man and Nature: The Spiritual Crisis of Modern Man*, Phanes Press, US, 1988.

[3] Seyyed Hossein Nasr, *A Young Muslim's Guide to the Modern World*, The Islamic Text Society, Cambridge, 1993, p. 145.

[4] Seyyed Hossein Nasr, *The Garden of Truth, The Vision and Promise of Sufism, Islam's Mystical Tradition*, Harper One, New York, 2007, p. xvi.

[5] Marshall G. Hodgson, *The Venture of Islam – Conscience and History in a World of Civilisation. Vol. 2, The Expansion of Islam in the Middle Periods*, University of Chicago Press, Chicago and London, 1974, p. 145.

[6] Martin Lings, *What is Sufism?* George Allen and Unwin, London, 1975, pp. 106–7. See also J. Nurbakhsh, *Sufism, Meaning, Knowledge and Unity*, Khaniqahi Nimatullahi Publications, New York, 1981; Reynold A. Nicholson, *The Mystics of Islam*, Routledge and Kegan Paul, London, 1997; Gai Eaton, *Islam and the Destiny of Man*, Islamic Texts Society, Cambridge, 1994.

[7] http://www.usc.edu/dept/MSA/newmuslim/karima.html, accessed at 30.11.2003.

[8] See Thomas W. Arnold, *The Preaching of Islam: A History of the Propagation of the Muslim Faith*, Archibald and Constable C., London, 1935.

[9] Dutton, op. cit., p. 163.

[10] Seyyed Hossein Nasr, *Islam and the Plight of Modern Man*, Longman, London, 1975, p. 49.

[11] Dutton, op. cit., p. 163; Ira M. Lapidus, *A History of Islamic Societies*, Cambridge University Press, Cambridge, 1988, pp. 445–6.

[12] Seyyed Hossein Nasr, 'Sufi Essays, George Allen and Unwin', London, 1972, pp. 43–4.

[13] Ibid., p. 44.

[14] Seyyed Hossein Nasr, *Islam and the Plight of Modern Man*, op. cit., pp. 3–17.

[15] Seyyed Hossein Nasr, 'Sufi Essays', op. cit., p. 49.

[16] See Margaret Smith, *Rabia the Mystic and Her Fellow-Saints in Islam*, Cambridge University Press, Cambridge, 1984; J. Nurbakhsh, *Sufi Women*, Khaniqahi Nimatullahi Publications, New York, 1983 and W. El-Sakkakini, *First among Sufis: The life and Thought of Rabia al-Adawiyya, the Woman Saint of Basra*, Octagon press, London, 1982.

[17] Y. Haddad and A. Lummis, *Islamic Values in the United States*, Oxford University press, 1987, pp. 22, 171.

[18] In this context it is worth referring to Ian Dallas, or Abdal Qadir al-Sufi, founder of the now worldwide movement, al-Murabitun. Born in Ayr, southwest Scotland in 1930 and educated both in Scotland and London, he became a successful writer, actor and playwright, very much immersed in the cultural and literary life of Britain in the 1950s and 1960s. He wrote a number of plays and literary adaptations for television and film scripts. He befriended famous people such as Kenneth Tynan, Ronald Laing, Bob Dylan, George Harrison and Eric Clapton. Despite his comfortable life he felt, like most of his generation in the 1960s and 1970s, that he was neither satisfied nor fulfilled and was very much yearning for spiritual attainment. A trip to North Africa in 1967 changed his life forever. There, he embraced Islam and took up the name Abdal Qadir after the great twelfth-century Sufi saint of Baghdad, Shayhk Abdal Qdir al-Jilani. In 1968, he returned to Morocco, met the spiritual teacher, Shaykh Muhammad ibn Habib, and joined his Habibiyya/Darqawiyya/Shadhiliyya Sufi order. The Shaykh then appointed him Muqaddam, or representative of the order in Britain. When he returned to England, he taught Islam and formed a group of English and American converts

first in London and then in Norwich. When Shaykh Muhammad ibn Habib, the leader of the tariqa died, Abdal Qadir al-Sufi succeeded him and became the leader of the order. His group, or movement, attracted English and American converts, especially in the 1970s and 1980s, but gradually, and especially in recent years, the numbers dwindled and the movement waned. This information is supplied by some one who is close to some members of the group. April, 2010.

[19] Loïc Le Pape, 'Communication Strategies and Public Commitments: The Example of a Sufi Order in Europe'. In Steano Allievi and Jorgen S. Nielsen (eds), *Muslim Networks and Transnational Communities in and across Europe*, Brill, Leiden, 2003, pp. 232–4.

[20] To some extent, there is an exception to this case, represented by the group of Abdal Qadir al-Sufi named al-Murabitun in Norwich. This group, as stated earlier, was originally formed by the Scottish playwright and actor, Ian Dallas, who converted to Islam in 1967. He gathered around him some English and America converts, initially in London, then moved to a permanent place in Norwich, where he established a disciplined, self-supported enclave under his authoritarian rule, rejecting much of British/Western modern culture and adopting an austere way of life. This secluded enterprise proved to be difficult to sustain, not only because it was difficult to completely shun the modern way of life but also because of the uncompromising views and domineering style of the leader. The group ultimately broke up into factions and the leader moved to Spain, where he set up a community of followers - Murabitun - a name derived from the eleventh-century Murabitun (Almoravid) in Morocco and Spain. Those who stayed loyal in Britain keep contact with him and continue to receive guidance from him; the majority of those who left him continue to live as Muslims and some joined other groups. Very few left Islam altogether. Al-Sufi travels a lot and seems to be successful in setting up communities loyal to him in many parts of the world; one of these is in Cape Town, South Africa, where he currently lives. Al-Sufi and his movement seem to have gone through two stages: in the first stage, he emphasized in his teaching the esoteric aspect of Islam, combined with an isolationist approach to the social environment on the grounds that it was morally bankrupt. In the second stage, he combined both the inner and outer aspects of the religion, or Sufism and Shariah, with an emphasis on reviving the Maliki fiqh as an authentic model to be followed. He also changed his strategy with regard to the social environment and instructed his followers to become more active within the wider society in order to achieve change from within. This change can only be achieved, according to him, through a radical transformation of the basic principles of British society and not through marrying the universal Islamic teachings with some Western values and principles. For him and his followers, British/Western society is morally, socially and economically diseased and has nothing to offer; it is because of these radical and uncompromising views that the movement has waned, not only in terms of its numbers but also in terms of its impact on the wider society. Having said this, the group is not violent in its approach to change, for them, change has to take place through peaceful rather than militant means. For example, the group condemns capitalism, especially the use of usury, and believes that it is the root of all current social, political and economic ills in the world. To solve these problems they advocate the replace-

ment of the current interest rate economic system with the Islamic economic/ trade system and revitalize the Zakat, which has been abandoned by Muslims in favour of the Western, capitalist system. The group is also active in promoting Islamic education since they believe that modern education falls short of providing children with their moral and spiritual needs. This information came through a personal interview with someone who has close contact with members of the group, Birmingham, July 2010. See also Ali Kose, Conversion to Islam, op. cit., pp. 175–88 and www.bewley.virtualave.net/saq.html, accessed at 26.2.2010.

[21] *British Muslims Monthly Survey*, Op. Cit, p. 8.

[22] For more information see the individual case studies in this book.

[23] Permission was granted by these individuals (and their siblings in the case of Gia Eaton and close friend in the case of Martin Lings). Permission was also sought and granted from both Hamza Yusuf and Tim Winter. It is worthwhile mentioning that some prominent convert scholars prefer to keep their conversion anonymous and have therefore refused to give permission to disclose their names or even to discuss their works and intellectual contributions, among them a respected professor of Islamic Studies who has published over twenty books on various Islamic issues! In these cases, the wish for privacy was respected.

[24] See an in-depth treatment of his work in chapter six of this book.

[25] Martin Lings died some years ago, and Gai Eaton passed away in April 2010. Their Works were, and continue to be, of crucial importance to Islam in general and British Islam in particular. For detailed treatment of their impact on British Islam, see chapters four and five in this book.

[26] Although Professor Waines is Canadian by birth, he has been living and working in Britain for over forty years. His works on Islamic faith have had an effect on British Islam in general.

[27] Laura was brought up in a family with a relaxed attitude to religion, converted to Islam when she was an undergraduate student in Scotland. Of her role as a convert she says: 'Part of being Muslim is to serve our communities and uphold justice, and I have always hoped in tiny ways my academic work could contribute positively: through teaching, through research and its determination, and in a broader sense, just by being a Muslim woman engaging in these subjects and the academy'. Personal communication, Birmingham, 16.12.2010.

[28] www.rferl.org./content/article/1052842.html, accessed at 13.8.2010.

[29] www.newmuslimsproject.net/meeting-point, accessed at 13.8.2010.

[30] www.newmuslimsproject.net/meeting-point, accessed at 13.8.2010.

[31] www.openmindsblogspot.com, accessed at 14.8.2010. See also www.muslimnews.co.uk/awards/index.php?page=2005/ihewitt and www.greenbelt.org.uk, (both accessed at 14.8.22010).

[32] www.yusufislam.com/biography/, accessed at 15.8.2010.

[33] Ibid.

[34] Ibid.

[35] Ibid.

[36] For more information on her story see her book entitled 'In the hands of the Taliban', Robson Books, London, 2001.

[37] See her website at www.yvonneridely.org, accessed at 15.8.2010.

[38] Cited in Margot Badran, 'Feminism and Conversion' in: Karin van Nieuwkerk (ed.), *Women Embracing Islam, Gender and Conversion in the West*, University of Texas Press, Austin, 2006, pp. 217–18.

[39] The Muslim News, 30 August 2002, p. 11.

[40] The Muslim News, 30 July 2004, p. 8; see also Islam online website.

[41] Sarah Joseph, 'editorial', *Emel magazine*, London, April 2006, p. 3.

[42] Ibid, p. 3.

[43] Interview with Sarah Joseph, Emel Magazine, by David Rowan, Evening Standard, July 20, 2005; it can also be seen at www.davidrowan.com/2005/07/interview-sarah-joseph-emel-magazine.html, accessed at 16.8.2010.

Chapter 4

[1] See René Guénon, *The Crisis of the Modern World*, SOPHIA Perennis, Hillsdale, NY, (first published 1941), 2001.

[2] Seyyed Hossein Nasr, *The Heart of Islam, Enduring Values for Humanity*, Harper San Francisco, New York, 2002, pp. 310–11.

[3] Shaykh Hamaza Yusuf, 'A Gentle Soul' in Sophia, *Journal of Traditional Studies, Vol 11*, No. 1, 2005, pp. 42–9.

[4] Gai Eaton, The Guardian on May 27, 2005 at www.guardian.co.uk/news/205. may/27/guardianobituaries.obituaries, accessed at 25.8.2010.

[5] Martin Lings, *A Return to the Spirit*, Fons Vita, Louisville, KY, Quinta Essentia, 2005, p. 2.

[6] Ibid., p. 2.

[7] Michael Fitzgerald, 'In Memoriam: Dr. Martin Lings' at www.worldwisdom.com, accessed at 22.8.2010, p. 90.

[8] Seyyed Hossein Nasr, 'Shaykh Abu Siraj al-Din (Martin Lings): A Tribute' in Sophia, op. cit., p. 31.

[9] Douglas Martin, 'Martin Lings, a Sufi Writer on Islamic Ideas, Dies at 96', The New York Times, May 29, 2005, at www.nytimes.com/2005/05/29/obituaries/29Lings.html?_=1, accessed at 25.8.2010.

[10] Michael Fitzgerald, op. cit, p. 92.

[11] For more information on the life and writings of René Guénon see: Robin Waterfield, René Guénon and the future of the West, Sophia Perennis, Hillsdale, NY, second edition, 2002.

[12] Martin Lings, *A Return to the Spirit*, op. cit., p 2.

[13] Ibid., pp. 2–3.

[14] Ibid., p. 3.

[15] Michael Fitzgerald, op. cit, pp. 90–1.

[16] Martin Lings, *A Return to the Spirit*, op. cit., p. 5.

[17] For more information on this issue see: Jean-Baptiste Aymard and Patrick Laude, Frithjof Schuon, Life and Teachings, op. cit., pp. 27–34.

[18] Martin Lings, *A Return to the Spirit*, op. cit., p. 8.

[19] The Hadith briefly states that one day while the Prophet was sitting with some of his companions, they heard him saying to himself, 'O my brethren!' which he

repeated three times. Then one of them asked him, 'Are not we your brethren?' 'No,' he says, 'you are my companions; my brethren are those who believe in me and love me without seeing me.' The Arabic version of the Hadith in Musnad Ahmad ibn Hanbal reads as thus: 'An Anas bin Malik, qala, qala rasulullah (saaws): Wadadtu anni laqitu ikhwani. Qal, qala ashab al-nabi (saaws): Awalaysa nahnu ikhwanuka? Qala antum ashab wa lakin ikhwani al-ladhina aamanu bi wa lam yarawni.' *Vol. 3*, p. 155 - Dar Sader, Beirut, no date.

[20] Martin Lings, *A Return to the Spirit*, op. cit., pp. 9–10.

[21] Seyyed Hossein Nasr, Foreward, in Jean-Baptiste Aymard and Patrick Laude, Frithjof Schuon, *Life and Teachings*, op. cit., pp. x-xi.

[22] See his biographers Aymard and Laude in their book Frithjof Schuon, Life and Teachings, op. cit., p. 1.

[23] See ibid., p. 1.

[24] Among them was Guénon's book 'East and West', which was rendered into English in 1941.

[25] Reza Shah-Kazemi, 'A Tribute to Martin Lings on the Occasion of his 90th Birthday'. Personal acquisition from the author, July 2010, pp. 1–2.

[26] Martin Lings, *Ancient Beliefs and Modern Superstitions*, *Archetype*, Cambridge, revised edition, 2004.

[27] Martin Lings, *The Eleventh Hour, The Spiritual Crisis of the Modern World in the light of Tradition and Prophecy*, *Archetype*, Cambridge, revised edition, 2002 (first edition was published in 1987).

[28] In this context, we may refer to the Hadith by the Prophet in which he says: 'He who omits one tenth of the Law in the beginning of Islam will be damned; but he who accomplishes one tenth of the Law at the end of Islam will be saved.' Quoted from Shah-Kazemi, 'A Message of Hope at the Eleventh Hour: Martin Lings, 1909–2005' in Sophia, *Journal of Traditional Studies, Vol. 11*, No. 1, 2005, p. 57. And a very well-known Qudsi Hadith which stresses: 'My Mercy Takes Precedence over My Wrath', and the Quranic verse VII: 156, which says: 'My mercy encompasses all things.'

[29] Ibid., p. 57.

[30] Martin Lings, *Symbol and Archetype, A Study of the Meaning of Existence*, Quinta Essentia, Cambridge, 1991, p. vii.

[31] Note that, despite the fact that the book is written from a Universalist perspective, it has two chapters related to the Islamic tradition and is infused with many Quranic verses that are admirably translated to fit into the overall theme of the book. This illustrates not only his deep and profound knowledge of Islam as a belief system but also his affinity to it.

[32] Martin Lings, *A Return to the Spirit: Questions and Answers*, Fons Vitae, Quinta Essentia, Louisville, KY, first published in 2005.

[33] Dr Shah-Kazemi also agrees with this analogy; see his 'A Message of Hope at the Eleventh Hour', op. cit., p. 54.

[34] Of this Shaykh Hamza Yusuf says: 'With a poet's pen, a metaphysician's mind and a saint's concerns. Dr Lings has left for us a profound posthumous farewell letter, filled with poignant insights gleaned from a lifetime of devotion, contemplation and concern about the human condition. He did in his life what he is urging the rest of us to do: return to the spirit.' See the jacket of *A Return to the Spirit*.

³⁵ See ibid.

³⁶ Martin Lings and Clinton Minnaar (eds.), *The Underlying Religion, An Introduction to the Perennial Philosophy*, World Wisdom, Bloomington, Ind, 2007.

³⁷ I am aware that there are many senior scholars in Philosophy departments who are either oblivious or ignorant of what the Perennial Philosophy means!

³⁸ In a private conversation a while ago about the works of Seyyed Hossein Nasr, Suha Taji-Farouki, Research Associate at the Institute of Ismaili studies and senior lecturer at Exeter University remarked that she found it difficult to follow some of the ideas in his writings and wished he could write more directly, so that the impact of his writings would be more widely felt. Personal communication, Birmingham, 1997. In her article on 'Seyyed Hossein Nasr: Defender of the Sacred and Islamic Traditionalism' Jane Smith refers to the same point to some extent when she says that Nasr appears to target certain audiences in his writings and writes for two different levels, see her article in Y. Haddad, Muslims of America, New York, Oxford University press, 1991, pp. 80–95.

³⁹ Martin Lings, *The Secret of Shakespeare, His Greatest Plays Seen in the Light of Sacred Art*, Archetype, Cambridge, 2002.

⁴⁰ Martin Lings, *Collected Poems*, Archetype, Cambridge, 2002.

⁴¹ The two quotes are from: www.radiusfoundation.org/lings-review.htm, accessed at 25.8.2010.

⁴² Shah-Kazemi, 'A Tribute to Martin Lings on the Occasion of his 90th Birthday,' op. cit., p. 13.

⁴³ The poem is cited from Shah-Kazemi, *A Message of Hope*, op. cit., p. 59.

⁴⁴ Martin Lings, *Muhammad, His Life Based on the Earliest Sources*, UNWIN, London, 1988 (first published in 1983 by Allen and Unwin).

⁴⁵ Ibid. See dust Jacket.

⁴⁶ Shah-Kazemi, op. cit., p. 5.

⁴⁷ See the quote at: www.mac.abc.se/~onesr/ez/dc/oml_e.htm accessed at 20.8.2010.

⁴⁸ Martin Lings, *A Sufi Saint of the Twentieth Century*, Shaikh Ahmad Al-Alawi, Allen and Unwin, London, 1961.

⁴⁹ Martin Lings, *What is Sufism?* Unwin Paperbacks, London, second edition, 1981 (first edition was published in 1971).

⁵⁰ Martin Lings, *A Sufi Saint of the Twentieth Century*, see the preface, pp. 9–10.

⁵¹ Ibid., p. 126.

⁵² See his concise chapter on the doctrine of the Oneness of Being in ibid., pp. 121–30.

⁵³ Shah-Kazemi, op. cit., p. 8.

⁵⁴ Martin Lings, *A Sufi Saint*, op. cit., p. 129.

⁵⁵ Shah-Kazemi, op. cit., p. 9.

⁵⁶ Martin Lings, *What is Sufism*, Op. Cit, pp. 15–16.

⁵⁷ Ibid., p. 22.

⁵⁸ The verse says: 'For each We have appointed a law and a path; and if God had wished He would have made you one people. But He hath made you as ye are that He may put to the test in what He hath given you. So vie with one another in good works. Unto God ye will all be brought back and He will then tell you about those things wherein ye differed.'

⁵⁹ Martin Lings, What is Sufism?, Op. Cit, p. 23.

[60] Three other important books on Islamic themes may also be mentioned. *The Book of Certainty*, published in 1970 by the Millat Book Centre, New Delhi, is his first written book and focuses mainly on explaining some of the Sufi principles from the traditional Quranic esoteric commentaries. The second is *Mecca from before the Genesis until now*, published by Archetype, Cambridge in 2004, a monograph that highlights the importance of the city of Mecca in the history of the three Abrahamic religions. The third is *The Holy Qur'an, Translation of Selected Verses*, which is unfinished as Lings passed away before he could complete it. The Royal Institute for Islamic Thought (Amman, Jordan) and the Islamic Texts Society (Cambridge) decided to publish what he had translated under the above title in 2007; it is a beautiful translation of some Quranic verses that could benefit those who want to know more about the Quran, especially from the spiritual perspective. This is in addition to dozens of articles on various Islamic subjects. As stated earlier, we cannot deal with them exhaustively within the constraints of this chapter.

[61] Martin Lings, *The Quranic Art of Calligraphy and Illumination*, first published by World of Islam Festival Trust in 1976, then by Scorpion, Essex, in 1987.

[62] Seyyed Hossein Nasr, 'Shaykh Abu Bakr Siraj al-Din: A Tribute', SOPHIA, *Journal of Traditional Studies*, op. cit., p. 32.

[63] For more on this subject see: Jean Sulzberger, 'Some Notes on Arab Calligraphy', in William Chittick,(ed.), *The Inner Journey, Views from the Islamic Tradition*, Morning Light Press, USA, 2007, pp. 78–81.

[64] Martin Lings, *The Quranic Art of Calligraphy and Illumination*, Op. Cit, p. 12.

[65] See www.themathesontrus.org/announce/?tag=reza-shah-kazemi, accessed at 25.8.2010.

[66] Shah-Kazemi, op. cit., p. 56.

Chapter 5

[1] See www.radicalmiddleway.co.uk/speakers/scholars/shaykh-hasan-le-gai-eaton, accessed at 25.08.2010.

[2] See www.seekersguidance.org/blog/2020/03/obituary-for-gai-eaton-remembering-the-uk, accessed at 08.10.2010.

[3] Gai Eaton, *A Bad Beginning and the Path to Islam*, Archetype, Cambridge, 2010, p. 23.

[4] For detailed account on his personal 'profane life' see ibid.

[5] Gai Eaton, *Islam and the Destiny of Man*, Islamic Texts Society, Cambridge, 1994, pp. 4–5.

[6] Gai Eaton, *A Bad Beginning and the Path to Islam*, op. cit., pp. 74–5.

[7] Gai Eaton, *Islam and the Destiny of Man*, op. cit., p. 6.

[8] Vedanta from the Traditional perspective is a doctrine of unity, and as such it is equivalent to the Islamic concept of Tawhid.

[9] Ibid., pp. 9–10.

[10] Gai Eaton, *A Bad Beginning*, op. cit., pp. 232–3.

[11] Ibid, p. 236.

[12] Gai Eaton, *Islam and the Destiny of Man*, op. cit., p. 11.

[13] Martin Lings had a great role to play in this, for after a long silence he received Eaton back permanently to his order.

[14] Gai Eaton, *A Bad Beginning and the Path to Islam*, op. cit., p. 351.

[15] Ibid., p. 353.

[16] Intreview with Gai Eaton, Emel, September/October, 2003; it can be seen at www. emel.com/article?id=18a_id-1164, accessed at 15.10.2010.

[17] Ibid.

[18] Ibid.

[19] Ibid.

[20] www.an-nisa.org/subpage.asp?id=323&mainid=78, accessed at 15.10.2010.

[21] See his talk on the issues of extremism, moderation and Islam that took place in London on 16 of December 2005 at www.youtub.com/watch?v=Iyvqfh2wupA, accessed at 16.10.2010.

[22] Gai Eaton, *The Richest Vein*, Sophia Perennis, Hillsdale, NY, 2005, p. 8.

[23] Ibid, pp. 17–18.

[24] Gai Eaton, *King of the Castle, Choice and Responsibility in the Modern World*, Islamic Texts Society, Cambridge, 1990, pp. 8–9.

[25] Ibid., p. 14.

[26] Ibid., p. 22.

[27] Ibid., p. 15.

[28] Gai Eaton, *Bad Beginning and the Path to Islam*, op. cit., p. 358.

[29] Gai Eaton, *Islam and the Destiny of Man*, op. cit., p. 8.

[30] Ibid., p. 40.

[31] Gai Eaton, *Remembering God, Reflections on Islam*, Islamic Texts Society, Cambridge, 2000, p. 39.

[32] Ibid., p. 41. The Quran is full of verses which illustrate that all in the heavens and the earth glorify God.

[33] Ibid., pp. 41–2.

[34] Ibid., p. 44.

[35] Ibid., pp. 51–2.

[36] Ibid., p. 230.

[37] Ibid., p. 232.

[38] Gai Eaton, *The Book of Hadith*, The book Foundation, Watsonville, California, Bristol, England, 2008.

[39] Jeremy Henzell-Thomas, from the introduction to *The Book of Hadith*, p. xxv.

[40] See in particular some of his works on various Islamic themes in William Chittick (ed.), The inner Journey, Views from the Islamic tradition, op. cit., pp. 10–18, 29–34, 56–61 and 191–8; also his short monographs: one on *The Concept of Justice in Islam*, The Book Foundation, London, 2004, the second on *The Concept of God in Islam*, the Islamic Cultural Centre, London, 2005. Some of his other works can also be found in various volumes of SOPHIA, The Journal of Traditional Studies.

Chapter 6

[1] See IOS magazine, October 2010, at www.iosminaret.org/vol-5/issue11/profile.php, accessed at 6.11.2010.

[2] Personal conversation with Tim Winter, Birmingham, May 2010.

[3] Cited from 'Beginning of the Hour', September 22, 2010 at www.moham-madthalif.blogspot.com/2010/09/timothy-winter-britains.most.html, accessed at 6.11.2010.

[4] Most of the above information is taken from his CV, which I managed to get hold of.

[5] Tim Winter, 'A Teenage Journey to Islam', WWW.masud.co.uk, accessed at 7.11.2010, p. 4.

[6] Cited from 'Beginning of the Hour', op. cit., p. 2

[7] Ibid., p. 2.

[8] Tim Winter, 'A Teenage Journey to Islam', op. cit., p. 3.

[9] See, for example, his 'Conversion as Nostalgia: Some Experiences of Islam', in M. Percy (ed.), Previous Convictions, Conversion in the Present Day, Society for Promoting Christian Knowledge, London, 2000, especially pp. 100–1; see also his 'The Trinity: A Muslim Perspective' at www.masud.co.uk, accessed at 7.11.2010, pp. 1–7.

[10] Tim Winter, 'The Trinity: A Muslim Perspective', at www.masud.co.uk, accessed at 10.11.2010, p. 2.

[11] Tim Winter, 'A Teenage Journey to Islam', op. cit, p. 3.

[12] Ibid, pp. 5–9.

[13] Ibid, pp. 8–9.

[14] Tim Winter, 'Love for others', Friday Khutbas, Cambridge Mosque, it can be seen at www.cambridgemosqueismoving.org.uk, accessed at 12.11.2010.

[15] See his speech 'Islam in the New Millennium', public lecture, Chicago, 1999. It can be seen at www.youtube.com/watch?v=fa_MdnXk8Gy@feature=related, accessed at 13.11.2010.

[16] See the leaflet: Cambridge Muslim College, Diploma in Contextual Islamic Studies and Leadership, Cambridge, May 2009.

[17] See the interview with Hamza Yusuf at www.youtube.com/watch?v=3RXrQr4mJ5 E8feature=related, accessed at 13.11.2010.

[18] Al-Busiri, The Mantle Adorned, Tim Winter (translator), Quilliam Press, London, 2009.

[19] See www.mantleadorned.com/author.htm, accessed at 14.11.2010.

[20] Abu Hamid al-Ghazali, Remembrance of Death and Afterlife, Tim Winter (translator), Islamic Texts Society, Cambridge, 1989.

[21] Abu Hamid al-Ghazali, *Disciplining the Soul and Breaking the Two Desires*, Tim Winter (translator), Islamic Texts Society, Cambridge, 1995.

[22] Al-Bayhaqi, *Seventy-Seven Branches of Faith*, Tim Winter (translator), Quilliam Press, London, 1990.

[23] Al-Asqalani, *Selections from Fath Al-Bari*, Tim Winter (translator), Muslim Academic Trust, Cambridge, 2000. Winter also translated from French an important book called *Unveiling Islam* that deals with some aspects of the faith; see Roger Du Pasquier (author) *Unveiling Islam*, Tim Winter (translator), Islamic Texts Society, Cambridge, 1992.

[24] See Tim Winter, (ed.), *The Cambridge Companion to Classical Islamic Theology*, Cambridge University Press, Cambridge, 2009.

[25] Tim Winter, 'The Saint with Seven Tombs' in William Chittick (ed.), *The Inner Journey, Views from the Islamic Tradition*, Op. Cit, pp. 244–51.

[26] Tim Winter, 'Islam, Irigaray, and the retrieval of gender' and 'Boys will be Boys', both of which can be found on his website www.masud.co.uk. See also his chapter 'Mary in Islam' in S. J. Boss, Mary: The Complete Resources, Continuum, London, 2007, pp. 479–502.

[27] Tim Winter et al (eds.) *Abraham's Children: Jews, Christians and Muslims in Conversation*, T&T Clark/ Continuum, London, 2006.

[28] Tim Winter and J. A. Williams (authors), *Understanding Islam and the Muslims*, Fons Vitae, Louisville, KY, 2002.

[29] See, for example, his description of Nasser: 'a man like Nasser, a butcher, a failed soldier, and a cynical demagogue, could have taken over a country as pivotal as Egypt, despite the vacuity of his beliefs.' To be found in his chapter 'The Poverty of Fanaticism' in Joseph Lumbard (ed.), *Islam, Fundamentalism and the Betrayal of Tradition*, World Wisdom, Bloomington, Ind, 2004, p. 284. I recall vividly the remark by David Waines, former professor of Islamic Studies at Lancaster University that 'he was taken aback by the description' when he read the article. Personal conversation, Lancaster, 1998.

[30] Tim Winter, 'Bombing without Moonlight, the Origins of Suicidal Terrorism', at www.masud.co.uk, accessed at 7.11.2010, p. 6. The article was then published as a book under the same title by Amal press, Bristol, England, 2008.

[31] Ibid., p. 7.

[32] Ibid., p. 7.

[33] Ibid., p. 9.

[34] Ibid., p. 10.

[35] Ibid., p. 14.

[36] Ibid., p. 18.

[37] Ibid., p. 22.

[38] Tim Winter, 'The Poverty of Fanaticism' in Joseph Lumbard (ed.), *Islam, Fundamentalism, and the Betrayal of Tradition*, World Wisdom, Bloomington, Ind, 2004, pp. 284–94.

[39] Ibid., p. 285.

[40] Ibid., p. 287.

[41] Tim Winter, 'Puritan Muslims', public interview, It can be viewed at www.youtube.com/watch?v=UgLQp4dcbBo@feature=relmfu, accessed at 5.11.2010.

[42] Tim Winter, 'Islam in the New Millennium', Op. Cit.

[43] Ibid.

[44] Tim Winter, 'British and Muslim?' at www.masud.co.uk, accessed at 6.11.2010, p. 4.

[45] Ibid., p. 7.

[46] Ibid., p. 8.

[47] Ibid., pp. 9–14.

[48] Ibid., pp.16–17.

[49] Tim Winter 'Muslim Loyalty and Belonging' at www.masud.co.uk, accessed at 6.11.2010, pp. 11–13. The article is reproduced in Seddon, Hussain and Malik (eds.), *British Muslims: Loyalty and Belonging*, The Islamic Foundation, Markfield, 2003, pp. 3–22.

[50] Tim Winter, 'Tradition or Extradition?' in Aftab Malik (ed.), *The Empire and the Crescent, Global Implications for a New American Century*, Amal Press, Bristol, England, 2003, p. 143.

51 Ibid., p. 154.

52 Ibid., pp. 154–5.

53 See, for example, his work with Harries and Solomon (eds.), *Abraham's Children: Jews, Christians and Muslims in Conversation*, Continuum, London, 2006.

54 Tim Winter, 'Thought for the Day', BBC Radio Four, May 15, 2009.

Chapter 7

1 See his sermon entitled 'Be Peace Makers' at www.youtube.com/watch?v= 3YjhqHmlOM, accessed at 2.11.2010.

2 Cited from Ann Sofie Roald, *New Muslims in the European Context, The Experience of Scandinavian Converts*, Brill, Leiden, 2004, p. 224.

3 Reza Shah-Kazemi, 'Shaykh Hamza Yusuf, A Response to Nadeem Azam', *Q-News*, London, August 1998, p. 19.

4 See his home page www.sheikhhamza.com/biography.aspx, accessed at 25.11.2010.

5 See his interview with Mark Lawson at www.youtube.com/watch?v=ZBukxf xvcQ9&NR=1, accessed at 3.12.2010.

6 Ibid.

7 Ibid.

8 Hamza Yusuf, 'A Gentle Soul' in SOPHIA, *The Journal of Traditional Studies*, op. cit., p. 42.

9 Predominantly English convert community set up by the Scottish writer and actor Ian Dallas, who converted to Islam in the 1970s. See the footnote in Chapter 3 of this book. The information regarding his membership of al-Sufi's group in England came from an interview with someone who knows closely some members of the group, Birmingham, April, 2010.

10 He stated that the main reason for leaving the group was that he wanted to learn Arabic in order to be able to read the original Islamic texts.

11 For more on his background see the unofficial biography of Hamza Yusuf at www.sheikhhamza.com/biography/, accessed 25.11.2010.

12 See www.education.com/video/data/20/video/us/2010/80/23/nr.muslim.college.cnn.htl, accessed at 29.11.2010.

13 See the College website at www.ZaytunaCollege.org, accessed at 20.10.2009.

14 Ibid.

15 See the Hadith in the Forty Hadith Qudsi, Selected and translated by E. Ibrahim, and D. Johnson-Davies, Dar Al-Koran Al-Kareem, Beirut and Damascus, 1980, p. 82.

16 See the Quran Chapter 4, Verse 34 which states '(husbands) are the protectors And maintainers of their (wives) Because Allah has given The one more (strength) Than the other, and because They support them From their means. Therefore the righteous women Are devoutly obedient, and guard In (the husband's) absence What Allah would have them guard. As to those women On whose part ye fear Disloyalty and ill conduct, Admonish them (first), (Next), refuse to share their beds, (And last) spank them (lightly); But if they return to obedience Seek not against them Means (of annoyance). For Allah is Most High,

Great (above you all)'. Cited from Abdullah Yusuf Ali, *The Meaning of the Holy Quran*, amana publications, Maryland, 2001, pp. 195–6.

[17] According to him, the Arabic word 'dharaba' has many different meanings; it can mean travel, struck, suffer humiliation and impoverishment or set example (in a metaphorical sense). For more on the meaning of the word, see his talk 'Removing the Silence on Domestic Violence' at www.youtube.com/watch?v=BDEKJDgox-u, accessed at 24.11.2010.

[18] See Ibid.

[19] See his interview with Mark Lawson, Op. Cit.

[20] See his interview at www.youtube.com/watch?v=pp4pbfiMf7c&feature=related, accessed at 3.12.2010.

[21] Ibid.

[22] See his interview with Mark Lawson, Op. Cit.

[23] Ibid.

[24] Ibid.

[25] See his Sermon 'Be Peace makers', Op. cit.

[26] Ibid.

[27] Reza Shah-Kazemi, 'A response to Nadeem Azam', op. cit., p. 18.

[28] See his interview on the BBC's 'Hard Talk' at www.youtube.com/watch?v=kqAkgo-s7bg&feature=related, accessed at 29.11.2010.

[29] See his public lecture 'Islam and the West' at www.youtube.com/watch?v=ttcA9kt09M&feature=related, accessed at 30.11.2010.

[30] See his 'Hard Talk' interview with the BBC, op. cit.

[31] See Hamza Yusuf, 'What the West can learn from Islam' at www.news.bbc.co.uk/1/hi/talking_point/3190931.stm, accessed at 20.11.2010.

[32] Ibid.

[33] Ibid. See also www.lastprophet.info/en/hamza-yusuf/ffrom-hamza-yusuf-s-view-point-what-can, accessed at 25.11.2010.

[34] See Hamza Yusuf, 'Seeing with Muslim Eyes' in Aftab Malik (ed.), The Empire and the Crescent, op. cit., pp. 107–11.

[35] On this point see his article 'A Time for Introspection' at www.muslim-canada.org/introspection.html, accessed at 12.11.2010.

[36] Hamza Yusuf, 'On A Night of Remembrance', *Q-News*, London, October 2003, pp. 40–1.

[37] See the Quran, Chapter 5:48 which says 'If Allah had so willed, He would have made you A single People, but (His Plan is) to test you in what He hath given you; so strive As in a race in all virtues'. See also Chapter 22:17.

[38] Hamza Yusuf, 'Buddha in the Quran?' in Reza Shah-Kazemi, *Common Ground between Islam and Buddhism*, Fons Vitae, Louisville, KY, 2010, p. 134.

[39] Cited in ibid., p. 143.

[40] Ibid., p. 133.

[41] Ibid., p. 131.

[42] See his talk at www.youtube.com/watch/v==mkw3lcMspoE&NR=1, accessed at 5.12.2010.

[43] See her book 'New Muslims in the European Context', op. cit., p. 229.

[44] See Shah-Kazemi, op. cit, p. 18.

[45] Personal interview, University of Birmingham, 6.12.2010.

[46] Roald, op. cit., p. 229.

[47] Some of his other works are: *Caesarean Moon Births: Calculations, Moon Sighting and Prophetic Way*, Fons Vitae, Louisville, KY, 2008; *Agenda to change our condition* (with Z. Shakir), Zaytuna, 2008. In addition to many articles and chapters in books, the most recent one is about 'Buddha in the Quran' in Shah-Kazemi, Islam and Buddhism, Fons Vitae, Louisville, KY, 2010, pp. 113–36.

[48] Hamza Yusuf, *Purification of the Heart, Signs, Symptoms, And Cures of the Spiritual Diseases of the Heart*, Translation and Commentary of Imam al-Mawlud's Matharat al-Qulub, USA, Starlatch, 2004.

[49] Hamza Yusuf, *The Creed of Imam al-Tahawi*, Fons Vitae, Louisville, KY, 2009.

[50] See www.zaytuna.org/tahawibooksap, accessed at 4.12.2010.

[51] See www.deen-intensive.com/mission-statment.html, accessed at 29.11.2010.

[52] Personal interview with Hamza Yusuf, Oxford, April 2010.

[53] See his book *The Islamist*, Penguin, London, 2007.

Conclusion

[1] Tim Winter, www.mpacuk.org/story/090910/uks-most-influential-muslim-agrees-foreign-pol, accessed at 6.11.2010.

[2] Reza Shah-Kazemi, www.radicalmiddleway.co.uk/speakers/scholars/shaykh-hasan-le-gai-eaton, accessed at 25.8.2010.

[3] This is especially the case with regard to Hamza Yusuf, who has been a pioneer in setting up the Deen Intensive Program and the Muslim College, which has been replicated here in Britain and other parts of Europe.

Bibliography

Ali, A. Y. (2001), *The Meaning of the Holy Quran*. Beltsville, MD: Amana Publications.

Allievi, S. (1996), 'The Muslim community in Italy', in G. Nonneman et al. (eds), *Muslim Communities in the New Europe*. Reading: Ithaca Press.

Ally, M. M. (1980), *History of Muslims in Britain, 1850–1980*. Unpublished MA dissertation: University of Birmingham.

Ansari, H. (2004), *The Infidel Within*. London: Hurst and Company.

Arnold, T. W. (1935), *The Preaching of Islam: A History of the Propagation of the Muslim faith*. London: Archibald and Constable C.

Asad, M. (1937), *Islam at the Crossroads*. Lahore: Arafat Press.

—. (2001), *This Law of Ours and Other Essays*. Kuala Lumpur: Islamic Book Trust.

—. (2003), *The Message of the Quran*. London: The Book Foundation.

—. (1980), *The Road to Mecca*. Gibraltar: Dar Al-Andalus, (first published 1954).

Attar, F. A.-D. (1990), *Muslim Saints and Mystics*. London: Arkana.

Austin, R. (1984), 'The Feminine Dimensions in ibn Arabi's Thought', *Muhyiddin ibn Arabi Society Journal*, 2.

Aymard, J.-B. and P. Laude. (2004), *Frithjof Schuon. Life and Teachings*. Albany: State University of New York Press.

Badran, M. (2006), 'Feminism and Conversion', in K. van Nieuwkerk (ed.), *Women Embracing Islam, Gender and Conversion in the West*. Austin: University of Texas Press.

Ballard, R. (1996), 'Islam and the Construction of Europe', in W. A. R. Shadid and P. S. van Koningsveld (eds), *Muslims in the Margin. Political Responses to the Presence of Islam in Western Europe*. the Netherlands: Kok Pharos Publishing House.

Bawany, B. A. (1967), *Islam-Our Choice*. Karachi: Abridged Edition.

Brice, K. (2011), '*A Minority within A Minority: A Report on Conversion to Islam in the United Kingdom*'. Swansea: Faith matters.

Burckhardt, T. (2009), *Art of Islam: Language and Meaning*. Bloomington, IN: World Wisdom.

—. (1992), *Fez: City of Islam*. Cambridge: Islamic Texts Society.

—. (2008), *An Introduction to Sufi Doctrine*. Bloomington, IN: World Wisdom.

—. (1999), *Moorish Culture in Spain*. Louisville, KY: Fons Vitae.

—. (1984), 'Traditional Science'. *Studies in Comparative Religion*, 16, 1–2.

—. (1983), *Universal Man, Abd al-Karim al-Jili: Extracts Translated with Commentary*. England: Beshara Publication.

—. (1984), 'The Void in Islamic Art', *Studies in Comparative Religion*, 16, 1–2.

Bushill-Matthews, L. (2008), *Welcome to Islam: A Convert's Tale*. London: Continuum.

Chishti, S. K. K. (1987), 'Female Spirituality in Islam', in S. H. Nasr (ed.), *Islamic Spirituality*. New York: Cross Road.

Chittick, W. (ed.) (2007), *The Inner Journey, Views from the Islamic Tradition*. USA: Morning Light Press.

Chodkiewicz, M. (1986), *The Seal of the Saints*. Paris: Gallimard.

Clark, P. (1986), *Marmaduke Pickthall: British Muslim*. London, Melbourne, New York: Quartet.

Clayer N. and E. Germain (eds) (2008), *Islam in Inter-War Europe*. London: Hurst and Company.

Cobbold, L. E. (2009), *Pilgrimage to Mecca* (New edition). London: Arabian publishing.

Daniel, N. (1975), *The Arabs and Medieval Europe*. London: Longman.

Dutton, Y. (1999), 'Conversion to Islam: Quranic Paradigm', in C. Lamb and M. Bryant (eds), *Religious Conversion, Contemporary Practices and Controversies*. London, New York: Cassell.

Eaton, G. (2010), *A Bad Beginning and the Path to Islam*. Cambridge: Archetype.

—. (2008), *The Book of Hadith*. Watsonville, California and Bristol, England: The Book Foundation.

—. (2005), *The Concept of God in Islam*. London: The Islamic Cultural Centre.

—. (2004), *The Concept of Justice in Islam*. London: The Book Foundation.

—. (1994), *Islam and the Destiny of Man*. Cambridge: Islamic Texts Society.

—. (1990), *King of the Castle, Choice and Responsibility in the Modern World*. Cambridge: The Islamic Texts Society.

—. (2000), *Remembering God, Reflections on Islam*. Cambridge: The Islamic Texts Society.

—. (2005), *The Richest Vein, Sophia Perennis*. New York: Hillsdale.

El-Sakkakini, W. (1982), *First Among Sufis: The Life and Thought of Rabia al-Adawiyya, the Woman Saint of Basra*. London: Octagon Press.

Facey, W. (2009), From Mayfair to Mecca, Lady Evelyn Cobbold's Pilgrimage in 1933. public lecture at IAIS, Exeter University, April.

Fitzgerald, M. 'In Memoriam: Dr Martin Lings', www.worldwisdom.com, accessed on 22.8.2010.

Fremantle, A. (1938), *Loyal Enemy*. London: Hutchinson and Co.

Geaves, R. (2010), *Islam in Victorian Britain, The Life and Times of Abdullah Quilliam*. Markfield: KUPE publication.

Gerholm T. and Lithman Y. G. (eds) (1988), *The New Islamic Presence in West Europe*. London and New York: Mansell Publishing Limited.

Guénon, R. (2004), *The Crisis of the Modern World (translated by Marco Pallis, Arthur Osborne and Richard C. Nicholson)*. Hillsdale, NY: Sophia Perennis (first published in French in 1946).

—. (2004), *East and West (translated by Martin Lings)*. Hillsdale, NY: Sophia Perennis, (first published in French in 1924).

—. (2001), *The Reign of Quantity and the Signs of the Times (translated by Lord Northbourne)*. Hillsdale, NY: Sophia Perennis (first published in French in 1945).

Haddad, Y. and Lummis, A. (1987), *Islamic Values in the United States*. New York: Oxford University press.

Haleem, H. (2003), 'Experiences, Needs and Potential of New Muslim Women in Britain', in H. Jawad and T. Benn (eds), *Muslim Women in the United Kingdom and Beyond, Experiences, and Images*. Leiden: Brill.

Headley, L. (1926), *The Affinity between the Original Church of Jesus Christ and Islam, trust for the Encouragement and Circulation of Muslim Religious Literature*. The Mosque, Woking.

—. (1923), *The Great Prophets of the World*. The Mosque, Woking.

—. (1914), *A Western Awakening to Islam*. The Mosque, Woking.

Henzell-Thomas, J. (2008), 'Introduction', in G. Eaton (ed.), *The Book of Hadith*. England: Bristol.

Herman, M. (1999), 'Roads to Mecca: Conversion Narratives of European and Euro-American Muslims'. *The Muslim Worm*, LXXXIX, 1.

Hodgson, M. G. (1974), *The Venture of Islam – Conscience and History in a World of Civilisation. Vol. 2, The Expansion of Islam in the Middle Periods*. Chicago and London: University of Chicago Press.

Hofmann, M. (1999), *Islam: The Alternative*. Beltsville, MD: Amana Publications.

—. (2007), *Islam and Quran*. Beltsville, MD: Amana Publications.

—. (2001), *Journey to Islam*. Markfield: The Islamic Foundation.

—. (1998), *Journey to Makkah*. Beltsville, MD: Amana Publications.

—. (2001), *Religion on the Rise, Islam in the Third Millennium*. Beltsville, MD: Amana Publications.

Hourani, A. (1991), *Islam in European Thought*. Cambridge: Cambridge University Press.

Husain, Ed. (2007), *The Islamist*. London: Penguin.

Ibrahim, E. and Johnson-Davies, D. (1980), (Selected and translated) *The Forty Hadith Qudsi*. Beirut and Damascus: Dar Al-Koran Al-Kareem.

Jawad, H. (1998), *The Rights of Women in Islam: An Authentic Approach*. London: Macmillan.

Joseph, S. (2006), *Editorial, Emel Magazine*. London, April.

Kose, A. (1996), *Conversion to Islam, A Study in Native British Converts*. London and New York: Kegan Paul international.

Lapidus, I. M. (1988), *A History of Islamic Societies*. Cambridge: Cambridge University Press.

Lewis, P. (1994), *Islamic Britain*. London: I.B. Tauris.

Lings, M. (2004), *Ancient Beliefs and Modern Superstitions* (revised edition). Cambridge: Archetype.

—. (1970), *The Book of Certainty*. New Delhi: The Millat Book Centre.

—. (2002), *Collected Poems*. Cambridge: Archetype.

—. (2002), *The Eleventh Hour, The Spiritual Crisis of the Modern World in the light of Tradition and Prophecy* (revised edition). Cambridge: Archetype (first edition was published in 1987).

—. (2007), *The Holy Qur'an, Translation of Selected Verses*. Cambridge: The Royal Institute for Islamic civilisation/The Islamic Texts Society.

—. (2004), *Mecca from before the Genesis Until Now*. Cambridge: Archetype.

—. (1988), *Muhammad, His Life Based on the Earliest Sources*. London: UNWIN(first published in 1983 by Allen and Unwin).

—. (1987), *The Quranic Art of Calligraphy and Illumination* (first published by World of Islam Festival Trust in 1976). Essex: Scorpion.

—. (2005), *A Return to the Spirit*. Quinta Essentia: Fons Vita.

—. (2002), *The Secret of Shakespeare, His Greatest Plays Seen in the Light of Sacred Art*. Cambridge: Archetype.

—. (1961), *A Sufi Saint of the Twentieth Century*, Shaikh Ahmad Al-Alawi. London: Allen and Unwin.

—. (1991), *Symbol and Archetype, A Study of the Meaning of Existence*. Cambridge: Quinta Essentia.

—. (1975), *What is Sufism?* London: George Allen and Unwin.

Lings, M. and Minnaar, C. (eds.) (2007), *The Underlying Religion, An Introduction to the Perennial Philosophy*. Bloomington, IN: World Wisdom.

Mansfield, P. (1982), *The Arabs*. London: Penguin Books.

Martin, D. 'Martin Lings, A Sufi writer on Islamic ideas, Dies at 96' The New York Times, May 29, 2005, at www.nytimes.com/2005/05/29/obituaries/29lings.html?=1, accessed on 25.8.2010.

Matar, N. I. (1993), '*The Renegade in the English Seventeenth-Century Imagination. Studies in English Literature 1500–1900*, 33.

—. (1994), 'Turning Turks: Conversion to Islam in English Renaissance Thought. *Durham University Journal*, LxxxI (1).

McGinty, A. (2006), *Becoming Muslim: Western Women's Coversion to Islam*. New York: Palgrave Macmillan.

Michon, J.-L. (1984), 'Titus Burckhardt in Fez 1972–1977'. *Studies in Comparative Religion*, 16, 1 and 2.

Murata, S. (1992), *The Tao of Islam*. Albany: State University of New York Press.

Nasr, S. H. (ed) (2005), *The Essential Frithjof Schuon*. Bloomington, IN: World Wisdom.

—. (2003), 'Foreword', in W. Stoddart (ed.), *The Essential Titus Burckhardt: Reflections on Sacred Art, Faiths and Civilsations*. Bloomington, IN: World Wisdom.

—. (2007), *The Garden of Truth, The Vision and Promise of Sufism, Islam's Mystical Tradition*. New York: Harper One.

—. (2004), *The Heart of Islam, Enduring Values for Humanity*. New York: Harper San Francisco.

—. *Islam and the Plight of Modern Man*. London: Longman.

—. (2003), *Islam: History, Religion, and Civilisation*. New York: Harper One.

—. (1988), *Man and Nature: The Spiritual Crisis of Modern Man*. US: Phanes Press.

—. (2005), 'Shaykh Abu Siraj al-Din (Martin Lings): A Tribute. *Sophia, Journal of Traditional Studoes*, 11, 1.

—. (1999), *Sufi Essays* (third edition). Chicago: ABC International Group, KAZI Publications.

—. (1987), *Traditional Islam in the Modern World*. London and New York: Kegan Paul International.

—. (1993), *A Young Muslim's Guide to the Modern World*. Cambridge: Islamic Texts Society.

Nicholson, R. A. (1997), *The Mystics of Islam*. London: Routledge and Kegan Paul.

Nielsen, J. (1991), *Muslims in West Europe*. Edinburgh: Edinburgh University Press.

—. (1995), *Muslims in West Europe* (second edition). Edinburgh: Edinburgh University Press.

—. (2004), *Muslims in West Europe* (third edition). Edinburgh: Edinburgh University Press.

Nurbakhsh, J. (1983), *Sufi Women*. New York: Khaniqahi-Nimatullahi Publications.

—. (1981), *Sufism, Meaning, Knowledge and Unity*. New York: Khaniqahi Nimatullahi Publications.

Pape, L. L. (2003), 'Communication Strategies and Public Commitments: the Example of a Sufi Order in Europe', in S. Allievi and J. S. Nielsen (eds), *Muslim Networks and Transnational Communities in and across Europe*. Leiden: Brill.

Pickthall, M. (1981), *The Cultural side of Islam* (second edition). New Delhi: Kitab Bhavan (first edition was published in 1927).

—. (1977), *The Meaning of the Glorious Quran, Text and Explanatory Translation,* translator's foreword. New York: The Muslim World League.

—. (no date), *The Position of Women in Islam.* Karachi: Umma Publishing House.

Ramadan, T. (2004), *Western Muslims and the Future of Islam.* Oxford: Oxford University Press.

Rambo, L. (1993), *Understanding Religious Conversion.* New Haven: Yale University Press.

Rambo, L. and C. Farhadian (1999), 'Converting: Stages of Religious Change', in C. Lamb and M. Bryant (eds), *Religious Conversion, Contemporary Practices and Controversies.* London, and New York: Cassell.

Rath, J. et al. (2001), *Western Europe and its Islam.* Leiden: Brill.

Ridely, Y. (2001), *In the hands of the Taliban.* London: Robson Books.

Roald, A. S. (2004), *New Muslims in the European Context, The Experience of Scandinavian Converts.* Leiden: Brill.

Rodinson, M. (1988), *Europe and the Mystique of Islam.* London: I.B. Tauris.

Rosenthal, E. (1931), *From Drury Lane to Mecca.* London: Sampson Low.

Schimmel, S. (1999), *My Soul is a Woman, the Feminine in Islam.* New York: Continuum.

—. (1975), *Mystical Dimensions of Islam.* Chapel Hill: The University of North Carolina press.

Schleifer, A. (1997), *Mary the Blessed Virgin of Islam.* Louisville: Fons Vitae.

Schuon, F. (1976), *Islam and the Perennial (translated by Peter Hobson and S. H. Nasr).* London: World of Islam Festival Publishing Company.

—. (1953), *The Transcendent Unity of Religions (translated by Peter Townsend).* London: Faber and Faber.

—. (1998), *Understanding Islam* Bloomington, IN: World Wisdom Books.

Shah-Kazemi, R. (2005), 'A Message of Hope at the Eleventh Hour: Martin Lings, 1909–2005', *Sophia, Journal of Traditional Studies,*11, 1.

—. (1998), *Shaykh Hamza Yusuf, A Response to Nadeem Azam.* London: Q-News.

—. (1999), 'A Tribute to Martin Lings on the Occasion of his 90th Birthday'. *SOPHIA, The Journal of Traditional Studies,* 5, 2.

—. (1996), *Women in Islam: A Reminder to the Taleban.* London: Dialogue.

Sherrard, P. (1987), *The Rape of Man and Nature: An Enquiry into the Origins and Consequences of Modern Science.* Ipswich: Golgonooza Press.

Smith, J. (1991), 'Seyyed Hossein Nasr: defender of the sacred and Islamic traditionalism', in H. Yvonne (ed.), *Muslims of America.* New York: Oxford University press.

Smith, M. (1984), *Rabia the Mystic and her Fellow Saints in Islam.* Cambridge: Cambridge University Press.

Sulzberger, J. (2007), 'Some notes on Arab calligraphy', in W. Chittick (ed.), *The Inner Journey, Views from the Islamic Tradition.* Morning Light Press.

Vertovec, S. and G. Peach (eds) (1997), *Islam in Europe. The Politics of Religion and Community.* Basingstoke: Macmillan.

Wadud, A. (2003), 'American Muslim Identity: Race and Ethnicity in Progressive Islam', in O. Safi (ed.), *Progressive Muslims, on Justice, Gender, and Pluralism.* Oxford: One World.

Waterfield, R. (2002), *René Guénon and the Future of the West.* Hillsdale, NY: Sophia Perennis.

Westerlund, D. and I. Svanberg (eds). (1999), *Islam Outside the Arab World.* New York: St. Martin's Press.

Winter, T. (translator), (1995), *Abu Hamid al-Ghazali, Disciplining the Soul and Breaking the Two Desires.* Cambridge: Islamic Texts Society.

—. (translator), (1989), *Abu Hamid al-Ghazali, Remembrance of Death and Afterlife.* Cambridge: Islamic Texts Society.

—. (translator), (2000), *Al-Asqalani, Selections from Fath Al-Bari.* Cambridge: Muslim Academic Trust.

—. (translator), (1990), *Al-Bayhaqi, Seventy-Seven Branches of Faith.* London: Quilliam Press.

—. (translator), (2009), *Al-Busiri, The Mantle Adorned.* London: Quilliam Press.

—. (2008), *Bombing without Moonlight, the Origins of Suicidal Terrorism.* Bristol, England: Amal Press.

—. (ed.) (2009), *The Cambridge Companion to Classical Islamic Theology* Cambridge: Cambridge University Press.

—. (2009), Cambridge Muslim College, Diploma in Contextual Islamic Studies and Leadership, Cambridge, May.

—. (2000), 'Conversion as Nostalgia: Some Experiences of Islam', in M. Percy (ed.), *Previous Convictions, Conversion in the Present Day.* London: Society for Promoting Christian Knowledge.

—. (2010), 'Islam and the New Millennium', public lecture, Chicago, 1999. It can be seen at www.youtube.com/watch?v=fa_MdnXk8Gy@feature=related. Accessed on 13.11.2010.

—. (2010), 'Islam, Irigaray, and the retrieval of gender', 'Boys will be Boys', 'British and Muslim?', 'Muslim Loyalty and Belonging', all can be found on his official website www.masud.co.uk.

—. (2010), 'Love for others', Friday Khutbas, Cambridge Mosque, Cambridge. It can be watched at www.cambridgemosqueismoving.org.uk. Accessed on 12.11.2010.

—. (2007), 'Mary in Islam', in S. J. Boss (ed.), *Mary: The Complete Resources.* London: Continuum.

—. (2003), 'Muslim loyalty and belonging', in M. S. Seddon, D. Hussain and N. Malik (eds.), *British Muslims: Loyalty and Belonging.* Markfield: Islamic Foundation.

—. (2005), *Muslim Songs of the British Isles.* London: Quilliam Press.

—. (2004), 'The poverty of fanaticism', in J. Lumbard (ed.), *Islam, Fundamentalism and the Betrayal of Tradition.* Bloomington, IN: World Wisdom.

—. (2007), 'The Saint with Seven Tombs', in W. Chittick (ed.), *The Inner Journey, Views from the Islamic Tradition.* USA: Morning Light Press.

—. (2009), 'Thought for the Day'. BBC Radio Four, May 15.

—. 'Tradition or extradition?' in A. Malik (ed.), *The Empire and the Crescent, Global Implications for a New American Century.* Bristol, England: AMAL Press.

—.(translator) (1992), Roger de Pasquier *Unveiling Islam.* Cambridge: Islamic Texts Society.

Winter, T. with Hamza Yusuf. (2010), YouTube, 13.11.2010.

Winter, T. and J. A. Williams (authors) (2002), *Understanding Islam and the Muslims.* Louisville: Fons Vitae.

Winter, T. et al. (eds.) (2006), *Abraham's Children: Jews, Christians and Muslims in Conversation*. Edinburgh: T&T Clark/Continuum.

—. (2004), 'Bombing without Moonlight, the Origins of Suicidal Terrorism', at www.masud.co.uk.

Yusuf, S. H. (2010), 'Be Peace makers', can be ssen at www.youtube.com/watch?v= pp4pbfiMf7c&feature=related (accessed 3.12.2010).

—. (2010), 'Buddha in the Quran?', in R. Shah-Kazemi, *Common Ground between Islam and Buddhism*. Louisville, KY: Fons Vitae.

—. (2008), *Caesarean Moon Births: Calculations, Moon Sighting and Prophetic Way*. Louisville, KY: Fons Vitae.

—. (translator and commentator), (2007), *The Creed of Imam al-Tahawi*. California: Zaytuna Institute.

—. (2005), 'A Gentle Soul'. *Sophia, Journal of Traditional Studies*, 11, 1.

—. (2010),'Hard Talk', BBC can be seen at www.youtube.com/watch?v=kqAkgo-s7bg&feature=related (accessed 29.11.2010).

—. (2010), 'Islam and the West', can be seen at www.youtube.com/watch?v=ttcA9k t09M&feature=related (accessed 30.11.2010).

—. (2003), 'On A Night of Remembrance'. London: Q-News, October.

—. (translator and commentator), (2004), *Purification of the Heart, Signs, Symptoms, and Cures of the Spiritual Diseases of the Heart, Imam al-Mawlud's Matharat al-Qulub*. USA: Starlatch.

—. (2010), 'Removing the Silence on Domestic Violence', can be seen at www.you-tube.com/watch?v=BDEKJDgxo-u (accessed 24.11.2010).

—. (2008), 'Seeing with Muslim Eyes', in A. Malik (ed.), *The Empire and the Crescent, Global Implications for a New American Century*. Bristol, England: AMAL Press.

—. 'A Time for Introspection', to be read at www.muslim-canada.org/introspection. html, accessed at 12.11.2010.

—. (2010), 'What the West can learn from Islam' can be seen at www.news.bbc. co.uk/1/hi/talking_point/3190931.stm (accessed 20.11.2010).

Yusuf, S. H. with Shakir, Z. (2008), *Agenda to Change our Condition*. California: Zaytuna.

Zebiri, K. (2008), *British Converts Choosing Alternative Lives*. Oxford: One World.

Personal Interviews

Personal Interview, Leicester April 2010.
Personal interview, Leicester, September 2010.
Personal Interview, Birmingham, July 2010.
Personal Interview, Birmingham, April, 2010.
Personal Communication, Birmingham, December 2010.
Personal Interview, Birmingham, December 2010.
Personal Conversation, Birmingham, May 2010.
Personal Interview, Oxford, April 2010.
Personal Communication, Lancaster, October 1997.
Personal Communication, Amsterdam, March 2003.
Personal Interview, Birmingham, September 2003.
Personal Conversation, Birmingham, 1997.
Personal Conversation, Lancaster, 1998.

Special Journals

The Islamic Review, January, Vol XXIII, No. 1, January 1935.
The Islamic Review, Vol XXII, No. 3, March 1934.
The Islamic Review, Vol. 2, No. 2, February 1914.
The Islamic Review, Vol XI, No. 6, June–July 1923.
The Islamic Review, Vol. III, No.1, January 1915.
The Islamic Review, Vol. XI, No. 1, September 1923.
The Islamic Review, Vol. XI,No. 12, December 1923.
The Muslim Outlook, Vol. II, No. 55, February 1926.
British Muslims Monthly Survey, 2002, Vol. 10:1, Centre for the Study of Islam and Christian-Muslim Relations, Department of Theology, University of Birmingham.

Newspapers

The Muslim News, 30 August 2002.
The Muslim News, 30 July 2004.
The Independent, 2 January 2009.
The Independent, 2 August 2007.
The Independent, Tuesday, 4 January 2011.

Internet Sources

http://thetruereligion.org/mum.htm
http://www.thetruereligion.org/yfm.htm
http://thetruereligion.org/mimima.htm
http://www.unn.ac.uk/societies/islamic/women/women3.htm
http://www.usc.edu/dept/MSA/newmusilm/karima.html
www.cis-ca.org/voices/g/Guénon-mn.htm.intor
www.cis-ca.org/voice/g/guenon-mn.htm
www.seriousseekers.com/Teachers%20Contributors/teachers_priority
www.allamaiqbal.com
www.informationislam.com/articles.aspx?cid=1&acid=207aid=150
www.islamonline.net/livedialogue/english/Guestcv.asp?hGuestID=ufM0Xx
www.geocities.com
www.islamonline.net/English/contemporary/2002/05/article3-a.shtml
www.worldwisdom.com/public/library/defult.aspx
www.religioperennis.org
http://revertmuslims.com/forum/index.php?showtopic=1309
http://www.euromuslim.net/index.php/islam-in-europe/country-profile/profile-of-the
www.absoluteastronomy.com/topics/Henry_Stanley,_3rd_Baron_Stanley_of_Al
www.wokingmuslim.org/pers/quilliam/rev-re12.htm
www.saudiaramcoworld.com/issue/200805/mayfair.to.makkah.htm
www.wokingmuslim.org/pers/ez_cobbold/index.htm
www.Masud.co.uk

www.lastprophet.info/en/tim-winter/the-first-british-guest-of-allah.html

www.wokingmuslim.org/pers/headley/headley-press.htm

www.wokingmuslim.org/pers/headley.htm

www.aaiil.org

www.masud.co.uk/ISLAM/bmh/BMM-AHM-pickthall_bio.htm

www.bewley.virtualave.net/saq.html

www.rferl.org./content/article/1052842.html

www.newmuslimsproject.net/meeting-point

www.openmindsblogspot.com

www.muslimnews.co.uk/awards/index.php?page=2005/ihewitt

www.greenbelt.org.uk

www.yusufislam.com/biography/

www.yvonneridely.org

www.davidrowan.com/2005/07/intreview-sarah-joseph-emel-magazine.html

www.guardian.co.uk/news/205.may/27/guardianobituaries.obituaries

www.worldwisdom.com

www.nytimes.com/2005/05/29/obituaries/29Lings.html?_=1

www.radiusfoundation.org/lings-review.htm

www.mac.abc.se/-onesr/ez/dc/oml_e.htm

www.themathesontrus.org/announce/?tag=reza-shah-kazemi

www.radicalmiddleway.co.uk/speakers/scholars/shaykh-hasan-le-gai-eaton

www.seekersguidance.org/blog/2020/03/obituary-for-gai-eaton-remembering-
    the-uk

www.emel.com/article?id=18a_id-1164

www.an-nisa.org/subpage.asp?id=323&mainid=78

www.iosminaret.org/vol-5/issue11/profile.php

www.mohammadthalif.blogspot.com/2010/09/timothy-winter-britains.most.html

www.mantleadorned.com/author.htm

www.youtube.com/watch?v=3YjhqHmlOM

www.sheikhhamza.com/biography.aspx

www.youtube.com/watch?v=ZBukxfxvcQ9&NR=1

www.education.com/video/data/20/video/us/2010/80/23/nr.muslim.college.
    cnn.htl

www.ZaytunaCollege.org

www.lastprophet.info/en/hamza-yusuf/ffrom-hamza-yusuf-s-viewpoint-what-can.

www.zaytuna.org/tahawibooksap

www.deen-intensive.com/mission-statment.html

www.mpacuk.org/story/090910/uks-most-influential-muslim-agrees-foreign-pol

www.radicalmiddleway.co.uk/speakers/scholars/shaykh-hasan-le-gai-eaton

www.youtub.com/watch?v=Iyvqfh2wupA

www.youtube.com/watch?v=3RXrQr4mJ5E8feature=related

www.youtube.com/watch?v=UgLQp4dcbBo@feature=relmfu

Subject Index

and Islam   47
pilgrimage to Mecca   48
wedding   47
conversion
    defined   1–2
    in Islamic context   2–3
*Conversion to Islam: A Study of Native British
        Converts* (Ali Kose)   14
Creed of Imam Al-Tahawi (Hamza Yusuf)   140
The Crescent (Abdul Rahman)   45–6
The Crisis of the Modern World (Abdul
        al-Wahid Yahya)   24, 85

divinity   97

Early British Convert Community
    Arabic inscription   43
    Elizabethan era   43–4
    Indian Muslim   44
    Islam
        declaration   43
        and living   43–4
    Muslim issues   44
The Earth's Complaint (Hasan Abdal
        Hakim)   111
Eastern Tradition and Modern Thought (Hasan
        Abdal Hakim)   107
Eaton, Charles Le Gai (Hasan Abdal Hakim)
    adab, cultivation of   105, 111
    An-Nisa Society   106
    British Muslim integration   105
    as consultant and editor   101
    conversions to Islam in south Asia   106
    criticism of modern thought   108
    education of   101
    eternal/spiritual values   111
    family and issues   101–2, 105
    harmony between God and human
        beings   111–12
    human salvation   109
    intellectual/academic
        contributions   112–13
    Islam and Europe/West   110
    Islamic radicalism   105
    Islamist extremism   106
    kindness and compassion   112
    metaphysical doctrine   103

moderation and avoidance of excess   112
modern/post-modern secular West   111
modern/Western life analysis   107
month of Ramadan   105
Muslims traders   106
outer course of   102
parents   101
patriarch of British Islam   101
political influence   110
Sacred Texts/Islamic history   106
Saudis and anti-Sufi attitude   105
seeker   101
spiritual vision   110
temptation and deviation   112
unrestrained life   104
views about religion   102
Western norms and thoughts   110
Eid al-fitr prayer at mosque   66
The Eleventh Hour (Abu Bakr Siraj
        al-Din)   91–2
Enid (Muhammad Marmaduke
        Pickthall)   65
esotericism and exotericism   74
extremism   74, 79

faith-based schools   81
Fez (Sidi Ibrahim Izz al-Din)   33
Fundamental Symbols of Sacred Science (Abdul
        al-Wahid Yahya)   25
Fusus al-Hikam (Sidi Ibrahim Izz
        al-Din)   34

The Grand Triad (Abdul al-Wahid Yahya)   25
Guénon, René (Sheikh Abdul Wahed Yahia)
    Catholic upbringing   23
    education   23
    metaphysical views   25
    philosophical and spiritual principles   25
    Sufi texts translation   23
    traditional religions   25
Gulf war   4

Hadith   132
Hanafi school of law   127
Hewitt, Ibrahim
    charity work   81
    faith schools   81
Hindu Vedanta   103